'Labour's record in government shows that Attlee and Blair were in the top rank of change-making prime ministers, and Wilson not far behind. An inspirational history.'
Alastair Campbell

'An outstanding book about Labour Party election performances over the course of more than a century – and even more importantly, an invaluable and terrific guide to Labour Party politics. Highly recommended.'
Peter Frankopan

'If Labour is to flourish in power, it needs to know much more about its history. Reading this book would be an excellent starting point for its leaders and followers.'
Anthony Seldon

'A timely and brilliantly illuminating book that offers much needed context to the 2024 general election. A must read.'
Steve Richards, BBC Radio 4 *Week in Westminster* and host of *Rock and Roll Politics*

VICTORY AT THE BALLOT BOX

The History of How Labour Built Britain

DOUGLAS BEATTIE

Elliott&Thompson

First published in 2024 as
How Labour Wins: (And Why It Loses) From 1900 to 2024
by Elliott and Thompson Limited
2 John Street
London WC1N 2ES
www.eandtbooks.com

Represented by:
Authorised Rep Compliance Ltd.
Ground Floor, 71 Lower Baggot Street
Dublin, D02 P593
Ireland
www.arccompliance.com

This paperback edition published in 2025

ISBN: 978-1-78396-850-3

9 8 7 6 5 4 3 2 1

A catalogue record for this book is available from the British Library.

Typeset in Poppins and Garamond Premier Pro by
SX Composing DTP, Rayleigh, Essex

Printed by CPI Group (UK) Ltd, Croydon, CR0 4YY

The nation wants food, work and homes.
Labour Manifesto 1945

CONTENTS

Introduction   **1**

Vote Notes: Key Facts on Labour's History   7

Chapter 1:   1893 – A Distinct Labour Group   11

Chapter 2:   1900 – The Khaki Two   15

Chapter 3:   1906 – A New Party in Parliament   20

Chapter 4:   1910 (January) – Does Labour Count?   26

Chapter 5:   1910 (December) – Labour Clears the Way   31

Chapter 6:   1918 – Everything Changes   35

Chapter 7:   1922 – Unrest and Development   42

Chapter 8:   1923 – 'Fail or Succeed' – Labour in Government   48

Chapter 9:   1924 – Red October   55

Chapter 10: 1929 – Striking Back   62

Chapter 11: 1931 – Depression and Betrayal   69

Chapter 12: 1935 – The Rising Tide   76

Chapter 13: 1945 – Winning the Peace   83

Chapter 14: 1950 – A Sharp Kick in the Pants   94

Chapter 15: 1951 – Forward or Backwards   104

Chapter 16: 1955 – Fighting Snow White   113

Chapter 17: 1959 – The Struggle Continues   123

Chapter 18: 1964 – The New Britain   133

Chapter 19: 1966 – Time for Decision   145

Chapter 20: 1970 – Now Britain's Strong   155

Chapter 21: 1974 (February) – Yesterday's Men?   166

Chapter 22: 1974 (October) – A Bumpy Ride   177

Chapter 23: 1979 – Sea Change   189

Chapter 24: 1983 – The New Hope   204

Chapter 25: 1987 – The Dream Ticket   217

Chapter 26: 1992 – Well All Right!   230

Chapter 27: 1997 – A New Dawn   245

Chapter 28: 2001 – The Quiet Landslide   259

Chapter 29: 2005 – We Can Unite Again   270

Chapter 30: 2010 – A Privilege to Serve   283

Chapter 31: 2015 – On the Brink   300

Chapter 32: 2017 – The Many Not the Few   315

Chapter 33: 2019 – Cutting the Flowers   332

Chapter 34: 2024 – All Change   347

Acknowledgements   363

Endnotes   365

Labour Leaders and their Constituencies   385

Index   389

About the Author   404

Introduction

General elections deal in the pursuit of power – deciding who wields it, on whose behalf and for what purpose. The Labour Party has long been at the forefront of that struggle at the ballot box, having gradually built its power at Westminster from the early years of the twentieth century.

There have been considerable victories and setbacks during that time. In 2024 the party stormed into government after 14 years out in the cold. It did so under Keir Starmer with a majority almost as big as that enjoyed by Tony Blair in 1997, and larger than anything Clement Attlee or Harold Wilson had been able to conjure in the past.

Remarkably, this followed one of the worst results in the party's history, at the general election of 2019. Shortly after that calamitous defeat I began to wonder about Labour's performance down the decades, what it stands for and what it is trying to achieve for the people of Britain.

The best way of doing this, I felt, was to take a new approach by examining the party's approach to each election since its inception. After all, Labour is very different to its opponents in Parliament because it has always sought primarily to rebalance the country in favour of the many not the few, to borrow a phrase.[1]

In so doing, it has built modern Britain and succeeded most often when it has a clear purpose and programme for government. In the short-lived minority administrations of 1924 and 1929–31 this was centred around the crisis of unemployment. In 1945 it was the execution of radical plans for the vast post-war reconstruction of society and industry.

Then, in the 1960s, Harold Wilson's technological and scientific vision for Britain across the second half of the twentieth century was the driving force, while between 1997 and 2010, under Tony Blair and Gordon Brown, there was again a sense that the country needed further remedial reconstruction. In 2024 Labour relied heavily on the theme of 'change', with the core messages of economic growth and national renewal.

It must also be accepted that in politics, if a party is to endure in the way Labour has, progress will be sought even in the embers of electoral defeat. It was a victory of a kind to get two MPs into Parliament in 1900, and to prosper at each election until taking power early in 1924.

Though still a large defeat in terms of seats, it was a victory too to bounce back in 1935 after being crushed four years earlier; all of this in no small part was preparing the ground for the historic landslide of 1945.

It is also worth remembering that the Labour Party and wider movement is a living thing. Walk down any street as day breaks or as night falls and Labour is there – in its members working in shops, driving trains and buses, keeping schools open, the lights on in our homes and carrying out shifts in hospitals. Labour is Britain and Britain can't do without Labour.

Yet though many today are aware of Blair and Brown, those who came before them are barely known at all. Each, however, made their mark and we all continue to live with their political legacies.

As Alastair Campbell, one of the most prominent figures in the Blair era, pointed out in a contribution to this book, 'to date only Clement Attlee, Harold Wilson, Tony Blair and Keir Starmer have won Parliamentary majorities as Labour leaders. This is a very hard country to win elections from the left.

'Two things which I think can be applied to all four – a sense of a better future than the present being created by their opponents; and fairness in their approach. Given Labour's relative failure in elections, set against the many successes of the Conservatives, their record in government cannot be understated.

'I would argue that both Attlee and Blair were in the top rank of change-making prime ministers, and Wilson not far behind. It is too early to say for Keir Starmer.'

Even Ramsay MacDonald, a name associated with treachery to the cause, cannot be dismissed and Campbell is right to point out that 'he broke the traditional dominance of Conservative and Liberal rule, and showed that Labour could govern effectively'.[2]

I was fascinated by how all of this had come about: how Labour had emerged, how the party had grown and supplanted the Liberals, how MacDonald had taken Labour into government.

How was it possible that Attlee and his ministers had ejected Winston Churchill from office, revolutionised Britain at the end of the Second World War and then been thrown out themselves just six years later? How had Wilson won four times and Blair scored a hat-trick of general election victories? All these stories and many more are told in the pages of this book.

Some of this is about capturing momentum and recognising the potential of the moment, especially when there is a demand for change, as was the case in 1945, 1997 and 2024. Labour is a party built on the empowering potential of change, but sometimes politics is simply about opportunity.

This book does not confine itself to the story of Labour, nor even the Conservatives, but out of necessity takes in the themes of modern Britain since 1900. In different guises the strands of this story seem to wash back at us time and again.

Unemployment, war, poverty, housing, the economy and Britain's place in the world are prime examples. Battles once raged over free trade and tariffs, but in more recent times these have been redrawn to consider the UK's trading position inside or outside the European Union.

Where Wilson and others struggled with Britain's balance of payments and a changing economy in the aftermath of empire, Gordon Brown battled the financial crash of 2008 and Starmer seeks to tame the economic dragons with 'fiscal rules'.

Labour and the other parties fight on many levels other than UK general elections, in local councils and devolved governments of one kind or another. However, Parliament in London remains the seat of the British government and for that reason the focus of this book is on Westminster.

It was my feeling that Labour seemed bewildered to lose in 2010 after 13 years in office, unsure of its future and what might befall the country under a Conservative–Liberal Democrat coalition. This also signalled the beginning of a highly turbulent era defined by post-financial crash austerity, the Scottish independence and Brexit referendums, as well as the Covid-19 pandemic and the short-lived Truss era of economic wildfires. For the Labour Party there was also the shock election of the left-wing backbencher Jeremy Corbyn as leader, followed by another sharp change of direction under Keir Starmer.

Curiously, general elections are both national events and highly personal. Campaigning is fun but it demands both mental and physical fortitude – in 2017, I covered 3,000 miles as a candidate in the Scottish rural seat where I grew up.

As a child I had watched the sitting Conservative MP touring my home town by car, hailing textile mill workers in an accent I recognised only from television news bulletins. Generally, it was not a place where people showed their political colours, a Tory stronghold dominated by farming and the feudal laird, though the town was packed with mill workers who produced some of the finest cloths in the world.

The jobs that sustained the town in the 1980s are gone now – much like the textile industry elsewhere on these isles, or the mining or the steel that once formed the nation's industrial spine. You could not be a teenager at that time and remain unaware of the situation in the country: how Britain seemed to be tearing itself apart.

In 1983, a young MP called Gordon Brown made his maiden speech in the House of Commons. Thinking of each era since 1900, his words are all too prescient: 'the grossest affront to human dignity and the gravest assault, on any view of social justice, is mass unemployment and its inevitable consequence, mass poverty'.[3]

The first election I voted in was 1992, a crushing defeat for Labour, which Neil Kinnock himself recalls in the pages of this book. Gordon Brown also explains here what it was like to oversee Labour's general election campaigns, while candidates and advisors from the 1970s to the present day give their take, as does a former Cabinet minister from the Blair era.

As I progressed with my research and writing, I came to feel that Labour figures from the past were reaching out from the pages of old books and newspapers to tell us that they are still here in the Britain of today.

I have tried throughout to give balanced accounts of Labour's fortunes under successive leaders. This is not a book written from the left, the right or the centre; it is written simply in the hope of bringing greater understanding of Labour's elections and telling the story of a party that has shaped Britain and its people for 125 years.

Across the 33 elections described in this volume, Labour has done best when it has been united and has had a leader able to calm the divisions that will always exist in political parties over the defining issues of the era.

Labour has also prospered when it has read the mood of the country and used that insight to shape popular policies that emancipate people, rather than pandering to populism.

It has done so, above all, when it has remained true to its roots. That means being faithful to the aspirations expressed over a century ago by Keir Hardie, to nurture the hopes and ease the hardships of the least well-off, while offering opportunity for all through the 'sunshine of socialism', as Hardie put it.[4]

Whether the opposing party is strong, well-led or in chaos, whether Labour is in power or opposition, whether grappling with economic crisis or international instability, it is remaining true to these values that provides the best chance for Labour to win.

Each leader has had their own approach, but all have tried their best to find the formula that would return the party to power. Every election is different, but each carries the possibility of success.

Labour's is a story of dogged determination, remarkable men and women, triumph, treachery, tradition, modernisation and so much more in the never-ending battle to serve and to build Britain into a country that allows the entire population to live good lives.

Vote Notes:
Key Facts on Labour's History

- Labour's first and present leaders are both called Keir – Keir Hardie and Keir Starmer.

- Harold Wilson was the youngest Cabinet minister of the twentieth century, aged just 31 on becoming president of the Board of Trade in 1947.

- Labour's biggest majority was won in 1997 – a 179-seat advantage. Its lowest was in 1964 – just four seats.

- The highest proportion of the vote won by Labour was 48.8 per cent in 1951, when the party also received the largest number of votes ever cast for it: 13,948,883.

- The highest percentage rise in the Labour vote between elections since universal suffrage in 1918 was 10.0 per cent between 1935 and 1945.

- The largest percentage fall in the Labour vote between elections was 7.9 per cent between 1979 and 1983.

- In 2000, Tony Blair's son Leo was the first baby born to a serving prime minister in 150 years.

- Labour has been led by two women – Margaret Beckett and Harriet Harman – both in interim positions.

- Jim Callaghan is the only Labour figure to have held all four great offices of state.

- Labour has had four leaders with the first name James, but former prime minister Jim Callaghan is not one of them! James (Keir Hardie), (Ramsay MacDonald), (Harold Wilson) and (Gordon Brown). Callaghan's first name was Leonard.

- Diane Abbott was the first black woman MP, elected for Labour in 1987 at the same time as Bernie Grant and Paul Boateng.

- Labour has won five landslide victories – 1945, 1966, 1997, 2001 and 2024.

- Labour has won a hat-trick of elections only once – 1997, 2001 and 2005, all under Tony Blair.

- Three of Labour's seven prime ministers were born in Scotland – Ramsay MacDonald, Tony Blair and Gordon Brown.

- Labour has won back-to-back election victories in 1945 and 1950, 1964 and 1966, 1974 (Feb) and 1974 (Oct).

- Labour has an election pact with the Co-operative Party. This arrangement goes back to the 1920s.

- Every Labour general election manifesto must be agreed at a 'Clause V' meeting involving the leadership, unions, national executive and others.

- Labour has had 23 leaders (including those in an acting capacity), but Ramsay MacDonald was the first to be styled 'leader' rather than simply chairman.

- The first woman Cabinet member in Britain was Labour's Margaret Bondfield, appointed minister of labour in 1929.

- Clement Attlee was the party's longest-serving leader over 20 years from 1935 to 1955.

- Labour's national logo is the red rose; this replaced a red flag motif in the 1980s, and before that the party used a symbol of torch, shovel and quill.

- The youngest Labour leader when taking the role was Ed Miliband, aged 40; the oldest was George Lansbury, aged 72.

- Jeremy Corbyn is the only former party leader ever to stand and win his seat as an independent candidate, becoming MP for Islington North in the 2024 general election.

- The largest ever Conservative-to-Labour swing in a general election was recorded in 2024, when former Conservative prime minister Liz Truss lost her South West Norfolk seat by a 25.9% swing.

- Prime Minister Keir Starmer has selected the highest number of women in key cabinet positions.

Chapter 1

1893 – A Distinct Labour Group

'The Liberal and Conservative Parties in this
country have long histories.'

Clement Attlee[1]

Today, general elections in the United Kingdom unfold through weeks of intense campaigning in what has become close to a presidential race to enter 10 Downing Street. All this is a far cry from the era in which what would become the Labour Party emerged at the start of the twentieth century.

On its website Labour says that *its formation was the result of many years of struggle by working class people, trade unionists and socialists, united by the goal of [having] working class voices represented in [the] British Parliament*.[2]

This summary significantly understates how extraordinary it was for a new party to emerge and take on the might of the Conservatives and the Liberals – neither of whose primary aim was to speak for working people.

Both parties were long established – growing out of the Tory Party and the Whigs in the mid-nineteenth century. While Conservatives were seen as representing the land-owning classes and the British establishment in its numerous forms, the Liberals promoted the growth of Parliamentary democracy and free trade.

The Liberals came to be known as the party of 'peace, economy and reform' and were attuned to the growing sense in Victorian society that all was not well; that many citizens lived under conditions of great hardship.

Numerous studies confirmed this, most notably *Life and Labour of the People in London* by the social reformer Charles Booth. Written in the 1880s, it demonstrated that more than 30 per cent of the population of London – and in some areas up to 60 per cent – lived at or below subsistence level. Poverty, wrote Booth, had become 'a national institution'.[3]

Liberalism favoured broad social reform, and in this regard the Third Reform Act of 1885 was key in that it gave the vote to an expanded electorate of almost six million men. At the same time, trade union membership was growing rapidly, while what was termed the 'new unionism' emerged, capturing a broader range of workers such as those in the docks, railways, transport and mines. By 1892, over a million and a half workers were members of a trade union.

These new unions were significantly more radical than their older artisan counterparts and began to reshape industrial relations in high-profile battles. In 1888, a thousand women and young girls employed at the Bryant and May match factory in East London walked out over grievances relating to desperately poor conditions. Weeks later, they returned to work victorious.

This was a stunning victory for organised labour, and one that helped inspire the London Dock Strike of 1889 which brought the most important port in the world to a standstill over demands for guaranteed minimum working hours and better pay. Dubbed the 'Dockers' Tanner', it won a deal of six pence an hour, and it had an electrifying effect, encouraging thousands of low-paid workers to join the trade union movement.

The industrial struggles did not always have such positive outcomes. The thousands of textile workers at Manningham Mills in Bradford, who walked out in 1891 to avert a 30 per cent reduction in their wages, were almost starved into submission in a five-month-long bitter dispute. During it, soldiers and the police were brought onto the streets with Liberal and Tory support.

It was an era when around 80 per cent of the adult population were manual workers, and the trade unions at this stage still supported the Liberals as the best means of gaining parliamentary representation. Although a small group of around a dozen working-class MPs known as Lib-Labs were backed by the unions, they took the Liberal whip while remaining free to speak out on labour issues.

As a result, there was a clear need for a political organisation which stood up for the rights and concerns of working people. The first major step towards that goal was taken in 1893, with the founding of the Independent Labour Party (ILP). Hardly a party in the traditional sense, it was a loose grouping that advocated for the working classes among the trade unions.

The establishment of the ILP changed the political dynamic, as it provided candidates, a new political direction, focused more clearly on the interests of the working class, and personnel – most prominently Keir Hardie and Ramsay MacDonald. It was one example of a growing sense among trade unionists and socialists that there were limits on the power of Liberalism to speak for the most oppressed in society.

Prompted by the Trades Union Congress, the Labour Representation Committee (LRC) was formed in February 1900. Even so, this did not yet represent a break with the Liberals. While it was to be 'a distinct Labour group in Parliament who should have their own whips, and agree upon their policy', as Keir Hardie's successful motion at the LRC's formation pointed out, it was necessary to 'embrace a readiness to cooperate with any party which for the time being may be engaged in promoting legislation in the direct interest of labour'.[4]

Hardie's stance in retaining ties with the Liberal Party was no accident: three of the men who would go on to lead Labour – MacDonald, George Lansbury and Arthur Henderson – had either worked for the Liberals or been members of the party, and those links would endure.

Chapter 2

1900 – The Khaki Two

'The object of these measures is to enable . . .
the Complete Emancipation of labour
from the Domination of Capitalism.'[1]

Labour Representation Committee manifesto

Seven months after the Labour Representation Committee was formed, it was faced with fighting a general election called by the veteran Conservative prime minister Lord Salisbury to capitalise on the major issue dominating politics at the time – the Boer War. Now largely forgotten, the conflict was fought against the two South African 'Boer' Republics, which resisted the British Empire's attempts to access gold mines and to incorporate them into a single British-ruled South African territory.

Though at the time Salisbury called the election it was thought the war was all but won, it would continue sporadically for another two years. In holding what came to be known as the Khaki Election (for the colour of the new British Army uniforms), the government hoped to benefit from a feeling of patriotic and pro-Imperial pride which dominated all classes.

With their main opponents, the Liberal Party, split internally over the war, the result was a landslide victory for the Conservative government, which won a 134-seat majority. They were backed by their Liberal Unionist allies, a faction which supported the war and opposed Irish Home Rule, a policy the mainstream Liberals strongly supported in the late nineteenth century.

For one rather straightforward reason the LRC could not win the election of 1900: it fielded only 15 candidates. Among these were Ramsay MacDonald, Philip Snowden and Fred Jowett, all of whom would play prominent roles in the coming years.

The more important point was that this new group, with its aim of securing greater political representation for advancing the interests of the working class, had taken part in the election and had done so with a degree of success.

The poll of 1900 would be a testbed for whether the LRC had any chance of unifying and representing all those factions which had sent delegates from across the country to its founding conference in London the previous February. The attendees had come not only from numerous unions, but also from the Independent Labour Party, the Social Democratic Federation and the Fabian Society.

As the *Guardian* put it at the time, the LRC existed to secure 'the return of a much larger number of members of Parliament in sympathy with the labour cause and prepared consistently and persistently to advocate it in that assembly'.[2] To this end the LRC had an elected executive committee whose primary duty was to collect information about candidates and prospective candidates who were sufficiently aligned with its beliefs and could be given the support of the labour movement in an election.

This remained an embryonic endeavour in 1900, one with limited funds provided by unions and affiliated societies and a skeletal organisational structure. It was said that 'the LRC could do no more for candidates than provide a small supply of leaflets and its best wishes' – making it all the more remarkable that two of these men were returned to parliament.[3]

The new LRC MPs were Keir Hardie, who won at Merthyr Tydfil, and Richard Bell at Derby. As Bell soon drifted wholly into the embrace of the Liberals, Hardie was essentially the only genuine LRC Member of the Commons. Both had triumphed in 'Double Member' constituencies, where voters could cast two votes, and in both Derby and Merthyr many split their ballots between LRC and Liberal candidates.

Hardie himself still viewed the LRC as nothing more than a pressure group for the rights of workers, rather than a fledgling party with its own set of policies. Indeed, in this election eight Lib-Lab MPs – who had the financial backing of trade unions but effectively took the Liberal whip – were also returned and this blurred the idea that the LRC was the only authentic voice of workers in the Commons.

Quite how the LRC had managed to gain two seats was a question Hardie had asked himself, writing 'how was it done? I don't know. My first clear recollection of anything is of scurrying across the station at Merthyr with a pork pie in one hand and a cup of tea in the other'.[4]

Having spent only a few hours in the South Wales constituency prior to the election, concentrating more on Preston where he was also standing, Hardie was met as though an old friend, not least for his strong anti-war views which chimed with those of the large Welsh mining community.

The *South Wales Daily Post* called Hardie's success 'the greatest possible surprise . . . an astonishing result'.[5] Still, there were obvious explanatory factors, not least the options open to electors in those constituencies, who were able to return two local MPs. In addition, the miners, though not yet affiliated to the LRC, would have known of Hardie's long-standing links to trade unions and his advocacy of better wages, improved conditions and voting rights.

Especially in an era of growing class consciousness, he was a good fit for Merthyr, though his return to the Commons – having been an independent Labour MP for West Ham South between 1892 and 1895

– was recorded without fanfare. The significant exception to this was the *Labour Leader*, a newspaper which Hardie himself edited. It reflected that in Hardie 'the party has absolute confidence', as someone who had 'never failed or faltered in his duty to the movement'.[6]

Ramsay MacDonald, writing as secretary, felt that the startling progress which had been made was due to the existence of the LRC as a focus for all sections of the labour movement, as well as the policies set out in the one-page manifesto which the committee had offered to voters.

This short document reflects wider themes relating to the Boer conflict. It contained pledges to abolish the standing army and allow the people to decide on issues of war and peace. There was also a commitment which would allow 'Legislative Independence for all parts of the Empire', plus the 'Nationalisation of Land and Railways', 'Better Houses' and 'Useful Work for the Unemployed'.[7]

These policies demonstrate the LRC's roots in liberalism, in the concerns over war and social improvements, but also highlight the differences – for instance, the LRC's stated aim that the means of production should be in the hands of the people. Though this was impractical in 1900, such an ambition demonstrated that the LRC could act as a focal point for labour in Parliament.

A year later the Law Lords upheld a judgment that unions could be sued and made to pay costs incurred by an employer during a strike. This 'Taff Vale' judgment is still spoken of today as a byword for any concerted threat to legitimate industrial action, and at the time it made strikes all but impossible.

The ruling concerned the short but bitterly fought dispute in which the Taff Vale Railway Company in South Wales took the Amalgamated Society of Railway Servants union to court and won a large sum in damages and costs. The judgment made the larger trade union movement realise that a strong presence in parliament was vital if they were to overturn Taff Vale and defend their rights more generally.

The Trades Union Congress (TUC) now began working towards an arrangement uniting the Labour Representation Committee and other socialist bodies so that they would jointly endorse parliamentary candidates at future elections. They were pushing at an open door, as the LRC had already given a taste of the power workers could hold in the Commons through MPs representing their interests.

1900 General Election Result

Date of Election – 28 September–4 October

Overall Turnout – 75.1%

Labour

Candidates – 15

MPs – 2

Votes – 62,698

Percentage share of the vote – 1.3%

Result – Conservative and Liberal Unionist majority

Highlight – This was nicknamed the Khaki election at the end of the Boer War, reflecting the new colour of British Army uniforms.

Chapter 3

1906 – A New Party in Parliament

'Organised labour as a political force
is already a menace to the easy-going
gentlemen of the old school . . .'[1]

Labour Conference report 1906.

The general election of 1906 is remembered as a great victory for the Liberal Party after long years of Conservative domination, but in the long term it was the accelerated progress of the LRC which would prove to be more significant.

Even at the time, journalists and politicians noted that the Liberal landslide had come about through a unique set of circumstances on which the party could not rely in future elections. While *The Times* made the case that the Conservatives (or Unionists as then known) still had a bright future, others did the same for Labour. Both sides predicted the demise of the Liberals, Keir Hardie himself declaring that it was 'obvious to everyone who took the slightest interest in public affairs that the old two-party system [was] breaking up'.[2] Hardie had good grounds for his comments, not least that 29 out of 50 LRC candidates had been successful in the election, a sensational improvement on the showing just six years earlier.

The issue which defined the election and dominated the politics of the period more generally was the question of protectionism versus free trade. Although it may seem a dry subject today, it was then a matter of huge concern, touching on the Empire, the functioning of the economy, taxation and the alleviation of poverty.

The principal idea behind protectionism was to place tariffs on imported goods, and so shield industry and agriculture while boosting the trading power of the British Empire as a single economic bloc. It was an argument that divided the Conservative Party, while Liberals were united in their desire for free trade as the best means of keeping prices stable and ensuring economic growth.

A minority Liberal government had taken office in December 1905 without an election, the Tory prime minister Arthur Balfour ceding power in the face of a divided party and a government all but paralysed over the proposed imposition of tariffs, a policy which he cautiously supported.

It may be strange that a prime minister should simply give up the seals of office, but Balfour had his reasons. Though his own government had been weakened over a controversial new Education Act and his long-running attempts to please both the Free Traders and pro-tariff figures in his party such as Joseph Chamberlain, Balfour felt that the Liberals faced greater problems.

He gambled that the formation of a Liberal government would highlight all their old factions and disagreements, particularly over Irish Home Rule. In the forthcoming election the voters would see these weaknesses, he hoped, and again turn to the Conservatives.

As a strategy, this turned out to be a grave miscalculation. Balfour had overlooked the core belief in free trade shared by all Liberals, including many of the Liberal Unionists, the Tories' allies in government. The Liberals were quickly able to form a stable Cabinet led by Henry Campbell-Bannerman, and shortly afterwards he called an early general election.

It was held over a four-week period from January to early February, the Liberals pushed a consistent pro-free trade message, crystallised in their 'Big Loaf, Small Loaf' campaign (which pressed their point that trade tariffs would cause prices to rise and so workers would only be able to afford a 'small loaf'). It was not a policy unique to them: free trade and cheap and plentiful food for the British working classes were just as important to the LRC, a point stressed in the party's manifesto, which described protectionism as a 'red herring' and 'no remedy for poverty and unemployment'.[3]

The LRC manifesto, an appeal made in the name of a million trade unionists, did not represent a full-throated socialist programme and was not vastly different to its Liberal counterpart. There were LRC commitments to tackle unemployment, the slums, neglect of the poor and the aged and creating better schools, but there was no call for widespread nationalisation nor any great attack on capitalism. The most pressing matter was that labour be properly represented in Parliament and this – rather than free trade – was by some distance the issue most often mentioned by LRC candidates. It was noted, moreover, that speeches made by senior LRC figures, including Ramsay MacDonald, could just as well have been made in the name of Campbell-Bannerman.

The lack of radicalism in the manifesto, milder in its calls for reform even than its counterpart of 1900, suited both the Liberals and the LRC given that the two parties had forged a mutually beneficial electoral agreement which would in effect see them jointly take on the Conservatives. This pact had been agreed early in 1903 at the top of each party and was not widely known outside leadership circles. The Liberals hoped by working with the LRC they might be able to keep labourism under the Liberal banner.

There was also the not insignificant matter of the £100,000 election fund the LRC had amassed from the unions, which dwarfed the sum held in the Liberal coffers. By 1905, almost 160 unions, with a membership of over 900,000 workers, had affiliated and quickly made the LRC the strongest political body in the country. Unsurprisingly the Liberals saw the value in a united front, believing that many working men who voted Tory could be persuaded to switch to the LRC, but not to Liberal candidates, who were seen as representing establishment interests.

It was Herbert Gladstone, the Liberal chief whip, and MacDonald, as LRC secretary, who brokered the agreement. MacDonald knew that the LRC was powerful only on paper at this stage, and that it had little chance of making major strides against candidates from the two big parties. The negotiations between the two men yielded a free run for the LRC in up to 50 seats in double-member constituencies, mainly held by Tories and located in and around Birmingham, Lancashire, London and the South, plus parts of Wales and the West Riding of Yorkshire.

MacDonald ensured that the selection of candidates was controlled from the centre by the ruling National Executive Committee, which led to a candidate body which was not overtly radically socialist. Meanwhile, Liberal leaders leaned on local parties to halt any opposition to LRC candidates who supported 'the general objects of the Liberal Party', while the LRC was to 'demonstrate friendliness' to Liberal candidates in seats where they were likely to win.[4]

Though advantageous to both sides, MacDonald clearly got the better of the deal. While the Liberals won the election and emerged into the 'blissful dawn' of a 128-seat majority over all other parties the LRC secured a much-enhanced group of MPs and an average of 37 per cent of the vote in these constituencies.[5]

While Hardie was returned at Merthyr, he was now joined in Parliament by those who would be important figures in the party in the years to come, among them MacDonald (Leicester), Arthur Henderson (Barnard Castle) and Philip Snowden (Blackburn).

A few days after the election result, the LRC MPs met for the first time in Parliament. The minutes of that gathering, in MacDonald's handwriting, show that the decision was taken to rename the organisation as the Labour Party. Officers and whips were appointed, a room was secured for the party's exclusive use and weekly meetings were scheduled. Perhaps most notable was the decision to sit on the Opposition side of the Commons, rather than with the Liberals on the Government side.

The Labour Party also elected a chairman, or leader. At first Hardie had appeared reluctant to run, stressing that he saw himself as a pioneer rather than a leader. Eventually, though, he allowed himself to be nominated and on a show of hands was tied with David Shackleton, a trade unionist who would go on to become a leading civil servant.

It was only when a formal ballot was held that Hardie emerged victorious – 15–14 – after the two candidates and MacDonald had cast their votes. By a whisker the newly named party had chosen as its first leader someone who was identifiably a socialist.

Even so, it remained unclear whether Labour – a broad coalition of trade unionists, reformers and revolutionaries – would be the gravediggers or the handmaidens of the Liberal Party. David Lloyd George, then president of the Board of Trade, said he believed working-class voters would stick with the Liberals if they were bold enough to embark on a programme of steady social reform.

Labour had flourished at the ballot box because of the pact with the Liberals, but at the same time it was striving for independence. As Snowden put it, the future was about seeing Labour 'strengthened to the extent of dominating if not directing the Government of the country'.[6]

1906 General Election Result

Date of Election – 12 January–7 February

Overall Turnout – 83.2%

Labour

Candidates – 51

MPs – 29

Votes – 329,748

Percentage share of the vote – 5.9%

Result – Liberal landslide

Highlight – This marked the last of the Liberal landslides, while Labour for the first time won large financial backing from the trade unions.

Chapter 4

1910 (January) – Does Labour Count?

'The hopeless condition of the Tory Party is one of the most remarkable features of present-day politics'.[1]

Arthur Henderson

The election of January 1910 is best remembered for the major constitutional crisis which was then enveloping Parliament and the monarchy. Yet it was Labour's threat to Liberal Party dominance that was the catalyst for the entire drama.

The Budget of 1909 was the trigger: having been passed by the Commons in April, it was then blocked by the House of Lords. Known as 'the People's Budget' the aim, as Chancellor David Lloyd George said, was 'raising money to wage implacable warfare against poverty and squalidness'.[2]

Lloyd George had often spoken out about the condition of the poor. Now, he warned that if the Liberals failed to act 'a new cry will arise for a land with a new party, and many of us will join that cry'.[3] It was a barely disguised warning of the emerging threat from Labour as the representatives of working people.

At this time the unelected Upper House was far from the revising chamber of today. The Lords saw themselves as being on a par with the Commons and were prepared to stand in the way of proposed Liberal reforms, either greatly modifying or sinking bills on education, the voting system, agriculture and rent reform in Ireland.

The peers had been outraged at Lloyd George's proposed budgetary measures – among them an increase in inheritance tax (25 per cent on estates over £1 million), hikes in income tax, a new super-tax on annual income over £5,000 and taxes at 20 per cent on income from the sale of land. Those most threatened by these measures, the very richest in society, turned to the Lords, with its inbuilt Conservative majority, to defend their wealth.

Today, finance Bills move through both Houses of Parliament without much fuss, but in 1909 the Budget was debated almost continuously, taking up nearly 75 days of Commons business before being passed by MPs in late November. It was then overwhelmingly rejected in the Lords.

On the 2nd of December the government won a vote stating that the peers had committed 'a breach of the Constitution and a usurpation of the rights of the Commons'.[4] In effect, the Lords had not only rejected the Budget but brought about a general election which would end up reshaping the structures of British politics.

Long planned by Liberal ministers, the election was held from the 15 January to the 10 February. Labour's pitch to the country – 'The Lords must go' – was unequivocal in its demand for democratic change. The question at hand, Labour said, was 'whether the Peers or the people are to rule this country'.[5]

It was no surprise to political observers that Labour supported the Liberals over such a crucial issue. The two parties had worked together in the election of 1906 via an electoral pact and the arrangement remained in place in 1910. The Liberals had also been as good as their word over a key issue for Labour. The 1906 Trades

Disputes Act, for which Labour MPs had lobbied the Liberal government hard, had reversed the 1901 Taff Vale decision stipulating that a union would be liable for costs and damages during a strike. It was an important victory, and one which maintained good relations between the parties.

The Lords did not involve themselves in this legislation, but in 1909 they upheld another landmark legal ruling, one which directly hampered not only the unions but Labour. The so-called Osborne Judgement concluded that there was nothing in law to suggest unions had any right of 'collecting and administering funds for political purposes'.[6] Outraged by this attack on their ability to fund themselves, it is little wonder that the Labour Party fell in behind the Liberals in taking on the powers of the Lords.

The election was called, Prime Minister Herbert Asquith said, to alleviate a 'momentous crisis', in which the Lords vetoed legislation when there was a Liberal government, but did not act likewise under the Tories. Getting to the heart of the matter, he added 'the claim of the House of Lords to control finance is novel, and a mere usurpation'.[7]

Over 1,300 candidates took part, battling for 670 seats, voted on by an electorate of seven and a half million men aged over 21 years. Labour fielded almost 80 candidates, the vast majority in single-member constituencies, under the cautious leadership of Arthur Henderson.

Again, it was impossible to win the election outright. Henderson's hope was for measured progress. It may seem odd that Labour went into the campaign with 45 MPs, having won 29 seats in the 1906 election. The simple reason for this was that in 1908 the hugely powerful Miners' Federation affiliated to the party allowing the Lib-Lab MPs sponsored by that union to take the Labour whip.

While Labour and the Liberals' approach broadly overlapped, on housing, unemployment, taxation and more, the issue of the Lords' behaviour was the key feature of the campaign. Here, backed in print by the Miners' and ILP manifestos, Labour was alone in calling not merely for reform, but abolition of the unelected second chamber.

The outcome of the election was a near dead heat. The Liberal Party had a total of 274 MPs, with their Conservative (and Liberal Unionist) opponents just two seats shy of that tally. This was a disappointment for both the big parties – the Liberal gains four years earlier had been wiped away, while the Tories had failed to return to office despite winning the popular vote.

The Conservatives' strong polling may seem surprising given that the other parties were defending the rights of the people against abuse of privilege, but the Tory warnings that Asquith's party and their allies were set on destroying the constitution by abolishing the Lords, in what amounted to a revolution, proved effective. Moreover, it is often overlooked that at the previous election the Conservatives had polled 43 per cent and were only undone by their divisions over trade. In short, the Tories remained a strong political force in the country, especially among the middle classes.

Labour and the Irish Parliamentary Party, with 71 seats, would ensure the Liberals remained in power. At the suggestion of the Commons' Speaker, the Labour MPs even crossed the floor to sit on the government side – although this was done to accommodate the different party groupings, not all of whom could sit on the opposition benches.

Labour lost eight seats and gained three in that January election, emerging with a total of 40 MPs. The votes came mainly from industrial areas with 120,000 votes in Lancashire and substantial support in the Midlands, Yorkshire, Durham, South Wales, Scotland and London.

Labour's performance in January 1910 can be read either as steady progress or simply treading water. It was, though, a poll held in highly unusual circumstances in which voters were being asked to judge the parliamentary system and British democracy itself.

Still a small party, it is noteworthy that Labour polled half a million votes – a solid increase on the 323,000 four years earlier. Labour had already come a long way since 1900, in terms of support and seats in the Commons, but the party remained somewhat under the wing of the Liberals. While this had been helpful in its first elections, it raised questions about Labour's long-term future as an independent political entity.

Keir Hardie himself remarked that the Party 'had almost ceased to count'.[8] The coming years would tell whether this was fair comment or not.

January 1910 General Election Result

Date of Election – 14 January–9 February

Overall Turnout – 86.8%

Labour

Candidates – 78

MPs – 40

Votes – 505,657

Percentage share of the vote – 7.6%

Result – Liberal minority government

Highlight – The House of Lords triggers a constitutional crisis and general election by rejecting the 'People's Budget'.

Chapter 5

1910 (December) – Labour Clears the Way

'Parliament has become the field upon which the great battles between capital and labour are to be fought'[1]

Labour Party leaflet

Labour's immediate task following the election of January 1910 was to support the minority Liberal government to enact the constitutional changes which would reform the House of Lords. This was the issue on which the second election of the year would be fought.

The Lords passed the People's Budget in April 1910 after the January election had given a popular mandate to the finance measures already agreed by the Commons. Yet that was not the end of the matter, as the Liberals then introduced a new Parliament Bill to curb the power of the second chamber once and for all.

Under its terms, the power of peers to block Finance Bills would be removed, and they would be able only to delay the passage of other legislation. The Lords in turn resisted, sparking a renewed crisis setting the unelected House of Parliament once more against the Commons' members sent directly by the people.

Herbert Asquith's Liberal government had already planned for this eventuality and proposed to create hundreds of new Liberal lords to guarantee a progressive majority in the Upper House. As the chancellor, David Lloyd George, put it 'we repudiate the claim put forward by 600 Tory Peers that they were born to control the destinies of 45,000,000 of their fellow citizens.'[2]

This was unprecedented. For the new Lords to be created en masse, the government required the active support of the Crown and the king, George V, who had been on the throne only a matter of months, was reluctant to give his consent. Faced with Asquith's threat of resignation, he relented, but there remained the problem of getting the Parliament Act through the Commons without a commanding majority. So, on 28 November, the prime minister was granted a dissolution of Parliament, meaning the second election of the year would take place over two weeks from early December.

The parties, Labour included, had been planning for this. In the aftermath of the January poll Ramsay MacDonald had written – 'we ought to assume . . . that a general election will be forced upon us almost at once and we ought to keep a very watchful eye upon the trend of events.'[3]

As in the previous election, Labour supported the overall Liberal position on the reform of the Lords, while taking a distinctly more radical line. The central message of its election posters was 'Labour Clears The Way', with images of the House of Lords being demolished by determined-looking shirt-sleeved men.

The party's manifesto repeated the call made in January that 'the Lords Must Go', telling the voters 'you are again being asked to return a majority pledged to remove the House of Lords as a block in the working of our Constitution. Do it, and do it emphatically'.[4]

The manifesto also included calls to deal with poverty and for MPs to be paid, a measure which would greatly help working-class men. Labour, led by the Scottish engineer George Barnes, also campaigned to reverse the Osborne Judgement, which prevented unions from using money for political ends.

This was already having an effect. Even the strongest local party branches like Manchester and Leeds were badly hit and, in some areas, they collapsed or were mothballed. Labour chose to run just 56 candidates at the December election, 22 fewer than in January. The best available strategy was to concentrate resources in seats already held, and particularly those where a strong vote had previously been recorded.

The wider question for Labour's leadership was its continued Liberal embrace. This troubled many, not only on Labour's socialist wing, but the immediate political reality was that, though the Liberals had been helped by Labour votes in the two previous elections, the Parliamentary Labour Party had clearly benefited still more from the tacit alliance. The Liberals in turn continued to see Labour as a junior partner, and in his election address (the manifesto) Asquith did not trouble himself even to mention them.

The Tories' message was striking by contrast. Their leader, Arthur Balfour, felt that Liberalism had been forced into its position against the Lords by 'their Socialist and [Irish] Nationalist allies' and that 'behind the Single Chamber conspiracy lurk Socialism and Home Rule'.[5]

The Conservatives were beginning to find their voice in attacking Labour, and would not have done so unless they thought there were votes to be won. It would be to no avail: across the two elections of 1910 Labour won 77 of 92 straight fights with the Tories and hardly any when a Liberal was on the ballot paper.

The Liberals again won the election in December, but only by a single seat, finishing with 272 MPs. It is not a result fondly remembered by any of the parties, having failed to shift the dial greatly from the position in January.

Labour's campaign was a success, but a qualified one. The party gained five seats and lost three, a net gain of two taking its total in the Commons to 42 MPs. Woolwich was won again by Will Crooks,

Bow and Bromley by George Lansbury, who triumphed after missing out in January, and Western Fife was won by William Adamson. The new Parliament also saw the party elect MacDonald, the long-serving secretary, as chairman in place of Barnes.

While the Osborne Judgement and relations with the Liberals would continue to create tensions inside Labour, with socialists and syndicalist union radicals worrying that the party was too timid and reformist, the party had now established itself as an important presence in Parliament. Liberalism had not simply melted away as some had hoped, but the Labour Party had clearly made great strides since its formation just ten years earlier.

1910 – General Election (December) – Result

Date of Election – 2 December–19 December

Overall Turnout – 81.6%

Labour

Candidates – 56

MPs – 42

Votes – 371,772

Percentage share of the vote – 6.4%

Result – Liberal minority

Highlight – Labour calls for the abolition of the House of Lords.

Chapter 6

1918 – Everything Changes

'The war has advanced state
socialism by half a century'

J. A. Hobson[1]

The 1918 election came at the end of the four years of the Great War, a vast collective trauma in which death touched every community in Britain. In a period of great pressure for Parliament and government, there were many significant changes, not least for the Labour Party.

An election had been due to take place in 1916, but it was postponed until the cessation of hostilities with Germany. Yet politics was not mothballed during the conflict, with matters continuing along party lines until May 1915. After that the Liberal government, headed by Herbert Asquith, came under intense pressure over the prosecution of the war, both on the Western Front and in the disastrous attempt to take the Dardanelles, a narrow strip of water off what is now Turkey.

As a result, the Tories demanded a coalition be formed. Into this new ministry came the Conservative leader, Andrew Bonar Law, and others from his party. So too did Arthur Henderson, once more leader of the Labour Party, and two more Labour men in junior government posts.

This placed Labour at the heart of the British political establishment for the first time. The party was hugely important in the wartime crisis: it had an affiliated membership of close to two million workers and the backing of 130 trade unions, all of which were vital to the war effort.

Though Henderson, a solid trade unionist, was seen as a safe pair of hands, Labour had its own internal divisions, which had been intensified by the conflict. The right of the party vocally supported Britain's involvement in the war; the left opposed not just this, but also the so-called 'fight to the finish' doctrine which had become mainstream.

The anti-war faction, which had its roots in the ILP group, was led by two great Labour stars: Ramsay MacDonald, who resigned as leader when the conflict began; and Keir Hardie. The intensity of feeling against those opposing hostilities with Germany led to MacDonald receiving much abuse, including letters addressed to 'Herr MacDonald'.

However, the prolonged nature of the conflict began to change minds. Henderson, who had previously said he was not in the Cabinet to please himself but 'to see the war through', resigned from the government –and by extension from the party leadership – in August 1917 over what he felt to be the hampering of efforts to reach an international peace settlement.[2]

His considerable energies were now focused on ending the war by advocating for a League of Nations and other levers for mediation in international disputes before they ran to conflict. Known as the Memorandum on War Aims it influenced not only British political leaders, but also the US president, Woodrow Wilson.

At the same time, Henderson pushed through the drafting of a new Labour constitution, at the heart of which was Clause IV and its commitment to 'secure for the producers by hand or by brain the full fruits of their industry' based on 'the common ownership of the means of production.'[3]

Clause IV was a deliberate strategy aimed to further bind the unions to Labour in the post-war period, but the constitution itself was important in establishing Labour as an independent and genuinely national organisation at the ballot box. Local constituency Labour parties would be created, allowing individuals beyond the trade unions and, notably, women to join. This was to prove a masterstroke, because when the country at last went to the polls in December 1918, the electorate had more than doubled in size since the election eight years previously.

The Representation of the People Act, which became law in February 1918, had extended the franchise to almost nine million women aged over 30 (who were either married or owned property), as well as all men aged 21. This huge shift, part passed to acknowledge the role of women in the war effort, appeared advantageous for Labour with the franchise now reaching much further into the working classes.

The other helpful step for the party was the passing of the Trade Union Act in 1913 which permitted unions again to collect a political levy from members. For Labour this meant a significant and consistent money stream it could devote to political purposes, electioneering and the support of candidates.

Externally too, events proved advantageous to Labour. David Lloyd George replaced Asquith as prime minister in late 1916, in what was effectively a political coup assisted by the Conservatives. Asquith remained Liberal leader but by the time of the election the two were in opposing camps and Liberalism had been decisively split.

By 1918 Labour had also left the coalition government, but only after Henderson and the National Executive demanded the parliamentary party do so. This period also marked a sea change in Labour's electoral strategy with the ending of the pact with the Liberals.

Held on 14 December, little more than a month after the formal armistice with Germany, the general election was the first to take place on a single day across the country. However, counting was not completed until after Christmas so that ballots cast by soldiers could be included.

Though the Coalition seemed to be in a dominant position, Lloyd George had taken no chances. Tory candidates and Coalition Liberals toured their constituencies with a short letter signed by Lloyd George and Bonar Law, the Conservative leader. This endorsed the candidates, signalling they had supported the war, and in so doing appealed to the overwhelming patriotic sentiment of the day. It became known as the 'coupon', and it all but guaranteed the bearer success in what was termed the 'Coupon Election'.

Labour's manifesto was entitled 'Labour's Call to the People', a recognition that much of the expanded electorate shared the party's goals. Its stated aim was to 'build a new world, and to build it by constitutional means [through] a programme of national and international justice'.[4]

Much of the manifesto was designed to further marginalise the Liberal Party. It overtly claimed Labour as the women's party, tied to the Co-operative Movement, which was dominated by women. At home, the focus was on land reform, and a million new houses for workers. On the international front there was the offer of reconstruction and peace, a contrast with the Coalition's determination to make Germany pay for the war. Labour also called for freedom for India as well as Ireland.

Perhaps given the timing, with the onset of the festive season and the end of the war, there was little enthusiasm among the public and only just over half the electorate voted. Together, the Coalition won comfortably, with over 470 seats – two thirds of the Commons. Conservatives again dominated with 332 MPs, though around 50 had not received the coupon and were not formally part of the Coalition. The opposition Asquith Liberals emerged with just 36 seats. Labour's respectable tally of 57 MPs represented a significant rise of 15 from their tally of members in December 1910.

Reflecting the work Henderson had done to remould Labour the party had fielded 388 candidates with just over 700 seats up for grabs. For the first time Labour could be considered a national party, even though outright victory would have required a political earthquake which not even the most faithful supporters believed possible.

Victory takes many forms, however, and the party more than trebled the vote share won at the previous election – scooping close to 2.5 million votes, thanks largely to the size and composition of the new electorate. Another significant step forward was that in 79 other constituencies Labour was second to the winner, ahead of the Liberal candidate.

The downside was that many leading Labour figures lost their seats – Henderson and MacDonald among them, in a reflection of the temperament of the time and the continuing divisions inside Labour about who had, and had not, supported the war. According to the *Book of the Labour Party*, a volume written in 1925, 'the spirit of unity which had gone [into] the building of the party had been ruthlessly shattered' by the war.[5]

None of this halted Labour's growth, with seats won in the Midlands, the North of England, South Wales and Scotland. Home to coal-mining, steelmaking, and manufacturing, these industrial heartlands, many cutting across urban areas, were becoming Labour's long-term powerbase.

The day-to-day working of the new Commons would crucially turn on Ireland. The old Irish Parliamentary Party, nationalists in favour of some form of home rule, were swept away by Sinn Féin and their demand for a full independent republic. Only two years earlier just such a republic had been proclaimed during the Easter Rising in Dublin, only to be snuffed out by British troops.

Led by Éamon de Valera, Sinn Féin, had fought the election on a pledge that his party would not take their seats in the Commons. They were as good as their word and the following month, in January 1919, formed a breakaway government in Dublin and declared independence.

Though it was never likely, had Sinn Féin with 73 seats decided to participate at Westminster, they would have been the biggest individual opposition group. The next largest caucus of MPs belonged to Labour, but the party did not assert that its chairman, William Adamson, should be regarded as leader of the opposition.

This position was instead taken by the independent Asquithian Liberals, though conventions around the role of the opposition were not as established as they are today. What was apparent was that Labour would be central in holding the government to account, confirming the speed of the party's advance from the political fringes in 1900.

One of the lessons of 1918 is that events shape elections and voters. In this case war in Europe was the principal factor. The Conservatives and Lloyd George Liberals were able to coalesce on their coupon offer of continuity, something which also chimed with the victorious national mood.

Though it may not have seemed so at the time Labour had the advantage of having left the coalition and offering a distinct programme to voters. It could do so confident that there was good reason, with the extended franchise and thirst for social reform, to believe the electoral tide was moving in their direction.

Having had candidates up and down the country, Labour was able to make an honest claim to be a potential party of power, rather than one sheltered by Liberalism. Leading Liberal figures, including Lloyd George, began to see the rise of Labour as almost inevitable. The split in the Liberal Party sapped Liberalism as a political force, robbing it of its cohesion, but opening the way for Labour to emerge as the dominant opposition to the Tories.

Though taken for granted today the reforms carried out by Henderson were crucial in providing a solid organisation for Labour and they would endure, almost untouched, to the present day. This, and the regained freedom of the unions to organise for political purposes meant that 1918 gave Labour a fertile base on which the party could grow in the coming years.

1918 General Election Result

Date of Election – 14 December

Overall Turnout 1918 – 57.2%

Labour

Candidates – 388

MPs – 57

Votes – 2,383,472

Percentage share of the vote – 22.2%

Result – Coalition victory

Highlight – Some women over the age of 30 get the vote and the first woman – Constance Markievicz –is elected to the Commons.

Chapter 7

1922 – Unrest and Development

'The workers are entitled to a better Britain
than they lived in before the war'.[1]

J. R. Clynes

Labour's development accelerated across the four general elections of the 1920s with the party emerging as the main opposition to the Conservatives, and then twice dramatically coming to power.

This seemed hardly possible in the period immediately after the 1918 election. Though Labour had improved its standing in the Commons with 57 MPs, the party had lost some star names, including Ramsay MacDonald, Arthur Henderson and George Lansbury.

In their absence the party was led by William Adamson, who was harshly described by the sharp-tongued Beatrice Webb as 'respectable but dull witted', and then John Robert (J. R.) Clynes, a mill worker from Lancashire.[2]

Their stewardship gave hope that further advancement might be possible. As memories of war faded, so too did Labour's divisions over the conflict, and there were signs the country was beginning to tire of the political arrangements which had taken it through wartime and the immediate post-war period.

This was just as well because these years saw a huge number of parliamentary by-elections, over 100 in total. Labour did not run candidates in all of them, but won notable victories, in 1919 at Bothwell, Spen Valley and Widnes, the last of which returned Henderson to the

Commons. There was more success the following year at Dartford and South Norfolk, with five more gains in 1921 and four across 1922.

Labour went into the general election of that year with 75 MPs and a party organisation which was working efficiently. There was now not only a full-time national organiser overseeing campaigning and elections but also a national organiser for women, though individual membership among women remained disappointingly low in places.

The party also aimed to have a full-time parliamentary agent in each constituency and a new structure, one still recognisable today, had been put in place from 1919. Under this, Labour split the country across nine regional districts such as North-Eastern, Midlands, London, Scotland, and Wales. In 1918, there were 215 local parties in operation, but by the time of the 1922 election this figure was over 500.

Labour's opponents looked upon these developments and viewed a party which seemed to be both expanding quickly and highly efficient. The other parties were also well aware of Labour's increasing potential, with its strong working-class support in large areas of the country.

Labour's leaders, whatever their private views, also portrayed themselves as responsible rather than revolutionary; their commitment was to reformist, gradual change, albeit it through state socialism.

It was a balance they needed to strike to capture still more of the electorate. There was reason to tread warily with the Bolshevik revolution, the overthrowing of the monarchy and the civil war that followed gripping Russia in the years from 1917. Under the heading 'Against Revolution', the party's 1922 manifesto stated that 'Labour's policy is to bring about a more equitable distribution of the nation's wealth by constitutional means. This is neither Bolshevism nor Communism, but common sense and justice. This is Labour's alternative to Reaction and Revolution'.[3]

This positioning was clever, as it allowed the party to remain true to the stated socialist aims of Clause IV, while appearing moderate at home and over foreign policy. For similar reasons, Labour blocked bids by the Communist Party of Great Britain to affiliate. That organisation, it was concluded, did not align with Labour's 'constitution, principles and programme'.[4]

Economic conditions in this period meant that the focus of the party and wider movement turned to industrial affairs. The boom of immediate post-war had quickly turned to a pronounced slump with rising inflation and unemployment standing at two million by 1922. Those in need of work protested – 'wanted in 1914 – not wanted now'.[5]

With an overall membership close to eight million workers by 1920 the unions, and in particular the miners, the largest industrial force in the country, were at the forefront of a wave of unrest. Their strength was further enhanced by membership of the Triple Alliance, alongside the railway and transport workers. Inactive during the war, this formidable bloc began working once again in concert, mainly to prevent wage reductions.

The mines and the railways had been in public hands during the years of conflict, but with the price of coal tumbling by 1921 the prime minister, Lloyd George, handed mining back to private owners to avoid having to implement a cut in wages.

In response, the Triple Alliance called a strike which had the power to bring the country to a virtual standstill. Labour's position in supporting the Triple Alliance and the miners and calling for the nationalisation of the mines and the railway matched that of an electorate that was largely sympathetic to the need to build a better society after the horrors of war. But after the government declared a state of emergency in April 1921, the unions pulled back at the last minute amid confusion and recriminations, on what became known as 'Black Friday'.

The other significant policy headache for the coalition government was ensuring the stability of Germany, a matter which dominated foreign policy long after 1918. As a result, Lloyd George was often abroad trying to dampen potential conflicts over territorial disputes. At the time the possibility of again sliding into war seemed very real.

However, in the autumn of 1922, the ground beneath the PM's feet gave way. Conservative MPs, weary of a growing scandal over honours given to the prime minister's friends and party funders, brought an end to the coalition government. Andrew Bonar Law became prime minister at the head of what was solely a Conservative administration. Soon after, he called a general election for 15 November.

Bonar Law received the mandate from the country he had hoped for, with 344 Tory MPs returned, an overall majority in the House of 73. Bonar Law's simple pitch to the nation was for 'tranquillity and stability both at home and abroad', in essence meaning peace and lower taxes.[6]

While the overall outcome of the 1922 election had not been a surprise, it was Labour's performance which caught the eye, with the party winning over four million votes – almost double that of the previous election. This surge led to gains in London and well beyond, with three seats in Derbyshire, five across Country Durham, seven in Wales and almost 20 in Scotland.

Labour now had a total of 142 MPs, winning a shade under 30 per cent of the vote. The Liberals, deeply divided between the Lloyd George and Asquith factions, failed collectively to surpass either Labour's number of seats or votes. Among Labour's MPs were 32 who had been elected on an ILP ticket, which included a militant contingent from Clydeside, quickly dubbed the 'wild men'.

Labour's upsurge was not only due to the Liberals' continuing difficulties. Since 1918, Labour had carved out a political space by being critical of the harsh peace terms imposed on Germany and warning about a growing militarism which could lead back to war, as well as highlighting the ongoing British brutality in Ireland.

In addition, after the Great War socialism was seen as the way forward by many people well beyond the working classes. The growing demands from the voters were around housing, social welfare, ownership of key industries and collective international security. Much of this formed the basis of what Labour would strive for in the decades to come.

The party began to draw not only Liberals but also Tories into its ranks. These included Stafford Cripps and Hugh Dalton, both of whom would be future stars, as well as a certain Clement Attlee. The changing face of Labour in Parliament was clear in 1922, with nine public schoolboys and more than twenty university graduates in its parliamentary ranks.

None of this had happened in isolation. As well as improving in organisation and winning by-election victories, Labour had also begun to make gains in local government, taking more than 400 seats in the 1919 local elections, and winning control of several councils. Its lack of reach in rural areas, however, remained a problem.

The general election of 1922 was not a victory for Labour, but it was a breakthrough. With the relegation of the Liberals to third place Labour was now tasked with providing the official opposition to a Conservative Party which enjoyed a comfortable majority.

While this was a challenge, it also opened up a new era of responsibility. Although it was not clear at the time, the election result was a staging post on Labour's path to power.

1922 General Election Result

Date of Election – 15 November

Overall Turnout 1922 – 73.0%

Labour

Candidates – 414

MPs – 142

Votes – 4,237,349

Percentage share of the vote – 29.5%

Result – Conservative victory

Highlight – Labour has almost 150 MPs and becomes the Official Opposition for the first time.

Chapter 8

1923 – 'Fail or Succeed' – Labour in Government

'We stand now at a moment when the sun of England seems menaced with final eclipse'

The English Review[1]

Wealthy new year revellers at top London venues waved goodbye to 1922 in style – 35,000 Christmas crackers were pulled at the Savoy and at the Piccadilly Hotel a female singer popped out of a huge champagne bottle to sing 'Auld Lang Syne'.

Terror would likely have struck the establishment clientele that night if they could have foreseen what was to come. Before 1923 was out an election would be held, bringing about what the Annual Register called 'a revolution in British politics' and ushering in the first Labour government.[2]

The figure who, more than any other, would make this a reality was James Ramsay MacDonald. Returned to the Commons for the South Wales seat of Aberavon in the November 1922 election, he was now a man in a hurry.

Having taken every step of the long march from the Memorial Hall in Farringdon, where Labour was founded in 1900, and endured the trauma of losing his seat in 1918 over his opposition to the First World War, MacDonald made an immediate impact.

When Labour MPs met in the days after the November 1922 election, J. R. Clynes had expected to continue in post, but with the support of the left-leaning Independent Labour Party group MacDonald squeaked home by five votes. Unquestionably, he was the most experienced and effective Parliamentarian in Labour's ranks.

While the party had been growing in strength since the close of the Great War, what they had lacked was a really substantial figure to lead them in Parliament. In the past MacDonald and others had simply been termed 'chairman', and this post revolved on a near yearly basis.

MacDonald was now styled 'chairman and leader', an important distinction. Now in his mid-fifties, he had many gifts as a politician: not only was he highly competent, but he was also blessed with considerable speaking ability, a rich Highland voice and abundant charm.

MacDonald's aim was to show he was a prime minister in waiting and his party ready for office. As he wrote at the time – 'the failure of the Labour party in the last Parliament was that it never was an Opposition, and was never led as an Opposition. It never impressed itself upon the country as an alternative Government'.[3]

He was also not afraid to act decisively, understanding the urgency of the moment as the dust settled on the 1922 election. While it had been customary for the outgoing PM and his party to take the role of Official Opposition, Labour under MacDonald asserted its right to this title as the largest opposition grouping.

Things now moved at pace for Labour's new leader. Bonar Law remained in office only a matter of months, until May 1923 when he was forced to resign, suffering from terminal cancer. He was replaced by Stanley Baldwin, and though the Conservatives had the cushion of a comfortable majority, Baldwin felt he needed to ask for a personal mandate from the electorate.

Baldwin sought to tackle the deep economic ills still stalking the country by deviating from his predecessor's free trade strategy. His plan to fight high unemployment by falling back on protectionism involved the imposition of tariffs, an issue which had haunted the Conservatives in the past.

Baldwin saw the main problem as Britain's over-exposure to competition. The Liberals disagreed, re-stating their absolute belief in free trade and in so doing unifying their splintered party once again, as both Lloyd George and Asquith put their names to the same manifesto.

Labour did much the same, declaring that tariffs 'poison the life of nations, lead to corruption in politics, promote trusts and monopolies, and impoverish the people'.[4] This criticism of profiteering while backing Liberal notions of free trade was typical MacDonald, appearing radical while at the same time swimming in mainstream political currents.

The election was held on 6 December. Crowds in Trafalgar Square cheered and booed declarations as they appeared on the giant *Daily Express* electric ticker tape bulletin. For the first time, it was also possible to hear the results come in at home as they were broadcast nationwide on BBC radio.

It soon became apparent that the country had rejected Baldwin's offer. He lost the Conservatives close to 90 seats, with only 258 Tories returned. The Liberals made substantial gains, rising to 158, but it was Labour who made the greatest progress – 191 candidates were elected, a gain of almost 50 seats on the previous year.

The party and the unions had concentrated funds on defending existing seats, but these were often in areas more generally sympathetic to Labour, and so it was natural that the Labour message, and some financial backing, seeped into nearby constituencies.

As a result, though the party's vote share climbed only slightly, there was an acceleration of gains in parts of the country where Labour already had a foothold – principally mining communities and areas of Scotland from the Clyde to the Forth, and inner and outer London towards Essex and the Midlands.

There were other reasons for Labour's improved showing, including the re-emergence of the *Daily Herald* newspaper (a forerunner of *The Sun*) under the control of the party and the Trades Union Congress. In a sea of Tory press, this gave Labour an impressive daily propaganda tool; the paper at the time boasted circulation figures close to 400,000 a day.

Labour also included in its manifesto a 'Programme of National Work' with what was described as a 'National System' for energy supply, transport, housing, town planning and more.[5] This meant the election was not fought on trade alone, but again on the prospect of building what Lloyd George had at the end of the war famously termed 'a country fit for heroes'.[6]

In foreign affairs Labour promised support for the fledgling League of Nations, and further diplomatic efforts to deal with the still troublesome issue of war reparations. Though not of immediate help at home in terms of filling the bellies of the poor, these were nonetheless important messages warmly received well beyond the party's core vote.

While the policies may have been straightforward, the result of the election was far less so. It was not clear who would govern, given that no single party had won a majority. The divisions between Baldwin and Asquith's parties on the question of trade – the reason for the election in the first place – were widely acknowledged and made any serious proposition of a Conservative–Liberal coalition all but unviable.

So, while few in Labour's ranks had expected to form a government, within days of the election moves were afoot to do so. The party's National Executive Committee and the TUC gave full backing to MacDonald and urged the parliamentary party to be ready to take office on its own.

Yet the Conservatives had the most MPs – almost 70 more than

Labour in second place – and Stanley Baldwin was not yet willing to cede power. He believed it might be possible to continue from a minority position, no doubt motivated in part by avoiding what he saw as the calamitous alternative of Labour in power.

Winston Churchill, then a losing Liberal candidate, warned of 'a serious national misfortunate', likening the prospect of a socialist government to defeat in war, while one Tory MP declared himself ready to lead the troops into the Commons to save the country.[7]

Such comments sparked further hope of a rekindled Tory–Liberal coalition, but in reality this was never likely. Baldwin's government attempted to limp on before being defeated by Labour and the Liberals in a vote on the King's Speech on 21 January 1924.

MacDonald, anticipating that Baldwin would resign the next day and ask the king to send for him, released a late-night statement to reporters. 'It is not a moment for elation,' it read, 'it is a terrible responsibility. We shall have to do our best to face it, fail or succeed.'[8]

The Labour leader grasped the politics of the moment: there was no triumphalism, but instead a simple pledge that his party would try to serve the country honestly. His principal concern was to demonstrate that Labour could govern competently and be trusted to continue doing so.

MacDonald was resolved that Labour should show the country that it was set on the path of respectability rather than revolution. The composition of his Cabinet – wholly upright, entirely male and to some degree not even of the party at all – showed this determination from the outset.

MacDonald was not only prime minister but also foreign secretary. While Philip Snowden was chancellor, Arthur Henderson insisted on the Home Office, Clynes was Leader of the Commons, Sidney Webb went to Trade, and Jimmy Thomas was colonial secretary.

These were all notable Labour figures, but MacDonald also appointed Viscount Haldane as lord chancellor, one of several former Liberals who had recently switched allegiance. Lord Parmoor, a former Tory, was Lord President of the Council, while some who were still Conservatives – Hugh Macmillan and Lord Chelmsford – also served. The only left-wing voices were those of John Wheatley at Health and Fred Jowett at the Office of Works.

The established political powers took some comfort from MacDonald's choice of personnel and the party's minority position in the Commons, which made its entry into office, from their perspective, as safe as it could be. To remain in post, MacDonald would have to rely on the support of the Liberals, who effectively held a power of veto which ruled out any prospect of radical legislation.

None of this extinguished the fears George V himself had about the new government. When the King raised concerns about the singing of the Red Flag at a recent Labour meeting, MacDonald sought to put him at his ease, saying that the use of that particular song – a socialist anthem dating from the 1880s which had become associated with the radical left of the Labour movement – was a custom from which he hoped in time to break.

There was some concern the incoming government would have revolutionary tendencies. The fear of many that the Bolshevik revolution which overthrew the Russian Tsar in 1917 might be repeated in Britain, with radical workers (and possibly the Labour party) at the vanguard, was real. In a way this was understandable, given that the situation in Russia remained high profile, with Vladimir Lenin having died just as Labour was about to take office.

This anxiety, though, was overblown. Labour ministers were instructed to wear full ceremonial Court dress, with top hats and frock coats, to receive the Seals of Office from His Majesty, and they willingly complied. 'I could not help marvelling at the strange turn of Fortune's wheel, that had brought MacDonald the starveling clerk, Thomas the engine-driver, Henderson the foundry labourer and Clynes the mill-hand to this pinnacle beside the man whose forebears had been kings for so many generations,' Clynes would later remark.[9]

Labour was falling into what some have called the 'aristocratic embrace', though this may be better termed an 'establishment embrace'. For some this was the start of a beautiful friendship and for others it was more akin to a stranglehold.

For all that, British politics would never be the same again. With the Labour Party in government the Conservative and Liberal hegemony which had been in place since the mid-nineteenth century was now at an end.

1923 General Election Result

Date of Election – 6 December

Overall Turnout 1923 – 71.1%

Labour

Candidates – 427

MPs – 191

Votes – 4,439,780

Percentage share of the vote – 30.5%

Result – Labour minority

Highlight – James Ramsay MacDonald becomes the first Labour prime minister.

Chapter 9

1924 – Red October

'How can I avoid the suspicion that the
whole thing is a political plot?'

Ramsay MacDonald[1]

Labour's first government lasted just nine months and fell in the autumn of 1924 at a general election brought about by scandal suggesting the party and its leadership were puppets of the Soviet government in Moscow.

Though Ramsay MacDonald had been clear that governing from such a minority position would be highly precarious, he could not have predicted the darkly dramatic circumstances which would force him from office.

By late October 1924, when the country went back to the polls, Labour could point only to some limited progress on unemployment, mainly around benefits and pensions. Matters were not helped by Chancellor Philip Snowden's ultra-cautious Budget, which was praised by opponents for cutting taxes without offering major funds to improve the lives of the worse-off members of the public.

The government's one great domestic success was the Housing Act, passed in August 1924. It had been the brainchild of the health minister, John Wheatley, and provided subsidies for building half a million decent homes for less well-off families. It proved to be the template for much of Britain's council housing in the decades to come.

It was in foreign affairs that the seeds of the government's demise were sown. Yet it was also here that MacDonald excelled over the course of his short ministry. The prime minister had long displayed a taste for international diplomacy, derived largely from his opposition to the Great War, and his aim in the years since had been to keep and cement the peace in Europe.

In July 1924 at a conference in London, MacDonald was central in the advancement of the Dawes Plan which ended the Franco-Belgian occupation of the Ruhr. This had been seized from Germany when it defaulted on the payment of war reparations, and the conference secured a new deal, helping quell tensions between European nations which had simmered since 1918.

What had initially seemed like another success turned out to be a calamitous misstep. A week after taking office, MacDonald formally recognised the Soviet Union, scarcely seven years after the Russian revolution which violently ended Tsarist rule and created the world's first communist state.

The Liberals were nervous at Labour's stance, and there was bitter opposition from the Conservatives and sections of the popular press. MacDonald's motivation had been sound enough, in aiming to dispel distrust and restore normal diplomatic and economic relations between the two countries.

Then, with Anglo-Soviet discussions over a trading treaty on the point of breakthrough, the *Workers' Weekly* – the official newspaper of the Communist Party of Great Britain – published an unsigned open letter to British troops.

The uncompromising message called on the Forces to 'definitely and categorically let it be known that neither in the class war nor a military war will you turn your guns upon your fellow workers, but instead will line up with your fellow workers in an attack upon the exploiters and capitalists . . .'[2]

The letter's effect was incendiary. In Parliament, questions were asked and charges of mutiny instigated against the paper's editor, J. R. Campbell, only to then be dropped. Once back from summer recess, though, Conservative and Liberal MPs demanded to know if the charges had been withdrawn by the government because of political interference from MacDonald himself.

The prime minister first said he had not been consulted at any stage on whether or not to prosecute Campbell, only to then muddy the waters by stating he had, in his initial statement, 'gone a little further than I ought to have gone'.[3]

In response, the Tories called for a vote of censure, and the Liberals demanded a select committee investigation of the Campbell case. MacDonald and his Cabinet viewed this as an attempt to humiliate the government and decided that both motions would be treated as confidence votes, a measure of how seriously MacDonald treated the accusation of being influenced by communist groups in league with a foreign power.

Labour ministers were also acutely aware that their lack of a Commons majority meant the government was unlikely to last a full Parliament. Weary at their inability to legislate and the attacks this provoked from their own left-wing, the Labour leadership saw an election as a possible way out of this straitjacket. As James Maxton, a high-profile left-wing MP said of the first Labour government – 'every day they were in led us further from socialism'.[4]

In early October, the vote of censure was defeated, but the House's overwhelming vote for the setting up of the select committee investigation sparked an immediate dissolution and election, the third in as many years.

For the first time the national campaign featured radio broadcasts by each of the party leaders. While Baldwin spoke quietly from the studio, his wife knitting by his side, MacDonald was heard noisily addressing a large gathering in Edinburgh.

The campaign took a dramatic turn with a coda to the Campbell case when on 25 October, just four days before polling day, the *Daily Mail* ran a fevered front-page headline: '*CIVIL WAR PLOT BY SOCIALISTS' MASTERS: MOSCOW ORDER TO OUR REDS*'.

The article claimed the uncovering of a so-called '*GREAT PLOT*' to paralyse the British military and spark a class-based civil war.[5] It highlighted Labour's policy of reconciliation with the USSR and came in the form of a letter purportedly written by Grigory Zinoviev, head of the Communist International to the Communist Party in Britain.

One of the strange aspects of the affair was that the 'Zinoviev Letter' arrived at the *Mail* via Britain's Secret Intelligence Service, and no original letter has ever been found. Stranger still Zinoviev denied being the author, instead calling it a forgery aimed at subverting the British general election.

Labour felt that the content and the timing pointed to state conspiracy, with sections of the establishment clearly involved in the publication of the text. Though now widely accepted as a forgery, most likely written by pro-Tsarist White Russians, it has scarred itself into the psyche of the party and become a byword for a smear campaign of the worst kind.

The election took place on Wednesday 29 October. The high turnout, at 77 per cent among a 20-million-strong electorate, showed public enthusiasm for the vote. Labour defended its competence in office around housing and was able to point towards progress on education. The party also made a specific pitch to women, not only on domestic issues but through the government's success in working for peace between nations.

This was part of a wider theme which aimed to contextualise their thinking towards the Soviet Union, the party stating that 'the Labour Government has refused to exclude from this general pacification the Russian people with whom it is essential to resume our trade and the interests of our unemployed and the country as a whole'.[6]

Labour made no direct mention of Campbell, though its opponents did not follow suit. The Conservatives suggested the calling of the election proved Labour's guilt over the dropped charges; the Liberals did likewise, criticising the treaty plans with the Soviets and a proposed British loan to Moscow.

Despite the calamity of the Campbell case, the election was by no means a disaster for Labour. The party offered more candidates – over 500 – and took more votes – more than five million – than ever before. Although the Zinoviev affair had not dented its vote, Labour unfortunately suffered a net drop of 40 seats – comprised of over 60 losses and 22 gains. In total Labour returned just 151 MPs. Those who were defeated included Manny Shinwell, Herbert Morrison and Margaret Bondfield, but most of the star names held on, so providing continuity in Parliament.

Most Labour seats were won in straight fights against Conservatives, though there were more than two dozen victories in three-cornered scraps where all the main parties could have triumphed. Perhaps most comforting of all – there was a distinct pattern of the party holding its safer seats.

Labour's biggest losses were in Scotland, Greater London and the North of England, notably Lancashire and Cheshire. In the Eastern region, there was also a pronounced slump, with the party being reduced to a single MP. On the upside there were gains in the North East, a contrast to the losses there at the previous election.

The overall outcome was an overwhelming Conservative victory, the Tories being returned to power with a majority of more than 200 seats, winning 47 per cent of the vote. It was a stunning turnaround on the previous year, but not unexpected given they already held the most seats in Parliament, while Labour could only have hoped to return as a minority, even under more favourable circumstances.

The Conservatives had wisely pitched a much broader set of policies than the previous year, and in so doing ditched any mention of protectionism. They offered 'strong and stable government',[7] a phrase still familiar today, as the alternative to what Baldwin negatively characterised as any further experiment with socialist government.

It was the Liberal vote which was squeezed to the point of collapse, the party being virtually wiped out across England and losing seats in Highland Scotland and in Wales. Asquith was defeated in his own constituency by Labour, and his party lost more than 100 seats to the Tories.

The middle classes, many of whom were traditional Liberals, had swung in behind the Conservatives, possibly as a result of fears of the Bolsheviks stirred up by the Campbell affair, and because the very fact of a Labour government had caused people to think of politics as a binary choice between socialism and conservatism.

The Zinoviev Letter opened the door to accusations that Labour was susceptible to the influence of communist governments overseas. Though it was not a reasonable charge against MacDonald or his ministry, it stuck, raising the question of whether a Labour government would ever again be trusted with the levers of power.

1924 General Election Result

Date of Election – 29 October

Overall Turnout – 77%

Labour

Candidates – 514

MPs – 151

Votes – 5,489,077

Percentage share of the vote – 33%

Result – Conservative majority

Highlight – The election is dominated by claims that the Labour government is under the influence of the Soviet regime in Moscow.

Chapter 10

1929 – Striking Back

'The Socialists now occupy the premier
position among the parties for the
first time in British politics.'[1]

The Scotsman, June 1929

In the five years after Labour was forced from office, the party and the country endured multiple hardships, the greatest of which was the inability of the Conservatives to make inroads into the high rate of unemployment.

Since the end of the First World War, unemployment had been rising steadily, first to one million and then to over 2.5 million by 1930. At no point did the government, led by Stanley Baldwin, instigate a national plan of any sort to deal with joblessness, contenting themselves instead with pointing vaguely to indistinct signs of recovery.

In an era without a meaningful welfare state, this was a crisis issue for millions of citizens. As the Labour leader, Ramsay MacDonald, put it in a radio address 'the threat of an ever-overhanging poverty' is 'the greatest problem of our civilisation'.[2]

Linked to this, and despite Britain's obvious industrial might, was the failing state of key sectors from which jobs might spring, particularly coal, steel and iron, which were performing poorly compared to foreign competitors.

There was a change in economic direction in April 1925 when the chancellor, Winston Churchill, returned sterling to the Gold Standard, a system which pegged the value of the pound to the price of gold. He hoped the confidence this showed to investors would provide stability and boost the economy.

In reality, the policy amounted to a devaluation, as gold was overvalued, and so manufacturers were forced to reduce costs. Churchill had undertaken the move despite being warned by leading economist John Maynard Keynes among others that returning to the Gold Standard would lead to rising unemployment, lower wages and strikes.

Three months later, the owners of the coal mines proposed a 13 per cent cut in wages, while at the same time lengthening the duration of miners' shifts.

Under pressure from the Miners' Federation and the TUC, Baldwin agreed to a nine-month subsidy of wages. Thereafter, he resisted calls for further assistance. After the Cabinet broke off negotiations with the TUC, on 4 May 1926, the General Strike began.

Estimates vary, but around 1.75 million workers took part. The miners were supported in their demands for 'not a penny off the pay, not a minute on the day' by workers on the railways, in transport, iron and steel as well as dockers, printers, those employed at power plants and much of the building trade.[3]

In an editorial titled 'King and Country' the *Daily Mail* claimed that a General Strike was 'not an industrial dispute. It is a revolutionary movement'.[4] This was hysterical propaganda. There was no attempt to bring down the government; rather the strike was an act of mass solidarity in defence of mining communities.

Pro-strike demonstrations took place in many towns and cities and soon public transport was crippled, food deliveries slowed and the country was brought to a virtual standstill. Troops were used to escort lorries carrying supplies, and thousands were arrested in clashes with baton-wielding police in London, Glasgow and other major population centres.

Though prepared to defend the miners MacDonald said he did 'not like general strikes' and told the Commons of his 'respect for the Constitution', while talking down all notions of Bolshevism.[5]

Labour's leaders were worried that the strike would be exploited by their political opponents and the media to portray the party as revolutionaries, just as had happened with the Zinoviev Letter and the Campbell Case at the previous election.

The General Strike lasted nine days and ended abruptly when the TUC capitulated – without first consulting the miners – believing that doing so would bring about a reopening of negotiations. Instead, Baldwin made it clear the pit owners remained in charge and the miners eventually went back to work in November on less pay for longer hours.

As the strike folded MacDonald appealed to the prime minister not to 'scrape the faces of trade unionists in the dust', calling for the Commons to 'make a declaration to the whole of the nation that it wants no crushing, that it wants no humiliation.'[6]

Instead, in victory the Conservative Party sought to maximise its gains. In July 1927, the Trade Disputes and Trade Union Act was passed, making large-scale industrial action illegal. Sympathy walkouts were outlawed and in echoes of the hated Osborne Judgement, unions again had to have the consent of members to use their money for political funding.

In an instant, Labour lost around a third of its subscriptions, making it harder to campaign and fight elections. Supported by the unions, the party responded with a programme called 'Labour and the Nation', advocating a living wage and the nationalisation of the land plus the coal, power and transport industries.

It would serve as the basis of the 1929 election platform, providing a clear set of policies and a commitment to social justice aimed at reassuring voters that Labour could govern effectively in their interests.

Baldwin called the election for 30 May 1929. The announcement came just weeks after a Budget speech by Churchill who – wearing his top hat – had walked through crowds from Downing Street to the Commons. There he outlined populist measures aimed at winning over voters, including the repeal of the betting tax, lower taxes on pubs and scrapping a tax on tea.

The prime minister meanwhile claimed trade was improving, that 'real prosperity is in sight', and that, 'hazardous socialist experiments would mean disaster'.[7] To his critics this was the mindset of a complacent leader in a time of crisis.

Though the Tories tried to blame the economic problems facing Britain on the General Strike, they knew that the political weather was against them, having suffered a series of by-election defeats in the course of the Parliament.

Labour, by contrast, had made a net gain of ten seats since 1924. This was no accident, given the significant work the party had undertaken to rebuild finances after three general elections in as many years and the determination of the party to fight in almost every seat.

In this period special funds were allocated for by-elections, and there was a major drive to increase individual membership and also develop local party organisations. While all this suggested Labour was in good shape for the election, the changing dynamics of the electorate made the vote particularly unpredictable.

The Equal Franchise Act of 1928 reduced the age at which women could vote, from 30 to 21 years, which at a stroke added more than five million to the electoral roll. It now totalled almost 29 million voters.

In all but a handful of constituencies women were in the majority. Each of the parties' election posters prominently featured women: Labour's depicted a closed factory next to a polling station, with workers of both sexes going to vote together.

The 1929 poll was nicknamed 'the Flapper Election', the newly franchised young women being known as Flappers, a slang term for those who wore shorter (knee-length) skirts, had bobbed hair and were generally in favour of more social freedoms.

They were expected to back Labour en masse, with one newspaper arguing that they were impressionable and that was why 'Socialists Want Votes For Flappers'.[8] Things were not so straightforward. Though Labour claimed to be appealing to women, the party had not gained as it might have expected since the extension of the franchise in 1918.

The Conservatives had a female membership in excess of half a million, while Labour was largely male dominated at every level, including the unions. It was also Baldwin's government that had passed the legislation which gave these women the vote.

More than that, the Tories had granted widows' pensions a few years earlier and their 1929 manifesto promised the further expansion of ante-natal clinics and an urgent enquiry into the causes of maternal mortality. Such policies characterising women as mothers may sound outdated now, but in the context of the time they would have been welcomed.

While the Tories were able to hold onto some marginal seats they had been tipped to lose in 1929, the election can only be seen as a stunning success for MacDonald and his Shadow Cabinet. As Philip Snowden put it, 'results have come quite up to our expectations. My most sanguine hopes have been realised.'[9]

Labour gained almost 140 seats – becoming the largest single party in the Commons for the first time with 288 MPs. The Conservatives had 28 seats fewer, while the Liberals won close to 60 seats. Labour would be in a minority government once more, but went into office with confidence.

The party had reached further into urban centres of population – in London alone 28 seats were gained, bringing the total to 54, as well as six in Birmingham, and similarly positive results in Lancashire, the West Midlands, Scotland and Wales.

Given that Labour had gone into the campaign well over 250 seats behind the Conservatives it was a remarkable outcome. However, the first-past-the-post electoral system threw up a bizarre quirk – it was the Tories who won the greatest number of votes cast (8.6 million, to Labour's 8.3 million).

Labour's victory had been years in the making – brought about in large part by an economic system which was failing ordinary citizens. The General Strike had been the most high-profile symptom, but the wider malaise could be traced back to the Great War and the slump that followed.

Labour's programme for government crystallised the solutions which were desperately sought by so many suffering economic hardship. The Liberals, who polled over five million votes, had a similar pitch to Labour about curing unemployment, but this served only to benefit MacDonald's party, which alone was viewed as representing a viable alternative to the Tories.

The Labour leader arrived back in London from his constituency in County Durham on 1 June to be greeted at King's Cross by a crowd of thousands carrying banners and wearing Labour rosettes. It took him half an hour to exit the station during which time 'For He's a Jolly Good Fellow' and the 'Red Flag' were sung.

Three days later Baldwin accepted defeat and went to see the king at Windsor to resign. In his stead came MacDonald, as leader of the largest party, for an audience lasting an hour, during which he submitted to His Majesty a proposed list of ministers.

From there, the new prime minister went to meet Labour's National Executive Committee at Transport House in London, where a decision was taken to open a 'victory and thanksgiving fund', to help the party rebuild its war chest on the back of a successful but costly election.

Days later MacDonald would be filmed with his Cabinet in Downing Street, smoking and chatting to Jimmy Thomas, Philip Snowden and many others who were returning, having served in the 1924 administration. Alongside them was Britain's first female Cabinet member, Margaret Bondfield.

A smiling prime minister introduced each of his senior ministers to the news cameras, telling the country and the world beyond that 'members of the Cabinet have been chosen for very hard work and because I believe the nation fully believes that they are perfectly competent to perform.'[10]

It was a claim which would be tested soon enough.

1929 – General Election – Result

Date of Election – 30 May

Overall Turnout – 76.3%

Labour

Candidates – 569

MPs – 288

Votes – 8,370,417

Percentage share of the vote – 37.1%

Result – Labour minority government (Labour as largest party)

Highlight – Nicknamed the 'Flapper Election', it was the first election in which women aged 21 and over had the vote.

Chapter 11

1931 – Depression and Betrayal

'If the Tories were an intelligent party they
would make MacDonald their leader'[1]

John Wheatley

For Labour, the election of 1931 was a catastrophe, forcing the party
from office just two-and-a-half years after its return to power, and creating an historic split which threatened to destroy it as a political entity.

The reason there was an election at all can be traced back to the
challenging issue of unemployment: this was the central concern when
Labour came to power in 1929, but it had been testing British politicians ever since the slump after the Great War.

When Labour took office, the jobless figure stood at one million. It had risen to almost three million by the summer of 1931,
and the increase showed no sign of slowing. Despite pledging to deal
with the matter urgently, the MacDonald government found itself
unable to alleviate the misery caused by the lack of work.

Across the Atlantic, in the United States, unemployment was
down and wages were up, and it had become commonplace for working
people to buy shares in what was thought to be an ever-rising market.
The seemingly unending era of prosperity proved to be an illusion. In
the second half of 1929, confidence quickly drained from the market,
causing investors to sell their holdings, leading to a disastrous fall in
share prices. The US economy was sent into a tailspin of historic proportions by what became known as the Wall Street Crash.

This sparked a global economic crisis, the Great Depression, during which America turned to protectionism, effectively closing off Britain's biggest marketplace and placing underperforming home industries under still greater strain.

That all this occurred when Labour was in power is something of a hard luck story, especially for a young party of the left. For the first six months, the government had been popular, and most observers thought it was moving in the right direction, not only on unemployment and housing, but along the wider theme of national development.

Once the economic decline deepened after the Crash, the government faced the escalating cost of paying for unemployment benefits, a vital lifeline to millions. Most workers were insured against unemployment in an arrangement which saw employees and the state pay into a national fund to keep them above the breadline.

Snowden, a Methodist teetotaller and orthodox chancellor, was a stickler for balanced budgets. In 1930 he used modest tax rises to combat the country's growing deficit but as Christmas approached, the government set up a Royal Commission to investigate the question of paying for the unemployment insurance fund. Six months later it reported, calling for a 30 per cent reduction in benefits.

In tandem a formal parliamentary committee was established to advise Snowden on how best to keep expenditure in check. It concluded that 1931 would see a £100 million deficit and proposed savings close to £70 million, all of which were to be found through hikes in unemployment insurance payments and the reduction in benefits.

The pressure on MacDonald and other ministers was considerable, with Snowden telling the Cabinet that 'the Budget prospect for 1931 is a grim one', amid signs the money markets were losing confidence in London and a banking crisis was spreading across Europe.[2]

Labour was in a bind, in that ensuring a basic standard of living and the welfare of workers was central to the party's credo. The government now met opposition from its own side, with the influential TUC General Council rejecting the planned cuts, and calling instead for new taxes on profits and incomes. This in turn prompted the prime minister to write back, saying 'I really personally find it absolutely impossible to overlook dread realities, as I am afraid you are doing'.[3]

The government, under severe pressure from the Bank of England and the City, indicated they would be willing to fund cuts to reduce debt and shore up the flagging pound. Ministers proposed not only reductions in unemployment benefit payments, but wage cuts for teachers, police and the armed forces.

In late August, MacDonald won a Cabinet vote confirming £76 million in savings, but only just, by 11 votes to 9. Those voting against indicated they would resign rather than implement the measures. Such a deep split at the top of government told the prime minister that his administration could not be maintained.

What followed is one of the great curiosities of British politics. George V, having returned from his summer retreat at Balmoral, consulted the opposition parties about what was now both a political and economic crisis. With MacDonald intent on resigning, it was suggested that if Labour could not implement the cuts, then the three main parties should come together under MacDonald to do so. According to his private secretary, George V told MacDonald 'that he was the only man to lead the country through this crisis . . .'[4]

It must have been hugely flattering for MacDonald to be thus informed by his king emperor, especially given his humble origins. What was being proposed was no less than the termination of the Labour government and the formation of a National Government in its stead.

In fact, MacDonald had foreshadowed this course of action two years earlier. In his first speech to MPs after the 1929 election the

Labour leader had wondered if it were possible for the parties to put 'our ideas into a common pool [so] we can bring out from that common pool legislation and administration that will be of substantial benefit for the nation as a whole.'[5]

Yet to his Labour ministers and the wider party the thought of joining forces with the Conservatives and Liberals, further abandoning and injuring the unemployed, was an outrage.

MacDonald resigned as Labour prime minister on 24 August 1931, claiming to be putting country before party. The leading members of the new National Government were sworn in the next day. Almost the whole Labour Party and the wider movement refused to support the new government and MacDonald was expelled along with the small number of MPs, Snowden included, who remained loyal to him.

It was a dark episode in Labour's history. More than anyone else, MacDonald had built the party into a powerful political force. There was a widely felt and acute sense of betrayal that he had submitted the resignation of the second Labour government without any proper consultation and accepted the king's offer to form a cross-party administration.

Disillusioned supporters defaced or destroyed images of their now former leader. As the popular rhyme of the time went:

'We'll hang Ramsay Mac on a sour apple tree

'We'll hang Snowden and Thomas to keep him company

'For that's the place where traitors ought to be'.[6]

Dominated by Conservatives, but with the charismatic MacDonald remaining as prime minister, the government took Britain off the Gold Standard on 21 September and pushed through a Budget which implemented the cuts to expenditure, including to unemployment benefit, which Labour had rejected.

To reinforce this MacDonald then went to the country asking for what was termed a 'doctor's mandate' – a prescription including tariffs on imports which ministers believed would heal the nation. Each of the parties – Conservative, Liberal, National Liberal and the rump National Labour under MacDonald – had their own manifestos but all carried the same opening statement from the prime minister.

The election was held on 27 October, barely two months after the government had been formed. The Labour Party, now for the third time under the leadership of Arthur Henderson, stood on a platform of publicly owned industries, price controls, free trade and reversal of the cuts.

This drew attacks from all sides. The Liberals accused Labour of planning to take the savings of the poor, MacDonald said the pound would be left virtually worthless, while Snowden went further in a radio broadcast, claiming Labour's plans were 'not socialism, it is Bolshevism run mad'.[7]

Given the attacks sustained by the first Labour government almost a decade earlier over the Zinoviev Letter, he would have understood well the potency of such an accusation; one which was welcomed and openly praised by the Tories.

It was an extraordinary time and an extraordinary election, with similarities to 1918 when a coalition had last come together in crisis. Just as in the Coupon Election, to be a candidate from one of the National parties in 1931 meant a high chance of success at the ballot box.

In almost 450 seats Labour had to take on National candidates of one description or another. This defined the election. It was not Labour versus Tory, but across the country it was Labour against the strength of a combined and united National coalition.

The National Government did not simply win the election – they were returned with a landslide majority of historic proportions, condemning Labour to the worst defeat in its history. The numbers are stark – collectively National candidates took more than 550 seats with around 67 per cent of the vote.

Of these, 470 MPs were Conservative, while the two wings of the Liberals accounted for 71 seats. MacDonald's National Labour entity saw only 13 of its candidates elected, having stood fewer than two dozen.

Labour lost 222 seats, suffering losses across the board. In Scotland, the party was left with just three MPs and in the Midlands over 40 seats were lost. The picture was similar in Lancashire and Yorkshire, while in London 45 seats were wrenched from the party's grasp. Outside the capital, the South of England was a Labour-free zone.

Only 52 MPs were returned and the Cabinet, Lansbury aside, were defeated as over two million votes drained away. Working people, who had brought Labour into power, now no longer believed the party could truly grip both the economic crisis and deal with unemployment.

The election of 1931 and the events which pulled Labour's second government apart have been hotly debated ever since. They were extremely difficult conditions in which to fight a campaign, and little could have been done to stave off the huge haemorrhaging of votes the party sustained.

The Labour government had not been a close-knit group, with senior ministers often working in silos rather than as team players. Had that not been so, had they had more confidence, as well as a different leader and chancellor, then a National Government might never have been formed. Certainly, MacDonald and Snowden were able to accommodate the idea of this grand coalition within their political outlook in a way others would not have entertained.

Though many at the time were shocked at the scale of Labour's losses, the party was not destroyed as some Tories had hoped might be the case. The groundwork of previous years, the structures and links to the unions were Labour's saviour. On the other hand, the cold reality remained: Labour had slid back to a position not much improved in terms of seats on that which it had occupied in 1910.

1931 – General Election – Result

Date of Election – Tuesday 27 October

Overall Turnout – 76.4%

Labour

Candidates – 517

MPs – 52

Votes – 6,649,630

Percentage share of the vote – 30.9%

Result – National government landslide

Highlight – An economic crisis with millions unemployed leads to an historic split in the Labour Party.

Chapter 12
1935 – The Rising Tide

'Labour asks the nation for a parliamentary
majority to promote Socialism at
home and peace abroad'.

Labour Party manifesto[1]

Labour went into this election aiming to demonstrate to the country that despite the deep wounds caused by the schism of 1931, it remained a force to be reckoned with – a party with its own unique ideas and commitment to bettering the lives of the working classes.

Much hard work had been undertaken to get the party back on its feet in the four years since the formation of the National Government and the expulsion from Labour of its former leader Ramsay MacDonald. The relatively small band of MPs, especially those on the front bench, had toiled continuously to counter the National parties, whose MPs outnumbered Labour by a ratio of ten to one.

They were led in the Commons by George Lansbury, the septuagenarian MP for Bow and Bromley, the sole remaining MP with a stature akin to Henderson, who had lost his seat at the previous election. Lansbury, who had led the high-profile Poplar Rates Rebellion – a tax protest by local councillors in a desperately poor borough, who refused to pass on higher rates demanded by London County Council – more than a decade earlier, was the perfect antidote to MacDonald.

He remained authentically socialist, having resisted the cuts in 1931 more vigorously than any other member of the Cabinet, and was still highly regarded by his constituents, on the left and across the wider labour movement. An inspirational speaker, on his watch Labour MPs were known to enter the voting lobbies singing 'The Red Flag'.

In this period of rebuilding, they would have to manage without the input of the ILP which chose to formally disaffiliate from the party in 1932, unhappy at what it saw as Labour's 'slow processes of gradual change'.[2]

For socialists the most pressing problem facing the country remained the still stubbornly high rate of unemployment. The situation was so grave that one in every four insured workers was seeking employment in 1932, with the jobless rate in some areas running at an astonishing 70 per cent. At this stage Labour offered little in the way of specific solutions, countering that these would emerge once the party was back in government. This was a source of frustration not only to the ILP – the Labour party's annual conference resolving in 1932 that the next Labour government must immediately adopt 'definite socialist legislation' and stand or fall by doing so.[3]

On this issue the government had introduced the Import Duties Act, a protectionist measure imposing a tariff of 10 per cent on most imports. Aside from this, ministers offered little more than blandishments, prompting the *New Statesman and Nation* magazine to quip 'the government has come to regard unemployment with public optimism and private fatalism'.[4]

While all this was unfolding at home, Hitler had come to power, rejecting the disarmament provisions of the Versailles Treaty as he set about rearming Germany, and introducing compulsory military service. Around the same time Italy's fascist leader, Benito Mussolini, had begun pursuing expansionist imperial policies.

At the time pacifism, rather than aggressive rearmament, was the dominant feature of international relations – an understandable reaction to the horrors of 1914–18.

Labour's stance of collective security under the League of Nations was reflected in its 'For Socialism and Peace' policy programme adopted in 1934, which called for large-scale economic reconstruction on the home front and diplomacy and peaceful relations between nations.

It also demanded a 'peace crusade', which was part of Lansbury's attempts to stop a drift towards another world war. This made the Labour leader an outlier among many of his colleagues, as by the mid-1930s much of the Parliamentary party was beginning to advocate resistance to acts of aggression.

The celebrations marking the Silver Jubilee of George V in May 1935 saw widescale pageantry not only in London but around the country. Weeks later, Stanley Baldwin, aged 67, elbowed the now ailing MacDonald out of Downing Street into the backwater post of Lord President.

While the National Government now had a Conservative at the helm, Labour was also about to make a change. Lansbury, an ardent pacifist with deeply held Christian beliefs, had faced strong attacks at Labour's annual conference.

Ernest Bevin, the prominent trade union leader, was furious that Lansbury had refused to back force by the League of Nations to stop Italy invading Abyssinia (present-day Ethiopia and Eritrea). After losing the conference vote on this issue and having previously said he would remain 'as long as my colleagues think it wise for me to be there', the Labour leader resigned.[5]

Two weeks later, Baldwin called an election for 14 November, partly to make capital out of Labour's disarray. This was compounded by the fact that Arthur Henderson, who had come back into the Commons in a by-election, was gravely ill and would soon pass away. To take them through the campaign, Labour MPs turned to Clement Attlee, the party's deputy leader.

With hindsight this seems like a natural progression. Attlee had made more speeches than anyone else on the front bench, and he had already held the leadership in 1933, albeit on a temporary basis, when he took over from the ailing Lansbury. Yet senior party figures had been expected to turn to Stafford Cripps or Herbert Morrison as Lansbury's successor.

The National Government had every reason to feel confident of winning a majority, given that it had been successful in over 40 of the 62 by-elections held since 1931.

Labour, by contrast, had won only eight, though the party was clearly bouncing back from its low point of 1931. It controlled London County Council for the first time and membership was on the rise – with 372,000 individual members in 1932 and nearly 420,000 by the time of the election.

In a joint manifesto – Conservative, National Liberal and MacDonald's National Labour – the governing parties placed international affairs above the domestic, declaring 'the League of Nations will remain the keystone of British foreign policy'. Peace, defence, armaments, imperial policy, trade, agriculture and fishing then followed before unemployment was addressed.

This was reinforced in a newsreel election film from each of the parties, Baldwin speaking of the 'desire to go on working to maintain world peace', and that 'our defence programme will be no more than is sufficient to make our country safe and enable us to fulfil our obligations.'[6]

Attlee set out a different priority, saying – 'the government seem to accept the position that some two million of our people cannot be found work. We in the Labour Party say that if this is the best that can be done under the present system then the present system must go.'[7]

Labour was by no means ignoring the growing threat in Europe and had called for collective security under the auspices of the League, as well as sanctions against Italy. The party's manifesto echoed many points being made by the National parties around the quest for international peace, though Labour diverged on the question of rearming – fearing that such a policy would hasten the same development elsewhere.

On this issue, more than unemployment, the election would turn. As the National Government-supporting *Daily Mirror* put it to readers on polling day: 'upon the government of this country, during the next few years, may depend the fate, not of England only, but of Europe, and therefore civilisation'.[8]

The paper discouraged any thought of reducing the government's majority and called on voters to trust the National parties, not only over peace and defence, but also to assist with unemployment, and economic recovery.

The electorate duly agreed, returning 387 Conservatives in a National Government total of 429 seats. Together these parties polled nearly 11.7 million votes, though overall their share was down 14 per cent on 1931.

Labour took over eight million votes, up almost two million on 1931, winning a shade under 38 per cent of the vote, the highest in the party's history so far. Attlee saw 154 MPs returned, a gain of over a hundred on the previous election, a figure which even just a few more votes would have made significantly higher still.

Over 500 seats were contested by Labour candidates and there were advances across the board – in Greater London, Yorkshire and Scotland, where the party gained 17 seats having been all but wiped out in 1931. The picture produced was similar in the Midlands and the North West.

That MacDonald was soundly beaten at Seaham by the redoubtable Emanuel 'Manny' Shinwell, who had held a minor post in the 1924 government, was a source of celebration. The election saw National Labour fall to just eight seats, with Jimmy Thomas the only surviving member of those who had split from Labour in 1931. Soon it would be consigned to history.

With the financial crisis that had brought it together now long past, the National Government remained strong. With evidence economic recovery was underway, sparked by a house-building boom, it had successfully pivoted to anxieties over foreign policy to sustain it, while continuing to attack Labour over economic competence.

Voters also looked upon Baldwin as someone with long years of experience in politics now ready to rearm Britain and prepared to stand up to international aggressors. Conversely, the public knew little about Attlee.

While 1935 was a defeat for Labour, it was also a qualified success. Given the scale of the rout in 1931, the party needed not only to hold its ground but to move forward. The vagaries of the electoral system, though, had worked against Labour's progress. Having won almost 40 per cent of the vote, the party was rewarded with just 25 per cent of the seats, while in 1929, with almost the same number of votes, Labour ended up with almost 290 MPs.

Yet the crucial point was that Labour – fighting alone under its own banner – had dispelled the notion that the MacDonald betrayal four years earlier had caused irreparable damage. 'The rising tide of Labour has again approached its previous high-water mark of 1929', was Attlee's optimistic assessment.[9]

The party retained its own distinct position of large-scale public ownership aimed at assisting the entire population. Significant numbers of voters had demonstrated their approval of this 'Socialist Reconstruction'.

All of this indicated there would be a real chance of returning to power at the next election, due to be held at the latest in 1940. Unfortunately, the gravest of international events postponed that poll and Labour would have to wait considerably longer to have the chance to prove itself again at the ballot box.

1935 – General Election – Result

Date of Election – Thursday 14 November

Overall Turnout – 71.1%

Labour

Candidates – 552

MPs – 154

Votes – 8,325,491

Percentage share of the vote – 37.9%

Result – National Government landslide

Highlight – With fascism rising in Europe the National Government wins its second landslide, despite Labour's improvement on the low point of 1931.

Chapter 13

1945 – Winning the Peace

'What kind of a world will come out of this war?'[1]

J. B. Priestley

The parliament elected in 1935 served for a full decade. In its first years, the government faced serious challenges, both domestically and in the international arena. Although the country emerged from the Depression, with unemployment falling to 1.5 million by 1937, the Jarrow Hunger March the previous year graphically demonstrated the searing effect it had had on already impoverished communities. The Labour movement had already suffered a fracture when the Independent Labour Party, disenchanted with Labour's economic stance, and calling for more radical policies such as a national minimum wage and widespread nationalisation, disaffiliated from the Labour Party in 1932.

Many former ILP members became attracted to the Communist Party and supported the Republican side in the Spanish Civil War, after its outbreak in 1936. The government's response to that, and to the Italian invasion of Abyssinia in 1936, was stuttering, a sign of disinclination to become involved in the cauldron of conflicts that was beginning to brew globally.

Normal political cycles were then totally pushed aside as those flashpoints ignited into another world war, the conflict spreading across much of the globe, but directly impacting the lives of millions of British civilians.

The outcome of the 1945 election for Labour was momentous, giving the party a landslide victory and its first majority government. The result was no accident, but was directly linked to the population's hopes for years of peace that would follow the Second World War.

Hostilities had begun in 1939, after the failure of long years of appeasement, the policy of trying to check, but not directly confront, Germany's territorial and military expansion. The aim had been to avoid another catastrophic mass conflict, but appeasement served instead only to embolden Adolf Hitler.

The policy's chief architect had been the prime minister, Neville Chamberlain, who headed the National Government, though he had the backing of much of the British establishment, which also favoured appeasement.

When Germany invaded Poland on 1 September 1939, Chamberlain made a procrastinating speech in Parliament, which greatly angered MPs on all sides. With the Labour leader, Clement Attlee, recovering from an operation, Arthur Greenwood was urged by a Conservative MP to 'speak for England', with further cries from the Labour benches to 'speak for the workers'.[2]

In the face of such strength of feeling, the prime minister felt forced to give an ultimatum to Germany to withdraw from Poland, a demand which was not met. Two days later, Britain declared war against Germany. Chamberlain remained in place at the head of a War Ministry, but without support from Labour and the Liberals he was forced out in May 1940.

Labour said it would join the War Ministry under a different Conservative leader, namely Winston Churchill, and so the party once again found itself occupying government positions during wartime, even more prominently so than in the 1914–18 conflict.

Into the small Churchill Cabinet came Attlee and Greenwood,

soon being joined by Ernest Bevin and Herbert Morrison, and later by Stafford Cripps, while a handful of others had more junior roles. Importantly, Labour's involvement offered a chance not only to serve but to shape policy; the theme of social and economic reconstruction – that things must change once peace returned – was pervasive.

All of these domestic policy concerns would develop in the background as the conflict grew and wore on. British troops were in place across Europe, the Mediterranean, the Middle East, North Africa and parts of Asia. At home, many cities came under intensive aerial bombardment from 1940 and millions of people, mainly children, were evacuated to rural areas.

At the same time, the government established oversight of the distribution of food, as well as mobilising labour into key industries to assist the war effort. It was the beginning of a reorganisation of society based on shared goals, including policies directing wages and controlling the cost of living.

Food prices were subsidised, and taxation was increased, with those on the highest incomes paying most. All of this played to the notion of a common wartime experience and a more level playing field in equal access to shelters, clothing, entertainment and food. The advent of rationing in early 1940, with bacon, butter and sugar the first to be restricted, and the system spreading to a wide range of everyday commodities as diverse, as tea, eggs, sweets and petrol, accentuated this sense of joint sacrifice.

War seemed simultaneously to end the scourge of unemployment, while improving wages and living standards; it brought about supplementary payments for pensioners and greatly increased domestic food production.

This was no coincidence, but part of a consistent set of policies by the government. The sense that it intended to continue with that trajectory was heightened with the publication in 1942 of the 'Social Insurance and Allied Services' report, an innocuous-sounding title that masked a radical intent.

It had been commissioned a year earlier by Arthur Greenwood, Labour's minister without portfolio and was written by the social economist Sir William Beveridge. The report would embed the idea that Britain must break the chains of social inequality by creating a welfare state, with a national health service at its core.

Beveridge focused on tackling what he called the 'five giants on the road to reconstruction' – want, disease, ignorance, squalor and idleness.[3] Not only was the Beveridge Report hugely popular with the public, but Conservative-supporting parts of the media variously judged it to be 'a plainly realisable project of national endeavour' and 'one of the most remarkable state documents ever drafted'.[4] Indeed, the scourge of 'ignorance' was tackled by Rab Butler, the Conservative education minister, who with Labour support pushed through the 1944 Education Act that introduced universal free secondary education.

The Beveridge Report's influence on Attlee and the Labour Party was huge, forming the foundation of their approach to what would be the most sensational general election of the century.

Once Germany surrendered, on 8 May 1945, Churchill was urged to hold a quick election to capitalise on his wartime popularity, just as Lloyd George had done in 1918. Although both he and Attlee wanted to see Japan defeated before a change of government, it was Labour who forced the issue.

At the party's annual conference shortly after the German capitulation, there was a sense of urgency. The Chair, Ellen Wilkinson, told a hall full of over 1,000 delegates – 'we want millions of houses, jobs for all and social security, but also educational opportunity for all . . . we are not interested in talk of coalitions. We fight for power, power for those who fought and worked and bled.'[5]

Though the National Executive wanted an immediate election, Attlee wrote to Churchill to say that Labour would stay in government no longer than October. The prime minister responded by calling the election for 5 July, so dissolving the coalition.

The electoral fight to reshape Britain in peacetime was now under-way. Most observers, Labour's high command included, expected a Conservative victory. This was despite Labour having been well ahead in the opinion polls for two years (although polling was in its infancy and not yet fully trusted as a reliable barometer of public opinion).

Labour's campaign was greatly aided by its manifesto 'Let Us Face The Future', a document which caught the public imagination, quickly selling over one and a half million copies.

It was a document not lacking in vision, calling the coming election 'the greatest test in our history of the judgement and common sense of our people'. Its core message was that collective struggle had won the war, not the actions of one man, or government and it was imperative that from that victory should flow prosperity for all.[6]

Labour argued that the people had effectively lost the peace fol-lowing the Great War, with industry remaining in private hands. Those mistakes would be avoided, the party argued, by backing Labour's vision for the country.

There was to be a programme to ensure full employment, pub-lic ownership of coal, gas and electricity, transport, iron and steel, as well as price controls, agricultural planning to provide ample food and the nationalisation of land. A national housing programme would be undertaken at pace, the school leaving age would rise to 16, there would be 'proper social security for all' and the crowning glory of a National Health Service 'free for all'.[7]

The aim was to build a socialist commonwealth, organised in the service of the entire population, engineered by a widescale reshaping of the Civil Service and government departments, including the creation of a new Ministry of Housing and Planning.

It was not that the Tories were unwilling to support such great changes. In a newsreel broadcast Churchill stated 'we must strive to give everybody greater security against poverty, unemployment, sickness and old age. Above all, we must tackle the housing problem with the same drive which we put into our war effort.'[8]

Churchill, who was greeted by cheering crowds on an extensive tour of the country, was very much the focus of his party's campaign. His popularity explains the shift in the polls which occurred in the run-up to votes being cast. Gallup surveys had Labour 20 per cent ahead early in 1945, a lead which had been whittled down to 8 per cent by the summer.

The Conservatives, though, faced the twin problems that not only was Labour's policy offering far more detailed, but they were seen as the party more naturally inclined to implement the profound social and economic change which the nation so ardently desired.

Around the country, voting took place between 8 a.m. and 9 p.m. before the ballot boxes were tied up, sealed with wax and taken to town halls or police stations. In a few areas, though, the election was staggered, with voting held up in some predominantly industrial constituencies in the North because of the annual Wakes Week holidays, when the factories closed down.

The delay was also vital for another reason, one which was said to be of great benefit to Labour: the votes of the many British servicemen overseas still had to be recorded. During this hiatus Churchill attended the Potsdam Conference with Attlee, where the post-war division of Germany and the reorganisation of Europe were discussed.

Ballot boxes were opened on the morning of 26 July, and the first indication of trouble for the Tories came quickly with the loss of Manchester Exchange, a seat which had been solidly blue for years. More soon followed, with the Conservatives tumbling to their worst defeat since the Liberal landslide of 1906.

Across the country Labour won a record 48 per cent of the vote, the swing to Attlee's party reaching almost 25 per cent in some English suburbs, a shift which delivered close to 400 seats and a majority of 146.

Other statistics were no less groundbreaking – close to 12 million people voted Labour, on a 73 per cent turnout. Churchill, the wartime leader and hero, had been routed by his rival in a manner which sent shockwaves around the world.

'*CHURCHILL IS DEFEATED IN LABOR LANDSLIDE*' is how the *New York Times* summed things up, while at home the *London Evening Standard* thundered – '*SOCIALISTS IN*', '*Britain swings to the left . . .*'[9,10] The *Daily Mirror* rather more soberly stated, '*ATTLEE TAKES OVER: SEES KING*', noting the new prime minister had been driven to the Palace by his wife.[11]

At that meeting Attlee told George VI 'I've won the election',[12] to which the king replied, 'I know, I heard it on the six o' clock news.' Typically measured, the new prime minister simply concluded that learning of his sweeping victory and then imparting this to the monarch had made for 'quite an interesting day'.[13]

The electoral map had changed dramatically since 1935. In almost every region of the country Labour increased its representation. None more so than in the capital: with 55 seats gained across the entire metropolitan area of London.

Lancashire and Cheshire saw almost 40 gains, there were 17 in Yorkshire and the same number in Scotland. The party was dominant in Birmingham and across the East and West Midlands, where it took more than half the seats.

There was a ring of red radiating outwards from London around Essex and up into East Anglia, including places such as Great Yarmouth, where previously all had been blue.

Further South, Labour took constituencies as far as Dover, and on the other side of the country there was an increased presence in South Wales, which spilled out into neighbouring English counties.

It was a truly national victory, with Labour taking seats that had long seemed beyond it, such as Taunton and Winchester. Into the Commons came many new Labour MPs, among them Barbara Castle, Harold Wilson, Michael Foot and James Callaghan.

Labour made significant gains among those voting for the first time, and among men generally. Notably the Conservatives also lost their advantage with female voters, among whom Labour gained a slight majority. The reaction to the collective war experience had enabled Labour to capture swathes of the middle classes, normally far outside the party's working-class base. In this, Beveridge was the keystone and Labour's manifesto the arch.

Many have asked, then and since, why Churchill lost, and how could he be unceremoniously turfed from office having just won the war. A better question is why Labour was able to win and to win so handsomely.

Fundamentally, this was because the British people in 1945 sought a society in which there would be shelter from the very real hardships experienced in previous decades.

Denis Healey, who addressed that 1945 Blackpool Conference in uniform as a young major returning from the fighting, later recalled, 'we all looked back to the '30s in the 1945 election, it was a period of mass unemployment, appalling housing, a large proportion of the population didn't have houses of their own to live in and of course there was no welfare state so that if you were poor, you suffered dreadfully.'[14]

Labour successfully cast itself as a party which offered a dramatic and decisive turn away from the long economic slump that stretched back to the early 1920s. Little wonder those old enough to remember such times wished to ensure the hardships did not return.

Sections of the press were vital in carrying this message of change. Labour was supported of course by the *Daily Herald*, while the *Daily Mirror*, widely read among the troops, was perhaps of greater significance. Although only explicitly backing Labour late in the campaign, the *Mirror* had done much to make socialism palatable, reassuring voters that men like Attlee and Bevin could be trusted because of their role in the wartime government, while also suggesting that nationalisation was nothing to fear.

Each day the newspaper carried on its front page a pro-Labour 'Vote For Them' or 'Vote For Him' slogan in relation to servicemen. It said the party's programme for government was typically British and was required because 'there must be something seriously wrong with a political and economic system which brought us so near to disaster'.[15]

At the time many people in Britain still looked at Russia as an ally and admired what seemed to be both military success in helping to defeat the Nazis, but also the Soviet system of planning. The feeling was that if this could be done in Moscow, it could be replicated at home.

The other side of this coin was the vulnerability of many Conservative MPs. *Guilty Men*, a widely read polemical book published in 1940 charged Chamberlain, Halifax, Baldwin and others with failing to confront Hitler in the build-up to war.

The pre-war proximity of others to senior Nazis was highlighted, with several sitting Tory MPs exposed as members of fascist organisations. In Fulham, the Labour candidate circulated images of Chamberlain embracing Hitler and Mussolini. Harold Macmillan, a rising Conservative star and future prime minister, reflected that 'it was not Churchill who lost the 1945 election, it was the ghost of Neville Chamberlain'.[16]

Linked to this was Labour's ability to portray itself as a patriotic party which had done the heavy lifting in the war and was set to do so again in peacetime. This socialism intertwined with a patriotism which sought to emancipate workers and their families, making a powerful combination.

These were not narratives which the Conservative leader accepted during an election campaign tainted with bitterness between two parties which had worked closely together in wartime. Much of this was played out in a series of evening radio broadcasts, which the BBC estimated to have been heard by as much as 45 per cent of the adult population.

In one such broadcast on 4 June, Churchill claimed that in order to implement their manifesto Labour would need to 'fall back on some form of Gestapo', the infamous Nazi secret police.[17]

It was an astonishing attack, though it is hard to say how much the accusation actually moved votes. A poll just before the campaign began revealed that almost 85 per cent of those asked had already decided which way they would cast their vote. Labour had caught a political wave and was now riding it triumphantly.

Attlee led a party whose time had most certainly arrived. Surrounded by supporters outside Transport House in central London and speaking steadily into a hand-held microphone, the new prime minister reflected on his party's historic victory.

Gratified by the result he remarked 'I am certain that this election is one in which the electors have thought deeply on the fundamental questions of the future, and they realise that Labour is the party of the future and that Labour's policy is the only policy that can lead us to peace abroad and social justice at home.'[18]

1945 – General Election – Result

Date of Election – Thursday 5 July

Overall Turnout – 72.8%

Labour

Candidates – 603

MPs – 393

Votes – 11,967,746

Percentage share of the vote – 48%

Result – Labour landslide

Highlight – Labour wins a landslide victory, removing Winston Churchill from office on a platform of transforming Britain after the war.

Chapter 14

1950 – A Sharp Kick in the Pants

'Though cowards flinch and traitors sneer,
we'll keep the red flag flying here'.[1]

'The Red Flag'

The opening act of Labour's first majority government was to sing their old battle hymn – 'The Red Flag' – in Parliament as a response to Churchill being greeted with 'For He's a Jolly Good Fellow' by the defeated Conservatives.

It was August 1945, and Labour was about to embark on its radical programme with a zeal which would have taken a considerable toll on the party by the time the country next went to the polls four and a half years later.

Throughout 1945 and the following year, more than 70 pieces of legislation were enacted, bringing a fifth of the British economy under state control. First came the nationalisation of the Bank of England, which would now report directly to ministers and Parliament.

The coal industry was next as over 800 private companies were replaced by a single public corporation – the National Coal Board. The government aimed to restock coal reserves, increase productivity, and boost employment and the living conditions in mining communities. Soon after civil aviation followed, with the formation of British European Airways, a corporation which had a monopoly over all short and medium haul British flights.

In early 1947 Cable and Wireless, the telecommunications

company which had kept the British Empire connected, was also nationalised. Railways and long-distance haulage were brought under public control, as well as inland waterways, docks and harbours, making a total of around a million workers into employees of the state.

Then in 1949 the gas industry was nationalised, with over 1,000 private companies merging under the wing of the state, in a move that aimed to develop and maintain an efficient gas supply.

By the end of the war each of these sectors had had some measure of public involvement. The Conservatives, therefore, did not raise significant objections to the programme, though when Labour signalled it would turn next to the iron and steel industries, there was stiff opposition from private companies and the Tories alike.

Underpinning it all was Labour's attempt to establish what was termed a Socialist Commonwealth of Great Britain. It was an idea that went well beyond industry, seeking to create what we today know as the 'Welfare State'.

Citizens would be provided, through national insurance contributions and general taxation, with a basic income if they became unemployed, sick or injured. Pensions would support the burden of old age, and there would be assistance for families with young children, for pregnant women, alongside maternity care, and provision for widowhood and funerals.

The jewel in this crown was the legislation passed in 1946 for the creation of the National Health Service, which began operating 18 months later. The two main parties shared some common ground that the development of such a service was needed; it was just that Labour went further in offering free, wholly comprehensive healthcare.

The midwife of the NHS was Labour's formidable health minister, Aneurin 'Nye' Bevan, at 47 the youngest member of the Attlee Cabinet. Moving the Bill for its second reading Bevan, with typical flair, had said the NHS 'will lift the shadow from millions of homes. It will keep very many people alive who might otherwise be dead.'

'It will relieve suffering. It will produce higher standards for the medical profession. It will be a great contribution towards the wellbeing of the common people of Great Britain.'[2]

In doing this, the Labour government was reforming the relationship of every citizen to the state. At the same time, though, it faced the monumental task of rebuilding a British economy shattered by the effects of the war and raising living standards back to at least pre-war levels.

When the war ended in 1945, the country had debts of almost £3.5 billion (£125 billion today) and a balance of payments deficit which would now be almost £125 billion. The negative balance had been caused by a huge drop in exports, and in response the government implemented austerity measures, with the continued rationing of commodities such as bread, meat and petrol, as well as wage controls, increased income taxes and restrictions on imports.

The US government provided a large loan to tide Britain over, but this was soon exhausted, without having provided any significant economic stimulus. The result was two sterling crises, as the pound came under severe pressure, and efforts to defend its value further drained national funds. The first came soon after the currency's convertibility was restored in July 1947, following on from a brutally hard winter which forced factories to cease production amid fuel shortages.

Then two years later, with the value of the pound – a symbol of national pride – tumbling against the dollar, Attlee's government took the drastic step of devaluing the currency. Though this made exports cheaper, it also helped hasten the idea that Britain was a diminished world power.

It was only when the United States decided to come back with a much wider financial assistance package, the European Recovery Programme, that Britain began to prosper once more. More commonly known as the Marshall Plan – after US Secretary of State General George C. Marshall who first proposed the idea – it was eagerly supported by Ernest Bevin, Labour's foreign secretary, who declared, 'Britain has been reborn.'[3]

In 1948, the first year of the Plan, Britain took the lion's share of this $2.7 billion grant, and by 1950, there had been a large rise in British exports, allowing the balance of payments account to be in slightly positive territory. Inflation was low, and the country was enjoying full employment, even in the most depressed areas.

It was in foreign policy that new ground was broken, as Labour attempted to keep Britain's place in a world now dominated by the United States and the Soviet Union, the two superpowers of the emerging Cold War. In 1947, the decision was taken to build a British atomic bomb. Britain also played a key early role in the creation of the North Atlantic Treaty Organization (NATO), established in 1949.

The challenges for the Attlee Cabinet in contending with major fractures in the Empire and beyond were if anything even greater. India and Pakistan were granted independence in 1947, the British withdrawal accompanied by the chaos of partition, with mass migration and violence along religious lines.

Burma and present-day Sri Lanka also became independent. In Palestine, unable either to contain growing violence between Jewish and Arab communities, or to find a solution satisfactory to both sides, Britain abruptly gave up its United Nations mandate in 1948. Shortly after, the new State of Israel was proclaimed. In strategically important Egypt, Labour proposed a staggered withdrawal of troops, while closer to home Ireland left the Commonwealth to become a republic.

Across a single parliament, a huge number of developments had taken place that would define Britain and its place in the world for decades to come. Yet the ministers carrying out these policies were in the main an ageing group of men (the only woman to serve in the Attlee Ministry was Ellen Wilkinson).

This 'Big Five' – Attlee as prime minister, Herbert Morrison (deputy PM and leader of the House), Hugh Dalton (chancellor of the exchequer, then of the Duchy of Lancaster), Ernest Bevin (foreign secretary) and Sir Stafford Cripps president of the Board of Trade, minister for economic affairs and then chancellor of the exchequer) – were by 1950 generally exhausted and in poor health. It was far from ideal preparation for a general election which would judge how the Labour government had performed since 1945. The attorney general, Sir Hartley Shawcross, had said 'we [Labour] are the masters at the moment, and not only at the moment, but for a very long time to come' – the election would also be a test of that claim.[4]

Speculation through the summer and autumn of 1949 that Attlee was planning to go to the country proved to be unfounded. Instead, the election came in February 1950, the very month that marked Labour's half century. Chancellor of the Exchequer Cripps had advised Attlee that to submit a spring Budget only to then hold an election would be quite improper.

The prime minister, confident of victory, predicted a majority of up to 100 seats. Other ministers were similarly optimistic, despite polls that showed the two main parties broadly neck and neck. With a working majority close to 150, and a party membership almost a million strong, it is easy to see why Labour was complacent about achieving an easy victory.

However, there were significant obstacles. The Conservatives had not been idle since their landslide defeat, and having questioned the wide extent of Labour's nationalisation programme, in 1947 they issued their own policy document entitled 'The Industrial Charter: A Statement of Conservative Industrial Policy'.

This accepted the basic reforms of the Attlee government, supported a mixed economy, opposed protectionism, and pledged to protect workers' rights, while challenging Labour's economic planning as too restrictive. While it is hard to tell how many voters were swayed by the Charter, a concise version sold over 2.5 million copies.

The Conservatives made considerable gains in the English municipal elections of 1947, then two years later took the most votes to tie with Labour in terms of seats in the London County Council elections.

All of this was assisted by a large reserve of party funds which ran to £1 million (around £29 million today). The Tories were able to employ a full-time party agent in more than 500 seats across England and Wales, and above this sat the intellectual driving force of Tory thought – the Research Department – under the watchful stewardship of Rab Butler.

Just as the Tories were changing, so was the electoral map, with the first major redistribution of seats since 1918, which redrew all but 90 or so constituencies. Overall, the number of seats in the Commons fell from 640 to 625, with a growth in suburban seats, at the expense of the inner cities, which had long been Labour's strongholds.

Polling day, 23 February, followed an unusually short campaign lasting just three weeks in duration. Throughout it, the parties concentrated for the first time on capturing floating voters, particularly those of the middle classes.

Labour highlighted its achievements in government, pointing out that 'the best medical care is available to everybody in the land' and that the party had 'ensured full employment and fair shares of the necessities of life'.[5] It was an attempt to seem both radical and reassuring; the implicit warning to the professional classes, dismayed though many of them might be over the persistent rationing and the rises in income tax, was that it would be foolhardy to turn away from Labour.

Churchill, of course, had a different message for voters saying, 'the choice before us is whether we should take another plunge into Socialist regimentation or, by a strong effort, regain the freedom, initiative and opportunity of British life.'[6]

The leader of the opposition was hedging his bets – claiming that state planning was itself profoundly un-British, while at the same campaigning on the promise of full employment, more housing, social security and the health service. Despite criticism of Labour's record, the Tories had no wish to return to a pre-1945 landscape.

Labour declared that it would go still further on nationalisation – not only implementing the Iron and Steel Act, but bringing water and the cement-making industry into public hands. The chemical industry would follow and sugar, still a rationed commodity, would also be taken out of private hands.

In response, Tate and Lyle launched an aggressive campaign featuring 'Mr Cube', a cartoon character seen on millions of sugar packets telling the public that 'state control will make a hole in your pocket and my packet'.[7] The core message was that only private enterprise would ensure there was no spike in prices. The Conservatives could not have dreamed up a greater marketing success. The Mr Cube campaign played to Churchill's theme of defending freedom, in this case the everyday freedom of being able to enjoy minor pleasures.

This was the major fault line between the parties in 1950: Labour believed its programme of change had proved effective, and wished to end further private monopolies where they were at odds with the public interest. The Conservatives, in contrast, supported by the Liberals, took a firm stand against more public ownership.

During the campaign, the Tories sought to portray Labour as ideologues focused only on nationalisation and planning, while most people just wished to live their lives unencumbered by rationing restrictions. Labour's high command, meanwhile, travelled extensively, engaging with voters in cities, towns, and villages, at factory gates, on housing estates and at town halls. Mr and Mrs Attlee undertook a 1,300-mile tour of marginal constituencies in their family car, with the prime minister doing crosswords while his wife drove to dozens of rallies and speaking engagements.

Once back in London the Labour leader used his party's final election broadcast to urge Britons to 'go forward along the road with us', capturing the idea that his party's work was ongoing, and perhaps a deliberate echo of 'This is the Road', the title of the Conservative manifesto.[8]

For many journalists the election lacked the spark and urgency of the 1945 campaign. This may in part have been because the country was at peace again and because the two main parties, sharing a broadly common outlook, were led by two respected elder statesmen. Yet there was no lack of excitement at the close of polling day which had begun in sunshine and for many ended in pouring rain. Voters were certainly enthusiastic, as the turnout reached 84 per cent, the highest ever recorded in a United Kingdom General Election.

The results were flashed up on screens to crowds watching in central London – with Labour soon racing into a commanding lead. Many of the party's leading lights went to bed believing that they had won a substantial victory only to discover, as the following day wore on, that the Conservatives had made up considerable ground in rural areas.

In the end Attlee's party was returned to power, but with a perilously slim overall majority of only five over all other parties, having lost 78 seats on a national swing of 1.3 per cent to the Conservatives.

Labour's seat total was 315, with the Tories on 298. Attlee's party took just over 46 per cent of the vote, well ahead of their rivals in a race which saw the highest turnout of any election since the war. Labour also amassed its biggest number of votes, at 13.27 million, a jump of almost 1.3 million votes on the previous election, though the Tory vote increased even more, shooting up by more than 2.5 million. Victory had been secured but at a cost: the Conservatives had clawed back a substantial amount of ground and the great landslide of 1945 had evaporated.

Understandably key Labour players sought to understand how this had happened. Dalton blamed rationing and the difficulties in the house-building programme, which had at first been slow, but would see over one million permanent homes constructed by 1951. Along with Morrison, he also felt that the long list of industries earmarked for further nationalisation had put off many voters.

Morrison went further still, grumbling about the negative effects of a 1948 speech in which Bevan had described the Conservatives as 'lower than vermin'.[9] The Tories and much of the media used this against Labour by suggesting Bevan was insulting Tory voters rather than just their MPs.

The Conservatives had also largely accepted what Labour had done in office in the immediate post-war, recognising that adapting to these new realities was their best hope of finding a route back to power. So, while Labour expended energy in the campaign defending a record which the Tories were, on the whole, not attacking, Churchill's party was able to create its own powerfully effective messages, with narratives around the erosion or restrictions of individual freedoms, using rationing and nationalisation as props.

Attlee himself felt that the voting reforms, which had redrawn seats to make constituencies more equal in terms of population, had been the key factor in Labour's decline. 'Undoubtedly this most honest attempt to give one vote one value hurt Labour very severely,' he wrote at the time.[10]

The boundary changes generally helped the Conservatives, worsening the effects of a suburban revolt against the government, with noticeable swings away from Labour across outer London, the Home Counties, Essex and beyond. The results showed women returning to the Conservatives and that almost 30 per cent of the working-class vote, and swathes of the middle classes, had swung in behind Churchill's party.

Attlee saw the king on 27 February and began forming his new administration. For Labour the most important point was that it still held power. Morrison underlined this in colourful language, quipping 'the British people are wonderful, they didn't mean to chuck us out, only to give us a sharp kick in the pants.'[11]

1950 – General Election – Result

Date of Election – Thursday 23 February

Overall Turnout – 83.9%

Labour

Candidates – 617

MPs – 315

Votes – 13,266,176

Percentage share of the vote – 46.8%

Result – Labour majority

Fact – Despite founding the NHS, building the welfare state and ensuring full employment, Labour is returned with only a small majority.

Chapter 15

1951 – Forward or Backwards

'We have gone a long way – a very
long way – against great difficulties.
Do not let us change direction now.'

Nye Bevan[1]

Despite predictions that another general election would follow shortly after Labour's narrow 1950 victory, the government survived for 20 months before seeking a more substantial mandate.

In homes across the nation on the evening of 19 September 1951, Clement Attlee's clipped, measured tones could be heard live on the airwaves from the BBC. His message to voters was that he needed greater support in Parliament to deal with the issues facing the government at home and overseas.

The dissolution, the prime minister told voters, would take place on 5 October, with the election being held 20 days later. Though the Conservatives held a substantial lead in the opinion polls, Labour hoped that the party's record since 1945 would see them returned again, and in increased numbers.

Having won a majority of just five over all other parties in 1950, many Labour backbenchers had actually been keen for some time that an election should be held, believing the longer they struggled to execute their legislative programme, the greater the longer-term damage would be.

Attlee, however, had considerations well beyond his own MPs

about the timing of the election. From early 1952, George VI was due to be overseas on a long Commonwealth tour and had become increasingly concerned that there should be no major upheaval while he was away.

The prime minister was happy to reassure the king of 'the need for avoiding any political crisis while Your Majesty was out of the country'.[2] Intentionally or otherwise, the king, who in the event was unable to undertake the planned journey due to serious ill health, was making the point that a change of government seemed possible, even probable.

Constitutionally, Attlee had no need to hold an election and had been advised against doing so by Herbert Morrison, the foreign secretary, who regarded himself as the party's specialist in such matters. In the end, the Labour leader pressed ahead, without consulting or informing many of his colleagues.

It proved an ill-starred decision. Though Labour still looked to 1945 as its lodestar, the public was increasingly resentful of the wartime constraints which remained in place in the form of rationing, including everyday items such as eggs, tea and bacon.

Labour was also suffering from the loss of many of those who had dominated the front bench in Parliament since the landslide victory in 1945. Bevin, the long-time foreign secretary, died in April 1951 while still in office (having been moved to the role of Lord Privy Seal), while Cripps, chancellor since 1947, retired in poor health in October 1950 and would also be dead within 18 months.

Attlee remained a spry figure, dashing off to the Scottish Labour Party Conference on the day the election was announced, yet even he had spent time in hospital. This changing of the guard would cause significant problems for the prime minister in dealing with tensions among his MPs.

Party management had been a constant concern given Labour's tiny majority since the 1950 election. Emboldened by having almost wiped out the 1945 Labour landslide, the Tories forced the Commons into many gruelling late sittings, with MPs compelled to be in place to vote.

A dinner in honour of the French president, Vincent Auriol, had to be abandoned, as ministers rushed back to the Commons to avoid Churchill overturning the Iron and Steel Act, which would establish a public body for those industries. On other occasions, MPs were brought to the division lobbies from their sickbeds.

Although the Labour whips were able in general to counter these tactics, they could not prevent the resignation of Aneurin Bevan as minister of labour in April 1951, along with John Freeman and Harold Wilson. Bevan, the MP for Ebbw Vale, was the shining star of the Labour left and as health minister had been pivotal in the formation of the NHS. For a time, Attlee had even viewed him as a future leader, before becoming wary of what he saw as the Welshman's volatile temperament.

The direct cause of Bevan's resignation was the proposal in the Budget of 1951 that NHS patients should be charged half the cost for their false teeth and spectacles. Bevan viewed this as a direct attack on the principle of a free health service which he held to be 'a piece of real socialism and 'a piece of real Christianity too'.[3]

The move to introduce charges was pushed by Hugh Gaitskell, a former academic and civil servant from the right of the party, who had become chancellor in October 1950, when Cripps was unable to continue in post. Gaitskell's appointment had been much to the distaste of Bevan, who had his own personal ambitions, but who also distrusted the new chancellor for his previous attempts to limit health spending by bringing it under the control of the Treasury.

Equal to the strength of Bevan's opposition to NHS fees was Gaitskell's belief that his view was correct, declaring the matter was 'a fight for the soul of the Labour Party', and that if Bevan won the argument the party might spend long years in opposition.[4]

Bevan's point, though, was reinforced by the coverage of the charges issue by the *Daily Express*. Gaitskell, the paper said, 'puts a charge of 50 per cent on teeth and spectacles. That is what the Tories would have done. Now the job is done for them.'[5]

As Bevan departed the front bench, the newspapers speculated that the gravity of the crisis inside Labour might force Attlee to dissolve Parliament. In the end Bevan made a passionate but poorly judged resignation speech and the prospect of an immediate election faded.

The other consideration behind Gaitskell's Budget calculations was the decision to enter the Korean War, which had broken out in June 1950. Communist North Korea, backed by Soviet Russia and China, invaded the south of the peninsula, triggering a United Nations intervention which was led by American forces, but supported by Britain.

With the Cold War deepening, the government had ordered an increase in spending on arms, with additional expenditure amounting to £4.5 billion, a figure so ambitious that it was never fully realised. The charges for teeth and glasses, in contrast, were only projected to raise around £25 million and it is therefore remarkable that Attlee and the Cabinet were unable to find a compromise which could have halted Bevan's resignation.

Bevan and the left had a deeper worry, the feeling that Gaitskell was signalling that Labour's active pursuit of socialism had ended with the creation of the NHS, the welfare state and the first wave of nationalisations. For Bevan, mere management of a mixed capitalist economy would be no substitute for the continued efforts required for a fuller transformation of society.

The row over the Budget and NHS charges exposed to the public the divisions emerging at the top of a party which had been broadly united since coming to office six years previously. It also highlighted a general feeling of drift, a sense that the government was beginning to lose its momentum.

Some of this unease was captured by voters interviewed for newsreels the day after the election announcement, with one middle-aged woman saying 'I think they have been in power for eighteen months and things have been gradually deteriorating.' Another thought the forthcoming election was 'the most encouraging news we have had for a very long time, it's essential to the country to have a change of government'.

Others were concerned not to lose the gains made since the war – a man standing beside a dray horse commented, 'I would like to see this party get in again because the simple reason (is) things have got a bit better now and I think they could do a lot better for the public.'[6]

Yet another, who claimed to be a Labour voter, grumbled to a polling company that the government had 'managed to take a lot of the joy and interest out of the atmosphere, it is not so much austerity but the general discontent'.[7] For many then, even though the promises of 1945 had been kept, everyday life remained drab. For the middle classes rising tax rates and the unavailability of goods presented twin sources of dissatisfaction.

The Conservatives pushed hard at this restlessness in the campaign, using the slogan – 'It's time for a change – Vote Conservative'.[8] Though Churchill could hardly be described as a new broom at this late stage in his long career, he was able to present himself as a unifier, and almost above party-political mudslinging.

The change the Tories promised took the shape of proposed tax cuts for individuals (tax rates were running at 48 per cent with a top rate of 98 per cent). A greater role for local government was also pledged, as well as reform of the House of Lords and a commitment to move speedily towards Scottish devolution.

Plans to build 300,000 homes a year echoed Labour's own commitment, as did prioritising the welfare of pensioners. The Conservatives pledged to repeal the Iron and Steel Act, but beyond that there was to be no move to return major industries to the private sector, nor to unpick the health service and social security.

Labour's offer was based on defending the things it had already achieved. There were no plans for further nationalisation, but the party pointed to full employment, and contrasted this with the struggles endured by many between the wars.

The point was pressed home in the party's manifesto: 'after six years of Labour rule and in spite of post-war difficulties, the standard of living of the vast majority of our people is higher than ever it was in the days of Tory rule. Never have the old folk been better cared for. Never had we so happy and healthy a young generation as we see in Britain to-day.'[9]

The party asked the public to consider who was best placed to ensure continuing peace, maintain full employment, increase economic production and bring down the cost of living in a just society. Would it be, 'Forward with Labour or Backwards with the Tories?'[10]

The other main strand of the campaign was defence. This was understandable, given both the high cost of the new arms programme and the threat posed to world peace by the Korean conflict. With the Second World War still very much a recent memory, there remained a genuine fear of a slide into another global conflict, one which would now be overshadowed by the atom bomb.

The Labour-supporting *Daily Mirror* ran a high-profile campaign against Churchill and his party, suggesting only Labour could be trusted to preserve peace and national security. On polling day, the paper carried the headline 'Whose Finger?' showing the image of a gun.

Churchill was outraged by the accusation that he was a warmonger, while Tory strategists knew the power this claim held and feared it would help further narrow polls just as voting was about to begin.

When the first results came in, Labour's hopes rose as the party raced into the lead, but the picture slowly changed as the hours wore on. The Tories first took the lead, and then by tea-time the next day (Friday 26 October) had secured victory. The final figures showed Labour on 295 seats, while the Tories had won 321 and the Liberals were on six.

Churchill was back as prime minister, but with a slender overall majority of just 17. While an improvement on Labour's 1950 majority, the Tories were left deflated, having believed a 40-seat cushion had been within their grasp. The press saw the outcome as a virtual stalemate, suggesting the new government would have to go back to the electorate before long.

Labour could take comfort from this and the fact that they had actually won the most votes, just under 14 million (48.8 per cent), slightly over 200,000 more than the Conservatives' total (48.0 per cent).

Labour votes piled up in the cities and industrial strongholds, where they became meaningless under the first-past-the-post system, but they had fallen away across crucial marginals in the Home Counties, East Anglia and Lancashire. Remarkably, Labour actually saw its vote increase in more than 500 constituencies.

The party garnered still more working-class support but, compared to 1950, lost out among the middle classes. Its support among men was lower than that in 1945, and across the entire country the average swing was tiny but uniform – roughly 1 per cent to the Conservatives.

Voters had switched from Labour with the luxury of knowing that doing so might bring a change of government but not a fundamental change in approach, with the Tories having committed themselves to governing for the entire population, rather than any narrow section.

Taken together, support for Labour and the Conservatives accounted for 97 per cent of the votes cast, underlining the fact that this was the high point of two-party politics. On the face of it, that should have been of some comfort to Attlee, but one aspect of the system hampered his party.

The Liberal vote had collapsed in 1950, when having put up nearly 500 candidates they won just nine seats. In more than 300 constituencies the party lost its deposit, by failing to exceed 12.5 per cent of the votes (as against the 5 per cent needed since 1985). This cost the party £150 a time – close to £1.25 million today. To avoid a repeat of these losses, the Liberals only contested just over 100 seats in 1951, while the Conservatives energetically set about capturing their supporters, helping Churchill's party to make gains in several suburban seats.

Overall, there was a feeling that Attlee's Cabinet had done its job, having delivered the main pillars of the 1945 manifesto and changed Britain beyond measure. Labour had given the impression of being content simply to consolidate in office what had already been achieved.

In the face of a resurgent and energised Conservative Party, this proved too narrow an offer. Attlee tendered his resignation to the king, so bringing down the curtain on a landmark six years of Labour majority rule, and 11 consecutive years when the party had formed part of the government.

The outbreak of the Korean War was probably the key factor in the demise of the Attlee administration, as it led to extensive and unaffordable spending commitments to rearm Britain. This placed significant strains on the economy and a society becoming ever more desperate to break free from wartime constraints.

Later, the Labour MP Richard Crossman, who would become a minister and celebrated diarist, blamed Attlee for the defeat, writing that 'if only he had held on, instead of appealing to the country in the trough of the [Korean] crisis, he would have reaped the benefit of the 1951 recovery'.[11]

All this was unfortunate for an exhausted Labour Party, as it allowed their opponents to take office on the cusp of a boom in prosperity and consumerism. The economy would soon improve. Britain's balance of payments was moving into surplus, and some rationing, such as on petrol, had already ceased.

'It looks as though those bastards can stay in as long as they like', Churchill had incorrectly observed during his years in opposition.[12] Now, though the tables were turned, the silver lining of this close-run election was the huge support Labour retained in the country. It was a reservoir of support which led those who now found themselves shadow ministers to speculate that they might soon be back in office.

1951 – General Election – Result

Date of Election – 25 October

Overall Turnout – 82.6%

Labour

Candidates – 617

MPs – 295

Votes – 13,948,883

Percentage share of the vote – 48.8%

Result – Conservative majority

Highlight – Labour receives almost 14 million votes – its highest share to date – but loses the election.

Chapter 16

1955 – Fighting Snow White

'The greatest social revolution in our history'.

Rab Butler on Labour's reforms since 1945.[1]

On a long-distance phone line at a remote railway station called Field, high in Canada's Rocky Mountains, Clement Attlee learned that a general election had been called for 26 May, bringing an abrupt end to his speaking tour of North America.

Labour's grand old man could hardly have been surprised. Speculation that Sir Anthony Eden, the new Conservative prime minister, would go to the country had been growing for weeks. Attlee, now aged 72, and set to lead his party into a fifth national election, pronounced himself confident of victory, but unhappy about the timing of the poll.

It was a point made by numerous other senior Labour figures. Eden, who had made his announcement in a broadcast from Chequers, claimed that an election was required because 'uncertainty at home and abroad about the political future is bad for our influence in world affairs, bad for trade, and unsettling in many ways.'[2]

Labour was unconvinced, suggesting instead that the prime minister was acting in bad faith by revealing the election date a few days before the Budget was due to take place. What Attlee and others suspected was that an untested Tory leader was planning giveaways which would encourage voters to look more favourably on his party at the ballot box.

On 19 April, the chancellor, Rab Butler, duly stood up in the House of Commons and delivered a headline-grabbing sixpence off the standard rate of income tax, coupled with rises in allowances for children, single people and married couples.

The Conservatives were hardly playing like gentlemen, they were playing to win. Attlee, having arrived in Winnipeg on his journey home remained upbeat, telling reporters that Butler's Budget was 'undoubtedly a pre-election move' but that he expected soon to be prime minister once again.[3]

Despite Attlee's optimism, Labour faced challenges on several fronts. The Conservatives had a fresh new leader who appeared in step with the upbeat mood in the country and what was being seen as a new Elizabethan Age, the young Queen Elizabeth having succeeded to the throne in 1952.

Her first prime minister was Winston Churchill, who served until the beginning of April 1955. Aged 80 and in failing health after a series of strokes, he gave way to his natural heir, Sir Anthony Eden, long his right-hand man as foreign secretary. Even at the last moment, Churchill found it a wrench to stand aside, saying 'I don't believe Anthony can do it.'[4]

Eden was a hugely experienced politician, who won the Military Cross in the Great War. A dashing, glamorous figure, he was also married to Churchill's niece. Attlee congratulated him on moving into Downing Street, wishing the new prime minister good health, but not a long stay in office.

Though of a different generation to Churchill, Eden's appointment did not signal a change in direction for the Tories. Since returning to power in 1951, they had continued to pursue Labour's policies, of full employment, social justice through the welfare state, while at the same time presiding over rising living standards. Their hope was to banish forever memories of the privations of the 1930s for which they were blamed, and in so doing reap an electoral dividend.

With a majority of just 17, the government had moved with caution, but had successfully executed manifesto pledges to de-nationalise the iron and steel industries, though public control was retained at Ebbw Vale, the largest plant in the country. The road haulage industry also moved back into private hands.

The major concern for ministers, however, lay in redressing a huge deficit of £400 million in the balance of payments. To deal with this imbalance between exports and imports officials at the Treasury came up with what was termed 'Operation ROBOT'. This system would make exports cheaper but imports more expensive, with the cost of food and raw materials spiking as a consequence.

Political reality trumped economics, and after much deliberation the idea was dropped. Churchill's most prominent advisor, Lord Cherwell, nicknamed 'The Prof', set out plainly the fear that ROBOT would lead to a marked rise in joblessness, saying: 'to rely on high prices and unemployment to reduce imports would put the Conservative Party out for a generation'.[5]

As it happened, things quickly began to improve, though this was not so much an economic miracle as a by-product of the end of the Korean War. This renewed growth in turn unshackled the British economy. With a growing sense of optimism, consumer spending boomed. Cars, fridges, televisions, and other household goods were no longer considered luxury items.

There would be new homes to accompany this: just as it was under Attlee, house building was a national priority, second only to defence. Conservatives took great pride that by 1953 they had made good on their target of building 300,000 properties a year, most of them council houses, outstripping the Labour Party.

The government's cause was also helped by the ending of all rationing in 1954, concluding a 14-year period of various restrictions which stemmed from the war. The Ministry of Food handed over several million tons of meat to private business, ration books were torn up and, in some cases, set alight. The Tories were making good on their 1951 promise to restore the basic freedoms for which voters clamoured.

While the Conservatives had a positive story to tell, Labour's activists met with apathy on the doorstep when pushing their own formidable record since 1945. The welfare state, nationalisation and full employment, issues which were once so totemic, now failed to cut through. The feeling was that these were battles, and victories, that lay in the past.

Labour's 1953 policy document 'Challenge to Britain' was symptomatic of the problem. It failed to break new ground, instead charting familiar territory: an extension of the welfare state, the return of iron and steel to public hands, as well as the nationalisation of engineering, chemicals and aircraft manufacturing. It would form the basis of the 1955 manifesto.

Labour faced another problem: while there were no extensive ideological differences between the top of the Labour and Conservative parties, deep divisions emerged across sections of Labour itself, among MPs, activists and trade union bosses.

This absorbed much of Labour's energy as the party battled to renew the definition of its socialism. The struggle focused on the former health minister, Nye Bevan, who had resigned from the government in 1951 over planned NHS charges and now emerged as the leader of a left-wing bloc of 'Bevanite' MPs with strong support across the grassroots of the movement.

The Bevanites sought to retain all the gains of the 1945 government

– control of industry, free public healthcare and the welfare state – and push nationalisation still further. They demanded industrial democracy, in which workers would take a lead, and were openly sceptical of following American foreign policy, and of nuclear weapons.

The battle came to a dramatic head at the party's annual conference in Morecambe in September 1952. Bevan and his allies – Barbara Castle, Harold Wilson, Tom Driberg, Ian Mikardo and Dick Crossman – were victorious, taking six of the seven seats on the ruling National Executive Committee.

Out went Herbert Morrison, Hugh Dalton and other stars, leaving some union leaders fuming. One was so angry that he shouted from the floor, 'after this, there'll be no more bloody money for this bloody party', his false teeth shooting out of his mouth during this tirade.[6]

The Bevanite group remained a minority among Labour MPs, albeit a powerful one. There were several other spats and Bevan resigned from the Shadow Cabinet in 1954, though the most serious discord came in March 1955 with the government's decision to manufacture a British hydrogen bomb.

Bevan and 62 other Labour MPs who abstained rather than voting with their party to support the policy had the whip withdrawn for a short time. When it was returned, it came with a warning that expulsion would be likely if Bevan did not change his ways. By this point a general election was close at hand.

Though Labour could point to strong gains made in the local elections of 1952 and 1953 in different parts of the country, they would go into the national contest behind in the polls and facing a Tory party which had not dropped a single seat they held in over 40 by elections contested since the country last went to the polls in 1951.

The Tory record was bolstered by rising wages and lower taxes, all of which heightened still further the sense that Britain had been unshackled. Labour also now faced a dilemma in how to attack Eden himself. Manny Shinwell, the Shadow Cabinet member and former minister, summed their problem up, saying 'at the last general election we had to fight Churchill. That was something to get our teeth into. But this time we are fighting Snow White and the Seven Dwarfs.'[7]

Once the campaign was underway Attlee was back on the road. Up and down the country he attended dozens of meetings and covered thousands of miles by car with his wife, Lady Attlee, at the wheel, just as she had been in the 1951 campaign.

Though the polls quickly narrowed, there were no real fireworks and journalists began to characterise it as a dull election. Attlee could see the danger. 'Wake up this election! The Tories hope to keep it quiet and sneak back into power before the nation realises what has happened', he told a rally in Glasgow.[8]

Though Eden was more prominent, often attracting crowds – mainly dominated by women – on his constituency visits, Churchill remained a visible presence. He retained his bite: a row broke out when the former Conservative prime minister distorted Attlee's words, suggesting the Labour leader had said it was an illusion to think of the hydrogen bomb as a deterrent.

It was untrue. Attlee had said Britain must not go around the world threatening to drop an H-Bomb as a means of quelling trouble. The Tories were trying to paint a picture of Labour as soft on Britain's defence in a nuclear age; Attlee was unwilling to let that lie and reprimanded Churchill for his remarks.

The row demonstrated that for all their mutual respect the pair could still clash in the heat of an election campaign. At one point Churchill described Attlee as a chameleon, only to be then reminded that while he had been loyal to his party, Sir Winston had switched colours from Conservative to Liberal and back again.

The Tories also tried suggesting that Labour would resurrect rationing if elected, even producing dummy ration books as a physical reminder of that little lamented era. Again, Attlee stood up to this, calling on Eden to renounce his party's claim and describing it as 'one of the dirtiest things they have ever put out.'[9]

The attacks on Attlee continued. Just before polling the *Daily Express* ran a cartoon showing a life-sized cut-out figure of the Labour leader, with holes for eyes and behind this a sly-looking Nye Bevan. Underneath ran the caption – 'You Can Trust Mr Attlee'. The implication was that Bevan was a left-wing stalking horse who, along with his followers, would take over should Labour come to power.

The attacks were of course misleading. Far from being extremist, the party manifesto, 'Forward with Labour', drew criticism for offering little more than a rehash of their 1951 programme.

The Conservative campaign was notable for its use of the comparatively new medium of television, its reach and role in portraying events in the life of the nation shown by its coverage of the Coronation, two years earlier, which had been viewed by many millions. The BBC was now regularly reaching audiences of up to six million, and the newly formed ITN was also proving a success.

Eden recognised TV's importance, using it for a novel type of election broadcast in which he took questions from a panel of journalists, including Hugh Cudlipp of the *Daily Mirror*.

A giant of Fleet Street, Cudlipp put to Eden: 'in the pre-war years there was the Toryism of the big majority, the Toryism of neglected housing, neglected national defence, slums and massive unemployment', then asking, 'what sort of Toryism can we expect from your government?'[10]

In response the prime minister answered: 'I hope and believe an intelligent and progressive Toryism that tries to build for the country on the basis of what we have been doing for the last three and half years.'[11]

Election night was also very much a live television event. There had been some TV coverage in 1950 and 1951, but now there were hours of live reports and analysis, the BBC's coverage being anchored by the prominent figure of Richard Dimbleby.

The general tone of this programme was very factual and analytical with little frivolity, but away from the cameras celebrations had begun soon after midnight at Conservative HQ in Victoria. Later in the morning, with only six seats left to declare, the BBC called the outcome with little fanfare, simply showing a graphic which read 'CONSERVATIVES IN'.[12]

The Tories were the first peacetime government since the nineteenth century to be returned with an increased majority. The final totals showed they had won 345 seats, Labour 277 and the Liberals remained far behind, still on six. The government was now comfortable in Parliament with a majority of 60.

Labour lost seats in central Scotland, the Midlands, East Anglia and the shires outside London on a sharp fall in turnout. In 1951, 82 per cent of voters had participated, now that figure was just 76 per cent.

Both the main parties saw their totals decrease – Labour losing 1.5 million votes and the Tories 400,000. Labour's general secretary, Morgan Phillips, was asked on TV if the drop in turnout accounted for the defeat. He replied: 'in some respects, yes . . . we feel that the overall reduction in the poll has been to our disadvantage.'[13]

Tory strategists also spotted that on a national swing towards them of under 2 per cent, it was Labour abstentions which had made the difference to the overall outcome. How different it might have been had the party not cut the number of full-time agents: Labour's national officer later listed more than 30 seats which might have been won with a greater ground organisation.

In an era when Labour and Conservative were the two dominant electoral blocs – accounting for 96 per cent of the votes cast in 1955 – it was more crucial than ever to muster their supporters to the polling stations.

There was really no third party to speak of, the Liberals again fielding little more than 100 candidates. A full slate may well have soaked up Tory votes outside the Labour heartlands and made the electoral picture more complex.

The newspapers were clear that the fault for the defeat lay at Labour's own door, citing divisions between what were now openly seen as the left and right wings of the party. Also, with the average age of the Shadow Cabinet touching 60, and many being closer to 70, there was a sense that a group of ageing and exhausted men had clung on for too long at the top.

The *Daily Mirror*, a key supporter, was especially scathing. It declared that Labour had failed because the leadership had failed to unite, to inspire or to organise. The paper called on Attlee to resign, castigating him for lacking warmth and talking like the leader of an old Boys' Brigade, rather than the leader of a major political party.

Although the accusations might have contained a grain of truth, Attlee, Morrison and the rest clearly sincerely believed in their prospectus for the country and wished to see it implemented.

Labour had changed Britain, and the approach of their political opponents, beyond measure. As Attlee put it the Tories 'have had to accept what we have done – many things which 20, 30 or 40 years ago would have been denounced as heresies and silly socialism.'[14]

Sadly for Labour, they were now not the ones reaping the electoral reward. Britain was entering an age of peace and relative prosperity, the Conservatives had again won the trust of the nation and it looked very much like the future belonged to Eden and his party.

1955– General Election – Result

Date of Election – 26 May

Overall Turnout – 76.8%

Labour

Candidates – 620

MPs – 277

Votes – 12,405,254

Percentage share of the vote – 46.4%

Result – Conservative majority

Highlight – The Conservatives become the only party ever to win over 50 % of the vote in Scotland.

Chapter 17

1959 – The Struggle Continues

'It is no good asking – what would Keir Hardie
have done?' We must have the top men
brought up in the present age'.

Clement Attlee[1]

Shortly after the 1955 defeat, the now 72-year-old Clement Attlee decided that 20 years as Labour leader was quite long enough and that it was time to make way for someone younger. His career at the top of the party had been long, stretching back to his time as deputy and interim leader in the 1930s, through the war as deputy prime minister, and then as prime minister in Labour governments which shaped much of modern Britain after the Second World War. It was a stellar record of service.

Even at this stage, his colleagues begged him to stay on. Ever modest and deeply loyal, he agreed. Although Attlee then suffered a mild stroke in the summer of 1955, he was in place at the party's annual conference in October. By early December, though in improving health, he finally decided to resign.

Later the same month he was replaced by Hugh Gaitskell, who had become the darling of the party's right and the trade union leaders. The leadership question was determined by a ballot of only Labour MPs, with Gaitskell comfortably beating his opponents, the left-wing Nye Bevan and Herbert Morrison, who had long coveted the position.

Gaitskell now informed the media that splits in his party were a thing of the past. Attlee reinforced this by congratulating Gaitskell and urging Bevan and his supporters to get behind the new leader and forget prior differences.

A year later, Bevan was shadow foreign secretary and three years after that deputy leader. As it turned out the pair worked well together, especially during the Suez Crisis, the international row which effectively ended Anthony Eden's premiership.

In 1956 the Egyptian leader, Colonel Gamal Abdel Nasser, nationalised the Suez Canal, the crucial strategic and economic waterway connecting the Mediterranean and the Red Sea. Britain was keen to retain her influence in the Middle East, both to ensure the region's stability and to guarantee a continuous flow of oil from Iraq and Kuwait, which alone accounted for nearly half of Britain's oil consumption.

Eden viewed Nasser as a dictator, and at the end of October Britain and France invaded Egypt in co-ordination with Israel, with the aim of regaining control of the Canal. It proved not only to be a military misadventure but a diplomatic calamity.

Having been kept in the dark the United States' president, Dwight Eisenhower, blasted Eden in an expletive-laden call from Washington. The United Nations complained of being ignored and the Soviet Union threatened to use missiles to return peace to the Middle East.

In the face of such intense opposition and fearing international isolation, Eden gave way and ordered a withdrawal. Gaitskell and Bevan went on the attack, the latter memorably telling a rally in Trafalgar Square 'Sir Anthony Eden has been pretending that he is now invading Egypt to strengthen the United Nations.'

'Every burglar of course could say the same thing; he could argue that he was entering the house to train the police. So, if Sir Anthony

Eden is sincere in what he is saying, and he may be, then he is too stupid to be a Prime Minister.'[2]

The whole episode was a humiliation for Britain and for Eden personally. In poor health, he stood down weeks later and in his stead came Harold Macmillan, who would prove to be a formidable opponent for Labour.

Born into a comfortable upper middle-class life and educated at Eton and Oxford, his political outlook was formed by the Great War, in which he was badly wounded fighting alongside enlisted men in the trenches as an infantry officer.

As an MP, Macmillan represented Stockton-on-Tees, a constituency where there was widespread deprivation and joblessness. He understood the needs of the working classes and had a sympathy to match, committing himself to the post-war consensus of full employment, the welfare state and nationalised industries.

On entering Downing Street in January 1957, he made a television address declaring: 'we have a difficult task before us in this country – all of us.'[3] That difficult task was the restoration of economic stability after the Suez crisis caused tens of millions of pounds to be wiped from Britain's reserves, and provoked intense speculation against the pound and a spike in inflation.

Labour responded to his appointment by demanding an immediate general election. The call went unheeded, and Macmillan was still in office as the economy improved over the next two years, with increased industrial production, rising wages and low unemployment. By 1957, he informed the nation 'let us be frank about it: most of our people have never had it so good.'[4]

Having had doubts that he had missed his best chance in not calling an election in 1958, Macmillan returned from his holidays in summer 1959 eager to have a dissolution. This was duly secured in early September with his party holding a seven-point opinion poll lead.

Rather improbably, Gaitskell was on a visit to Moscow with Bevan at this point. Arrangements were quickly made to return on a Soviet airliner, the pair pronouncing themselves confident of victory and eager to get on with the contest which would take place on 8 October.

For the first time in almost a decade, Labour's leaders felt they had a real chance of returning to power. There was some evidence to back up their confidence; the party had proven that during the electoral cycle it could get itself ahead in the polls, having been 13 points in front when Eden fell from grace.

The shift to a Tory lead since then was partly due to the improving economic conditions which naturally assisted the party in power. Also, six months before the election was announced the government had cut 3.75p from the standard rate of income tax and an additional 2.5p from the lower rates. Purchase tax and duty on beer were also reduced. Just as in 1955, it was a classic giveaway, timed to have a positive effect in the run-up to a national poll.

Labour, for its part, seemed determined to avoid allegations it was a disunited party and Bevan told the 1957 conference that he opposed unilateral nuclear disarmament and that a Labour foreign secretary must not be sent 'naked into the conference chamber' to negotiate with world powers.[5] Though the majority view across the party, it was a moment which left his followers aghast and feeling isolated.

Long overdue, deficiencies in Labour's organising techniques had also been addressed, with attempts made to appoint more party agents and to target resources towards marginal seats. A review was carried out into the stinging defeat of 1955, led by Harold Wilson, one of Bevan's early followers, and by this stage shadow chancellor.

After each election, the Conservatives had undertaken a root and branch investigation of the outcome. Wilson's, in contrast, was the first by Labour. The report made over 40 recommendations and slammed the party structures for being 'still at the penny-farthing stage in a jet-propelled era'.[6] It also pointed to inefficiency at party HQ and raised concerns about the falling number of individual members, down from just over a million in 1952 to fewer than 850,000 three years later.

A further series of policy papers after Gaitskell became leader focused more on achieving social equality than the nationalisation agenda of the Attlee era. So too, did *The Future of Socialism*, a book written by Anthony Crosland, a former and future Labour MP with an academic background. His idea was that Labour, in opposing the evils of capitalism, was becoming outdated and that pursuing equality was perfectly possible without dismantling the structures of capitalism. Much of his thinking would filter through to the 1959 Labour manifesto.

Labour believed that at the next election, the pendulum would swing back their way as voters felt it was time for a change. Given that no party had won three elections in a row after serving full terms since the Napoleonic Wars, it was a reasonable assumption.

However, Macmillan went to the country not only armed with the right economic conditions and with the polls running in his favour, but the prime minister had also now been christened 'Supermac' by the *London Evening Standard*. Though intended as irony, the nickname soon caught on and helped bolster Macmillan's public image.

Having already been in power for eight years and now asking for another term, the government went with the simple but powerful slogan 'Life's better with the Conservatives. Don't let Labour ruin it'.[7]

This message was displayed on election posters accompanied by the image of a happy family around a dining table consuming butter, milk cheese and jam. It was another attempt to contrast the ration-book past under Labour with the benefits of the now-flourishing economy. The Tory manifesto trumpeted a long list of what had been done under their rule, including tax cuts, the building of considerably more homes and the provision of additional school places.

In contrast, Labour's poster, a picture of a smiling Gaitskell with the accompanying text 'we want a Britain where production expands year by year and the growing wealth is fairly shared throughout the nation', was unlikely to set pulses racing.[8]

The party did better with 'Remember Suez – Vote Labour', 'Make Sure Your Job is Safe – Vote Labour' and 'Britain Belongs to You', all of which sought to remind voters that not everyone was doing well. What, Labour asked, of the widow with children, the sick, the near half a million unemployed, and the millions in their old age without adequate pensions?

Labour proposed to raise the basic state pension to end pensioner poverty. There was a pledge to get rid of the 11-plus exam, bring in a system of comprehensive school education and spend 1 per cent of national income each year to help underdeveloped countries. Nationalisation also remained part of the agenda, but in a limited fashion, Gaitskell proposing only that steel and road haulage would come back into public hands.

A fortnight before polling day, the media was beginning to sense that a Conservative victory was becoming less likely, as opinion polls showed between 15 and 20 per cent of the electorate were still undecided. With a battleground of fewer than 150 marginal seats this seemed to set the election on a knife-edge.

The *Economist* magazine went as far as to state that there was a real possibility of Gaitskell becoming prime minister. The Labour leader told his rallies that victory was within reach, something reflected in his confident TV appearances during which he bashed the government over Suez and told the country that Labour was setting the agenda.

Television had now reached around 70 per cent of all British homes and was becoming an ever more important part of electioneering. Labour's own broadcasts were innovative and slick, often taking the form of a news magazine show. These were fronted by Tony Benn, the Labour MP still then known as Anthony Wedgwood Benn.

The series was called 'Britain Belongs to You' and was styled 'A Campaign Report direct from Labour's Radio and TV Operations Room in London'. Labour MPs played the role of reporters, interviewing a range of people from different walks of life, including senior party figures.

On one occasion Gaitskell appeared by live link from Newcastle, saying 'most of the places that I have been to in this tour seem to be more concerned about pensions and the cost of living, housing and health and things like that.'

'But up here on Tyneside they have got something else that they are worrying about – and it's jobs. You see here you have unemployment which is substantially higher than it was a year ago and pretty well twice what it was two years ago.'[9] The Labour leader promised help to build factories and push firms into areas, not only the North East but in Lancashire, where hundreds of mills were closing.

The Labour strategy also included a diet of daily press conferences, an innovation which allowed the party to speak to the media – and therefore the voters – about whichever topics it wished to highlight. This was so successful that the Conservatives, who had spent almost £500,000 (£9.75 million today) on advertising in the months leading to the election, were forced to follow suit.

Despite a strong campaign Labour made a significant blunder, and it came from the very top. Gaitskell, who had attracted crowds of up to 20,000 to his rallies, made the error at a crucial stage. The context was tax, and how the cost of Labour's manifesto promises might be met. With ten days to go until polling Gaitskell claimed that economic growth would be secured and would pay for the party's spending plans without the need for any income tax rises.

However, just three days later, the Labour leader suddenly pledged his government would end purchase tax – a levy on a range of goods deemed to be luxury items. It was a bombshell which blew a hole in the credibility of Labour's proposals, allowing the Tories to attack, claiming the electorate were being offered bribes by spivs. Bevan was so distraught that he said of Gaitskell, 'he's thrown it away – he's lost the election.'[10]

Polling day around the country continued the warm temperatures of the summer. Over London the clear conditions were exploited by a Tory-supporting businessman to trail smoke from a plane writing the words 'Back Mac' across the capital's sky. In Bedford, the sunshine encouraged a wasp to sting a man while in the polling booth casting his vote. That mishap aside, polling day was reported to be generally quiet.

At nighttime the traditional crowds gathered in central London, while West End hotels had electronic scoreboards and teleprinters to entertain well-heeled guests. Most of the country tuned in to television which, as in 1955, was providing hour-by-hour coverage.

As results began to trickle in, a picture emerged of a North/South divide across English constituencies; there was a swing to Labour in places like Manchester, but in favour of the Conservatives in suburban seats outside London. Then, with not many more than 100 results declared, the BBC predicted that Macmillan would have a majority of about the same figure. This was to prove remarkably accurate.

Not long afterwards Gaitskell was asked about this forecast at his Leeds South count. He refused to be drawn, airily suggesting that he had not yet had the luxury of studying any results. Had he done so, he would have seen the Tories picking up several seats from Labour, with the tide clearly going against his party.

The final result showed Labour on 258 seats, a net loss of 19 seats, while the Conservatives had reached 365 seats, an increase of 20, which took their majority to a round 100, just as the BBC had predicted. The Liberals, though often cutting into the vote of both the main parties, were squeezed out, and ended exactly where they had begun, with six seats.

A national swing to the Tories of 1 per cent accounted for the overall result, but in some areas – including Scotland and South Wales – Labour improved its position and made gains. However, in the West Midlands the party had lost more than half a dozen seats.

By the early hours of the morning, with over half the 630 seats having declared, Gaitskell was back before the television cameras. 'It seems clear that there is going to be another Conservative government and therefore I must concede, in this sense, victory to our opponents', he said with considerable grace.[11]

This was a first for British democracy, a political leader conceding defeat to the watching millions on television. The Tories had not only recovered from their landslide defeat of 1945, but over the course of the 1950s had built their own majority into three figures. That this had occurred so soon after the Suez debacle was even more remarkable.

In large part they had Macmillan to thank, a confident and skilful leader able to portray himself as a man of the times, keeping Britain and the British people prosperous. By contrast, Labour had been painted as a party which was becoming outdated, still focused on class divisions rather than the benefits of widespread social change.

Memories of the 1930s had by now faded and the sizable advances Labour had secured in health, homes, jobs and education were simply accepted as part of British life no matter which party was in power.

At the margins Suez, for all its toxicity, may have played a part in Labour's defeat. Many working-class voters supported Eden's military action and Labour's popularity among manual workers fell to 57 per cent and dropped too among non-manual workers. There was a slight increase in support for Labour among women, and the party was more popular with those of pensionable age, but the young tended to split evenly for the two main parties.

Labour's share of the vote fell from 46 to 43 per cent while that of the Tories fell only slightly to 49 per cent. Set against the backdrop of three consecutive defeats across a largely barren decade many openly asked 'Must Labour Lose?', the title of a book soon being dedicated to that very question.

Gaitskell, who the weekend before the election had felt confident enough to draw up his Cabinet, evidently did not think so. In defeat he urged supporters to look beyond the result and 'not to be too despondent, or too dismayed, we have lost the battle, but the struggle continues and in the end we shall win'.[12]

1959– General Election Result

Date of Election – 8 October

Overall Turnout – 78.7%

Labour

Candidates – 621

MPs – 258

Votes – 12,216,172

Percentage share of the vote – 43.8%

Result – Conservative majority

Highlight – Election night results are broadcast live by both the BBC and ITV for the first time.

Chapter 18

1964 – The New Britain

'An outdated Conservative Britain ruled from the
grouse moors or a modern Socialist Britain'.

Harold Wilson[1]

On the afternoon of Friday 16 October 1964, Harold Wilson took a call from the queen's private secretary asking that he come at once to Buckingham Palace to officially be installed as the third prime minister in Labour's history.

It was the final act of a nail-biting election which had seen his party scrape to victory by a handful of seats, an achievement which could hardly have been foreseen in the aftermath of the wounding defeat five years earlier.

In 1959, Labour looked to be in serious trouble, having lost three times in a row to the rejuvenated Conservatives. The truth was that although Labour did have its problems with the electorate – 30 per cent of wage earners at that election voting against the party – these were not as great as believed at the time.

Nevertheless, the road to redemption at the polls was a hard one. It began in November 1959, a month after the defeat which had seen the Tories increase their majority to 100 seats. As so often, the drama unfolded at Labour's annual conference. Hugh Gaitskell, using his leader's speech in Blackpool as an election post-mortem, attacked the long-held commitment to public ownership which had been part of Labour's constitution since 1918.

Referred to simply as 'Clause IV' this vowed to 'secure for the workers by hand or by brain the full fruits of their industry and the most equitable distribution thereof that may be possible upon the basis of the common ownership of the means of production'.[2] Gaitskell wished to remove the passage, believing its message was holding Labour back by putting off voters.

Many objected, including the conference chair Barbara Castle and Harold Wilson the shadow chancellor. The strongest denunciation came from Nye Bevan, by now deputy leader of the party. From the platform he told delegates: 'the overwhelming majority of the Labour Party will not acquiesce in the jettisoning of the concept of progressive public ownership'.

Then, growing more passionate, he declared to the hall 'when we realise that all the tides of history are flowing in our direction, that we are not beaten, that we represent the future. Then, when we say it and mean it, we shall lead our people to where they deserve to be led.'[3]

Clause IV was retained with the support of the trade unions, though sections of the media – *The Times* and others who tended to back the Conservatives – felt that Labour was sacrificing the chance of a fresh start.

Bevan's intervention was to be his last great speech to the party. He would die from cancer in the summer of 1960 at the age of 62, sparking an outpouring of grief in Parliament, in South Wales and the country beyond.

It was the first of two tragedies to befall Labour during the 1959–64 Parliament and Bevan's passing had consequences. The left, in search of a new figurehead, alighted on Harold Wilson who, somewhat reluctantly, challenged Gaitskell for the leadership in late 1960.

Gaitskell, as was always likely, won comfortably, but was coming to be seen as rather out of touch. The feeling was most marked around the re-emergence of an anti-war movement within Labour's ranks, which saw the party adopt a position of unilateral nuclear disarmament at the 1960 conference. Gaitskell was furious and vowed to 'fight and fight and fight again to save the party we love', successfully overturning the decision a year later.[4]

The debate over nuclear weapons was in keeping with the times: the sixties was a decade of profound liberalising change across much of British society in the law, media, religion, music and youth culture. Accompanying this was a waning of deference and a growing assertion of individual rights.

In the first two years after the 1959 election the prime minister, Harold Macmillan, was at his most commanding, both at home and abroad, where he accepted that Commonwealth countries should gain independence from the Empire. Thereafter his popularity, and that of the government, began to dwindle. As so often, the central issue was the economy, which by late 1960 was suffering an adverse balance of payments, with rising inflation and fears of growing unemployment.

In 1961, the government tried to restore the economy to health through deflationary measures including spending cuts, increases in indirect taxation and hikes in the Bank of England base rate. The Conservatives also brought in what was termed a 'pay pause', which in reality represented a freeze, keeping wage increases in line with the nation's meagre productivity rate.

Well into 1962 when the pause itself was abandoned, the economy stubbornly showed no further signs of growth. It was the beginning of the end of what had been a period of optimism, and the change in sentiment became obvious to the Tories when they were defeated by the Liberals on a huge swing in the Orpington by-election that March.

The result was seen as a straw in the wind for the coming general election and when Labour won the Middlesborough West by-election three months later, with a 22 per cent fall in the Tory vote, Macmillan reacted by dispatching a third of his Cabinet, replacing them with younger MPs. Dubbed the 'night of the long knives' the sudden sackings shocked the country and dented Macmillan's gentlemanly image.

There was a gathering sense of a prime minister in a panic. Macmillan's actions sparked anger, and a revolt among his MPs, which was only quelled when Labour tabled a vote of no confidence in the government.

Worse was to follow when it was revealed in early 1963 that the minister for war, John Profumo, had been conducting an affair with a model and 'showgirl', Christine Keeler. Prostitution was alleged, but the bigger issue was that another of Keeler's lovers was a Soviet intelligence officer.

Much was made in the Commons and the media of the obvious national security risks and matters were made worse when Profumo was later exposed as having lied to Parliament over the affair and was forced to resign. The crisis tarnished not only his reputation but that of the Conservative Party.

The Profumo affair made the government look out of step with the people, untrustworthy and even faintly ridiculous. The ridicule took very real shape in the form of a stage and television satire boom driven by young university graduates who had the establishment, and particularly ministers, in their sights.

Ailing and exhausted by the scandal, Macmillan decided to call it a day. The Conservatives stuck to tradition and found a new leader without bothering to hold any form of election even among their own MPs.

They turned to Alec Douglas-Home, a Scottish earl with a hereditary place in the House of Lords. Though he then renounced his peerage and won a seat in the Commons, it was an appointment that did nothing to dispel the image of the Tories as a party run by posh old men in tweeds who hunted game.

Labour, in contrast, had a leader very much of the era in Harold Wilson. With his northern charm and grammar-school background he was the antithesis of Douglas-Home. A celebrated Oxford scholar and highly capable civil servant, he had been a young protégé of Clement Attlee. Seen mainly as a centre-left figure he had risen quickly through the Parliamentary ranks.

Wilson was aged just 46 when he took over, beating the then deputy leader, George Brown, and shadow chancellor, James Callaghan, in the ballot among Labour MPs. Immediately, he called for unity and promised to focus on leading the party to victory.

Wilson, though, was very much an accidental leader. The contest only occurred after Gaitskell died suddenly in January 1963. Aged just 56, his passing shocked the nation, with the BBC reporting that it came 'as Labour appears poised for victory at the next election thanks largely to Mr Gaitskell's efforts to make the party "relevant and realistic".'[5]

It is impossible to know whether Gaitskell would have won the coming election, had he lived, but it is certain that Wilson imbued Labour with fresh energy. In his address to delegates at the party conference in 1963 the Labour leader said a new Britain was being re-cast in a coming technological and scientific revolution and that Labour was 're-defining and re-stating our socialism' in those terms.

However, that would only happen, he said, if the party and the country embraced a depth of economic and social change. He went on to say that a Britain 'that is going to be forged in the white heat of this revolution, will be no place for restrictive practices or for outdated methods on either side of industry.'[6]

The speech was important because it offered a path back to power, and in pivoting to science Wilson had taken Labour beyond debates about public ownership, giving the white lab coat as much prominence as working overalls in the mind of the British worker. Wilson appeared reassuring and at the same time radical, well beyond his core vote.

The electoral prospects for Labour when Macmillan resigned seemed rosy, with an opinion poll lead of 20 per cent. The unexpected twist was that the public warmed to Douglas-Home, with the new Tory leader being seen as someone who was both unflappable and experienced, especially in foreign affairs.

Though many felt a Labour win to be in the bag, Wilson took nothing for granted, and was out touring the country through the hard winter months to April 1964. The party meanwhile stepped up its campaigning activity in the constituencies, but despite all this the late summer polls showed a distinct shift back towards the Tories. By September, on the back of a more favourable economic outlook, the government was ahead.

The Conservatives waited until virtually the last moment before calling the election for Thursday 15 October – five years and one week after the country had last voted. This was confirmed by Douglas-Home on 15 September, after he flew to Balmoral to ask his personal friend, the queen, to dissolve Parliament.

In truth, campaigning was already underway and before going to Scotland the prime minister had appeared in Kent, where he variously spoke from the top of a haycart, a Conservative club balcony and later in front of a theatre; all a world away from the image Labour and Wilson were cultivating.

Before the election had officially been called, Labour held a mass rally at the Empire Pool in Wembley; where, in front of 20,000 supporters, Wilson struck the keynote, saying 'the choice we offer . . . is between standing still, clinging to a tired philosophy of a day that is gone, or moving forward in partnership and unity to a dynamic, expanding, confident and above all purposive new Britain'.[7]

Though the government would go into the election with a 94-seat majority it did so having suffered a net loss of five by-elections since 1959. In all but two of the 22 by-elections during that period, Labour's share of the vote increased.

In local elections earlier in the year Labour had made a net gain of over 150 seats and in the first elections to the new Greater London Council Labour took 64 of the 100 seats. Generally, the party was enjoying a swing of around 7 per cent, which if replicated in a general election would deliver a majority of around 100 seats.

There was every reason to be confident and Labour's manifesto, boldly titled 'The New Britain', reflected that optimism. The slogan was also used on posters and in election broadcasts, along with the message 'Let's GO with Labour and we'll get things done', which was even turned into a song and released as a single.[8]

Promising to end what Labour called 'thirteen wasted years' of Tory misrule, the party held out the guarantee of full employment, industrial growth, a halt to rising prices and a lasting solution to the balance of payments deficit. This would come about through what was termed a National Plan to modernise the economy.

To implement this, a new Ministry of Economic Affairs would be created, alongside major expansion programmes for the existing nationalised industries. Iron and steel, which had been nationalised and then de-nationalised after the war, would again come back into public hands, but that was as far as Labour went on the issue of public ownership.

A Ministry for Technology would be set up, and a major overhaul of the tax system would take place to make things fairer for those not on the highest incomes. Labour also promised to reorganise secondary schools fully along comprehensive lines, and to cut class sizes. It also committed itself to the building of around 400,000 homes each year, a figure matching the Tory offer. Prescription charges were to be abolished.

On the economy Labour appealed to voters to take the chance to reverse the economic decline of the Conservative years. This had come to be characterised as 'Stop-Go' economics, the cycle of deflationary (stop) and inflationary (go) measures aimed at controlling inflation and maintaining full employment.

In one of his few memorable phrases of the campaign, Douglas-Home countered that Wilson was offering 'a menu without prices'.[9] It was intended as a warning to voters that Labour should not be trusted with their money, but was laughed off by Wilson who ridiculed the Tory leader for being unable to grasp economic matters, after Douglas-Home revealed that he used matchsticks to help him count.

The Conservative manifesto was soberly titled 'Prosperity with a Purpose' and relied heavily on a defence of the party's record in office, particularly the improvement in living standards. Opinion polls showed time and again that voters were concerned mainly about domestic issues such as the cost of living, education and housing.

For a while, Britain's proposed entry into the European Common Market had looked as though it would be a major campaign theme. However, by the time the country went to the polls the issue had faded into the background.

Macmillan had tried to secure British entry into the forerunner of the European Union only for France's President Charles de Gaulle to veto the application in January 1963. Labour was opposed to membership because it would undermine trade with the Commonwealth, and accused the Tories of allowing this relationship to decline.

As polling day approached, Wilson remained most prominent in Labour's campaigning, while Douglas-Home relied on support from numerous Cabinet colleagues. At the close of the campaign, the opinion polls were tight, though they indicated that across the most marginal seats Labour was only about 2 per cent in front; the difficulty was that for a decisive victory Wilson required an overall swing of closer to 5 per cent.

On election day the longest spell of dry weather in years broke and much of the country was damp and grey. Election night itself was far from dull with early declarations from the larger urban centres putting Labour significantly in front. Just after midnight Wilson's party had made almost two dozen gains, with 180 seats accounted for. At this stage experts in the BBC studio predicted that Labour would win with an overall majority of as many as 40 seats.

Yet as the hours wore on, the tide turned significantly back towards the Conservatives, causing some confusion about the likely outcome of the election. When Wilson arrived at Transport House, Labour's central London headquarters, the following afternoon he told expectant supporters that they would have to wait longer still to be sure of victory.

By mid-afternoon Labour were just three seats short of an overall majority with only a dozen or so results to come. The key gain was in Meriden in the West Midlands, which was won with a majority of 300 votes, leaving supporters ecstatic.

The drama quickly shifted to Downing Street where Douglas-Home emerged to both cheers and boos, announcing that he was going to see the queen. Shortly afterwards, with the news that Labour had held Penistone in Yorkshire and could not be beaten, it was Wilson who set off for the Palace.

The BBC flashed up a graphic showing 'LABOUR IN', but just as this was appearing on screen, the telephone rang in the studio. The anchorman, Richard Dimbleby, answered the call, then announced, 'I've just been told that China has exploded an atomic bomb – everything's happening today isn't it.'[10]

The timing of the test – making China the second communist nuclear power – is interesting in the context of the election which had also seen the Soviet leader, Nikita Khrushchev, removed from power, just as Britons were going to vote. The instability in the international arena was a concern for Labour, as it might make the electorate reluctant to change government.

It is possible that had these two events happened a few days earlier they may have swung things back towards the Tories, with their more strident defence policies and Douglas-Home's perceived strength in foreign affairs.

The final tally showed Labour with 317 seats, 13 ahead of the Conservatives. This gave Wilson a four-seat working majority on the back of 60 gains. It was a very similar picture to Labour's 1950 victory and, just as then, predictions soon followed that another election would be necessary.

Labour won 44 per cent of the vote, which was actually a small fall compared to the 1959 figure, while the Tories managed 43 per cent, a drop of nearly 6 per cent. Labour's national agent was quick to point out that a more decisive win would have been achieved had they captured a few hundred more votes across marginal seats.

In what was a very tight race, Labour had also been assisted by a significant rise in support for the Liberals. Though there was no great revival for the party it did surpass its target of three million votes, a tally which hurt Douglas-Home more than Wilson.

Instead of basing its offering on an appeal to ideology, Labour had instead captured the idea of change, presenting a plan of action that would propel Britain through the second half of the century. The party's socialism was not so much cast off, as worn lightly.

All of this struck a chord with voters who increasingly viewed the Tories as too remote and unlikely to maintain the improved living standards they had achieved during the previous decade, especially with unemployment nearing one million by 1963.

The Conservative brand had also suffered significant damage, not just through the Profumo affair, but also in the humiliating French rejection of the UK's bid to join the EEC, something the satirists did not allow to pass without comment.

Resentment also simmered in the Tory ranks over the antiquated way they had chosen Douglas-Home to replace Macmillan. That anger spilled into the public domain in a damning *Spectator* magazine article written some months before the election by Iain Macleod, who had been a senior figure in Macmillan's government.

In the aftermath of the election, the *Guardian* reported that Douglas-Home 'seemed to evaporate into the afternoon sunshine', on leaving Buckingham Palace by the North Gateway, a side route to avoid the crowds. Wilson had then arrived smiling and wearing a red rose, accompanied by his wife.

So ended the long Tory years which had begun in 1951 with the ousting of the great Attlee post-war reforming governments. As the newspaper elegantly put it: 'Sir Alec drove in, but it was Mr Wilson who drove out.'[11]

1964– General Election Result

Date of Election – Thursday 15 October

Overall Turnout – 77.1%

Labour

Candidates – 628

MPs – 317

Votes – 12,205,808

Percentage share of the vote – 44.1%

Result – Labour majority

Highlight – Labour under Harold Wilson stands on a platform of harnessing a technological revolution and a 'New Britain'.

Chapter 19

1966 – Time for Decision

'We are asking for a mandate to carry through
the radical reconstruction of our national life . . .'

Labour manifesto 1966[1]

With the slogan 'You Know Labour Government Works', Harold Wilson took the greatest gamble of his political career by calling a general election in March 1966, less than 18 months after coming to power. He aimed at a significant increase in his slender Commons majority, but the stakes could not have been higher; the election would make or break the youngest prime minister in 70 years.

Since its victory in autumn 1964, Labour had managed to govern alone with a majority which had dropped to as low as three. Wilson seemingly never considered any arrangement with the Liberals which might have eased the tight parliamentary arithmetic.

From the outset, things had been difficult for his government. On Labour's first day in office, official figures revealed an £800m deficit (over £13.5 billion today) in the balance of payments, Britain's trading figures with the rest of the world. Though the Queen's Speech set out measures to address this, the government quickly faced a full sterling crisis.

Advised to devalue the pound, which had been pegged at $2.80 for the previous 15 years, Wilson demurred, believing that doing so would be a grave blow to Britain's standing and that of his government. He opted instead for increasing charges on imports and tax rises. The announcement did not calm sentiment against sterling, and further turbulence followed, forcing a rise in the Bank of England base rates.

This was extremely damaging for a government elected on a pledge of ushering in an era of sustained growth in place of the Stop-Go Tory years, but Wilson was understandably determined his party was not going to take the blame for the economic weakness inherited from their opponents.

Instead, he championed the setting-up of a Department for Economic Affairs – intended to give the PM a closer handle on the levers of the economy, bypassing the Treasury and reducing its political clout – and a Ministry of Technology which would feed ideas into Labour's National Plan. This was published in 1965, targeting an extraordinarily ambitious 25 per cent growth in Gross Domestic Product (GDP) by 1970.

To achieve this, more wealth would have to be produced at home, combined with a drive to increase exports. At the same time ministers hoped to control inflation and maintain full employment by limiting prices and wages, something which angered the left of the party and trade unions.

Wilson was the driving force behind much of this, in an effort to prove his government's grasp of economics and that he could make good on the pledge to steer Britain into the promised era of (technological and scientific) modernity. He was seeking to protect his reputation as a politician of substance, one able to stand up to the Treasury and the Bank of England.

More than that, Wilson was determined to find the political space needed to entrench his government in power so that, if another election had to be fought, there would be a strong record to defend which would carry them to victory.

Though economics dominated, the government faced other significant issues during the parliament. NHS prescription charges were abolished, as promised, early in 1965 and in the same year the government supported moves towards ending capital punishment.

The Rent Act of 1965 had given greater security to tenants and the Redundancy Payments Act provided compensation and protection for workers who had lost their jobs or were threatened with redundancy. There was also a landmark change with the passing of the Race Relations Act, which made racial discrimination illegal and set up a Race Relations Board.

Returning the iron and steel industries to the public realm proved more troublesome. The difficulty of forcing this through with a small majority, and dissent from the right-wing of his own party, meant Wilson shelved the plans.

Overseas, Wilson faced a major crisis in Rhodesia (now Zimbabwe) where the prime minister, Ian Smith, was determined to resist voting reforms which would have ended the white minority government in a country with an overwhelmingly black population. On the wider international front, the prime minister rejected advances from the United States' president, Lyndon Johnson, to bring even a handful of British troops into the Vietnam War.

Amid all these difficulties, it was little wonder that hints of an early election, both from Downing Street and in the press, regularly surfaced in 1965. These were eventually shut down by the prime minister at Labour's annual conference in Blackpool that year.

Wilson made the point that the government had not been idle, carrying 65 Bills through Parliament in just over eight months. 'We intend to get on with the job you gave us to do. I believe that is what you want. I believe that is what the country wants', he told delegates.[2]

Behind Wilson's comments lay not only a desire to show that Labour could govern successfully, but also the fact that, as ever in politics, his opponents had not stood still. In July, Alec Douglas-Home surprised the Conservative Party by suddenly announcing his intention to step down from the leadership.

Within days a new leader was in place, and for the first time his appointment came after an election among Tory MPs. Ted Heath was a figure quite unlike his predecessor. The son of a carpenter from Kent and grammar-school educated like Wilson, he seemed almost classless.

Heath's vision embraced cutting taxes, Britain joining the EEC, reforming the trade unions and the targeting of welfare towards those most in need. These ideas came out of a policy review called *Putting Britain Right Ahead* – part of an effort to chart a course back to office.

Yet research undertaken by the party found that voters still saw them as lacking new ideas and as representative mainly of the upper echelons of society. Tory strategists could hardly fail to notice, too, that Heath's own polling figures were far from impressive.

In January and February 1966, Conservative morale was said to be at its lowest point since being removed from power. By now the prospect of a general election was very much in sight, thanks to a resounding by-election victory for Labour at Kingston upon Hull North.

Until the last moment, it had been predicted that this marginal seat would fall to the Tories, but Labour's majority in fact increased by more than 4,000 votes. With the economy growing, unemployment low and wages rising faster than prices, the political outlook was good. Labour led in the polls and Wilson was a commanding figure whose popularity was even greater than that of his party.

On 28 February, fresh from meeting the Soviet leader, Leonid Brezhnev, in Moscow, Wilson told his Cabinet that it was time to ask for a stronger mandate to govern. With his wife Mary he went for a stroll in St James's Park before the country was told at six o'clock that there would be an election.

Parliament was to be dissolved ten days later, with the election following on 31 March. It was a moment of frustration for the Conservatives who had hoped Wilson would wait until the autumn, so allowing the public extra time to become better acquainted with Mr Heath.

Labour went into the campaign with a 10 per cent lead in the polls, but wary of voter apathy. To counter this they relentlessly attacked the record of the Tories in office from 1951 as 'thirteen wasted years' while also portraying Heath as a threat to the welfare state and the settlement of 1945.

As well as setting out Labour's successes, the prime minister also made the case for an enhanced majority. 'This is the make-or-break year', Wilson told the BBC, 'there's a great deal we have got to carry through, especially to make the country sound economically.'

'We cannot be put in the position where we can't get through essential legislation and, of course, with a majority of three the chances of people who hold it up, waste time to frustrate the government legislative intentions, are enormous.'[3]

The bookies had Labour down as strong favourites, something Heath himself acknowledged, saying 'the odds are against us, but we shall fight every inch of the way and we shall put our policies forward positively and we shall attack the weaknesses of this government.'[4]

Wilson based himself in Downing Street, so deliberately keeping the party's HQ, Transport House, at arm's length. This was not a new tactic; since coming into office he had largely excluded the party machine and the National Executive from policy and decision-making.

Unusually, Wilson also decided not to involve himself in the day-to-day skirmishes of the campaign, but rather to remain above the fray in the hope of conveying an impression of simply getting on with the job of running the country. It was a surprising move, given that the Labour leader was more popular than Heath and, in the end, he relented and took a more active part in the campaign from mid-March.

The campaign was instead largely fronted by Jim Callaghan, the chancellor, who was at the sharp end of morning press conferences, while the deputy leader, George Brown, undertook an extensive tour of the country, as he had done in 1964.

That this was no easy task was illustrated in *The Hecklers*, a documentary by the American filmmaker Joseph Strick. It captured the deep anger of voters during public meetings which at times descended into fist fights with forced removals from the hustings.

In Birmingham, a noose was waved at Wilson. There was a particular context. Two years earlier against a backdrop of factory closures in the nearby seat of Smethwick, the Tory candidate Peter Griffiths had beaten Labour's Patrick Gordon Walker, after criticising immigration levels from the Commonwealth. Griffiths refused to condemn the manifest racism in the unofficial election slogan: 'If you want a nigger for a neighbour, vote Labour'.[5]

At an open-air meeting featured in the film Quintin Hogg, a senior Conservative, uses his walking stick to smash a Labour placard featuring the prime minister's image with Hogg then telling his audience – 'take a look at that poster, the one with the ugly face.'[6]

Though only a snapshot, the film undermines the notion of a country at ease with itself in an era of consensus politics. Clearly many voters, not only the young, had strong views about which party should govern and the direction Britain should take as a result.

Labour certainly advocated a clear vision of the future, telling voters they had only just begun to clean up the economic mess left by the Conservatives and should be allowed to complete the task. The party's election material reflected this point, with posters displaying Wilson's pipe and asking for 'FIVE YEARS TO FINISH THE JOB'.

The manifesto, 'Time for Decision', stressed the need for economic planning to boost the regions, and a renewed commitment to bring the private steel monopoly into public ownership, as well as the aircraft industry. It set a target to build half a million homes by 1970, and promised more roads, a new National Freight Authority for road and rail usage and a National Ports Authority to modernise the docks.

An Open University, 'the University of the Air', was to be established and, provided it did not harm the Commonwealth, Britain should again push to join the EEC. To pay in part for all these new programmes, there would be substantial cuts to the defence budget.

In all of this there was a coherence and a rhythm – the repeated suggestion that Labour would change Britain for the better. The announcement in Callaghan's so-called 'little-Budget' at the beginning of March that preparations would begin immediately to move to a decimal currency was further evidence of this.

The Conservatives attempted to match Labour with a dynamic-sounding manifesto, 'Action Not Words'. Drawing on *Putting Britain Right Ahead*, it proposed legislation to limit the power of the trade unions, changes to the welfare state, lower taxes and low inflation as a priority.

The Tories, too, offered an extensive house-building programme and their commitment to a British future inside the EEC was firmer than Labour's. Selling all of this to the public proved to be difficult for Heath; during the campaign he often appeared unhappy, wooden and unsure in comparison with Wilson's buoyant persona.

Not that the prime minister was always favourably received by the public. On a visit to a school in Slough he was hit in the eye by a stink bomb. Though slightly injured he did not press charges, quipping instead that the 15-year-old schoolboy responsible for the prank should be playing cricket for England. It was a line devoured by the newspapers. Not for the last time Wilson had turned adversity into advantage.

The polls remained steady throughout the campaign, with Labour hovering close to 50 per cent during March, and the Conservatives around ten points behind. The veteran pollster Bob McKenzie said there had been 'no campaign in history where we've had so little movement.'[7]

As campaigning entered the final stages expectation grew that Labour would remain in power. When the polls closed at 9 p.m. on 31 March, confirmation of this was not long in coming.

Half an hour after voting ended the BBC went live with their election night coverage. Just after 10 p.m. Cheltenham declared; the Conservatives held on, but with a swing to Labour of almost 3 per cent. Within the hour, no less a figure than the High Sheriff of Devon stepped forward and amid cheers in the civic hall told the nation that 'Mrs Gwyneth Dunwoody is elected Member for Exeter.'[8]

Labour had its first gain and Dunwoody, the daughter of Labour's former general secretary, Morgan Phillips, was engulfed by delighted supporters. Heath must have known his hopes were fading fast, as even in the 1945 landslide Labour had not captured this corner of the West Country.

Minutes later, back in the BBC studio, the political scientist David Butler explained that 'when you have had 18 seats [declared] and every one of them has swung to the government in power you can say without a shadow of a doubt that the Labour Party has, in fact, won this election.'[9]

Shortly after 2 a.m., with a 100-seat majority being predicted, Wilson was tucked up in bed. Heath, meanwhile, was in his flat at the Albany building in Mayfair considering whether to make a concession speech. He was right to wait. Labour's progress slowed as results came in from rural locations.

Labour's advances did not stop though, and unlike in 1964 seats continued to change hands – from northeast Scotland to the Borders, Lancashire, the Midlands, the South East and South West of England. Places as diverse as Caithness and Sutherland, Hampstead and Lancaster all fell to Labour for the first time. At noon the next day, the 315th seat came in for Wilson, securing a majority.

Heath then emerged to make a short statement, telling waiting reporters that 'it is now clear the Labour Party will form the next government', then adding that he intended to go on leading his party.[10]

Meanwhile, the prime minister was on the train back to London from his Merseyside constituency. Having departed Liverpool Lime Street to the sound of a bagpiper playing 'Scotland the Brave', Wilson was greeted at Euston Station by cheering, television cameras and a burst of photographers' flashbulbs. Clad in his distinctive Gannex overcoat, he offered a wave and a smile but nothing more for the media.

Labour's final total was 364 with the Conservatives on 253 and the Liberals capturing a dozen seats. This delivered a majority of 98 for Wilson, tipping the victory into landslide territory. Labour had done particularly well in the cities, in Hull, Newcastle, Birmingham and elsewhere, while winning a swing across the country of 3 per cent.

At 76 per cent of the electorate, though, the turnout was the lowest at a general election since the war, in a worrying indication of disenchantment with politics. Even so, Labour won across both gender and class lines, with slightly more women voting for Wilson than Heath. There was strong support among both skilled and unskilled workers, the 25–34 age group moved more decisively to Labour than in 1964, the party won significant backing from the over-65s and even among the better off support also increased.

The campaign and its result were an accentuated version of 1964. At the end of a short parliament, voters searching for stability were really given no pressing reason to switch sides.

Labour continually pushed the idea that they had to be given time to put the country on the right road, blaming past Conservative governments for creating Britain's economic problems, its balance of payments deficit and pockets of rising unemployment. Wilson was presented as the antidote, a leader with a plan and the ability to implement it.

The Tories suffered from a less well-defined offering, and the drawback that Wilson had cannily called the election before their leader could establish himself in the public's minds. By comparison Wilson was already prime minister and seemed like a safe bet. Findings from surveys conducted shortly after the election bear this out; voters viewed Wilson as a stronger leader than his main opponent.

Heath could also not shake off the perception that the Conservatives were out of touch, a party run by and in the interests of the upper classes. Memories of Macmillan's pay pause and the Profumo scandal still dogged the party.

The second landslide in Labour's history was described by the prime minister as 'the greatest peacetime victory for any party since 1906', when the Liberals had been swept back into office at what had seemed like the beginning of a golden era.[11] Wilson was now the single dominant figure in British politics and seemed set fair to govern for many years to come.

1966– General Election Result

Date of Election – Thursday 31 March
Overall Turnout – 75.8%
Labour
Candidates – 622
MPs – 364
Votes – 13,096,629
Percentage share of the vote – 48%
Result – Labour landslide
Highlight – Harold Wilson wins the second landslide in Labour's history.

Chapter 20

1970 – Now Britain's Strong

'At the beginning of the campaign
we were sure we would win. We were
quite unprepared for defeat.'

Marcia Williams, political secretary to Harold Wilson.[1]

With ice cream sales booming, parks full of sunbathers, and the lowest rainfall in a decade, Britain went to the polls in June 1970. Harold Wilson was making the most of his opportunity, with public opinion showing Labour ahead for the first time in three years.

Having won a landslide in 1966, Wilson had sought to demonstrate sound economic management and to prove that Labour was the natural party of government, well-suited to steering a prosperous Britain in the second half of the twentieth century.

This road had not been easy. Less than two months after being elected, his government found itself embroiled in a pay dispute with the National Union of Seamen, which brought merchant shipping to a standstill.

There was a wider context than simply dealing with a single industrial dispute. Wilson was worried that to capitulate to the seamen would completely undermine the government's prices and incomes policy which aimed to reduce inflation by limiting wage rises to 3.5 per cent.

The strike concluded at the beginning of July with concessions on all sides, but the aftermath of the agreement proved damaging. The publication of a government Bill establishing further strict controls over wage settlements in turn provoked the resignation of Frank Cousins, the technology minister, who went back to leading the powerful Transport and General Workers' Union.

In the same month, sterling fell to its lowest level for nearly two years, partly depressed by the industrial unrest. As speculation against the pound grew, Labour was presented with a difficult choice: it could devalue the currency or deflate the economy.

The Cabinet was divided, but the prime minister remained opposed to devaluation. Instead, he managed to persuade enough key ministers, including the chancellor Jim Callaghan, that deflationary measures should be the priority. The result was higher indirect taxes, sharp cuts in public spending and a wages and prices freeze. There was a further consequence, as George Brown's much-vaunted National Plan was all but abandoned.

By the end of 1966 the balance of payments began to improve, and a surplus was recorded in the early part of 1967. The good news for Labour, though, did not last. As the weeks and months passed, speculative pressure on sterling mounted.

Foreign creditors and the markets remained unconvinced that the deflationary package of measures taken in 1966 had done enough to rebalance the economy and end the persistent trade deficits. The situation was not helped by a dockers' strike which stopped exports leaving the country.

The closure of the Suez Canal as a result of the Six-Day War between an Arab coalition and Israel in June 1967, also disrupted trade and led to Arab countries selling sterling. Central banks and the International Monetary Fund then signalled they would no longer be willing to prop up the pound.

In the background Britain's second attempt to join the European

Economic Community continued to have an impact. Wilson made a formal application in May 1967, only to see it vetoed by the French president Charles de Gaulle who, while overseeing his own booming domestic economy, claimed Britain was not compatible with the Common Market.

The devaluation of the pound, previously an unthinkable prospect, became a reality in November 1967, after the Bank of England was forced to spend £200 million in gold and foreign currency reserves in its defence on one day alone. Callaghan had little choice but to announce that the government was lowering the exchange rate against the US dollar from $2.80 to $2.40 (a near 15 per cent devaluation).

The immediate aim was to make exports cheaper, and so encourage other countries to buy more goods from Britain. It was hoped this would in turn secure economic growth and full employment, while sustaining the United Kingdom's international standing. The price to be paid for this was interest rate rises and spending cuts. In truth, devaluation was a full-scale political humiliation, which involved a complete reversal of Wilson's previous position on the issue.

Addressing millions of viewers on television, the Labour leader tried to sell the government's new strategy, explaining that 'From now on the pound abroad is worth 14 per cent or so less in terms of other currencies. It does not mean, of course, that the pound here in Britain, in your pocket or purse, or in your bank has been devalued.'[2]

The intention was to explain and reassure, but these remarks would be used time and again against Wilson in future by his political opponents and they would come to haunt him.

At the start of 1968, the prospects for Labour looked bleak. In just over three years since Wilson first became prime minister, the government had been hampered by continuous economic crises. There had been by-election successes for the Conservatives, and in November

1967, the Scottish National Party caused a huge upset by winning Hamilton, a previously rock-solid Labour seat.

Labour also suffered reversals in the 1968 municipal elections, losing close to 600 seats, while in London the Tories returned to power for the first time since the 1930s. Although as a result, the Conservatives found themselves in the happy position of being 20 points in front in the opinion polls, their leader, Ted Heath, suffered the setback of having to dismiss his shadow defence minister, Enoch Powell, in April 1968 over the racist nature of what became known as the 'Rivers of Blood' speech to Tory activists.

The Tories, too, faced the challenge of the undoubted strides the Labour government had made in the social sphere. The voting age was lowered to 18, capital punishment abolished, and sex between men aged over 21 was legalised in England and Wales. In Parliament ministers also brought in the forerunner of a system of Select Committees to better scrutinise the work of government.

Meanwhile, the issue of America's war in Vietnam, which provoked at times violent protests on British streets, troubled ministers. It also angered the left of the party, as many grassroots activists were disillusioned by the government's support for the United States. There were tensions closer to home, too, with Wilson taking the controversial decision in 1969 to send British troops into Northern Ireland, where violence had escalated between nationalist and unionist communities.

However, it continued to be the economy which defined political fortunes. In 1968, more working days were lost to strikes (many of them unofficial) than in any of the previous five years. In the main the walkouts were provoked by rising inflation and the cost of living.

In response, the government published a White Paper – a form of policy document produced by governments that set out their proposals for future legislation – called 'In Place of Strife'. The title was a deliberate echo of 'In Place of Fear', Nye Bevan's case for socialism from the early 1950s. Its proposals included the imposition of a four-week cooling-off period before a strike could begin, during which unions would be forced to ballot members about taking action.

In presenting the White Paper to MPs in March 1969 its author, the employment secretary Barbara Castle, argued that it would protect the unions and place them again fully at the heart of British democracy. Though unspoken, its other aim was to outflank Heath who was preparing his own reforms, which were expected to be draconian by comparison.

Though the *Daily Mirror* described Castle's ideas as 'Bloody Good Sense', the unions did not see it that way, nor did many Labour MPs including some in the Cabinet. With acrimony growing, and Wilson at one point threatening to resign, Castle gave way, things were smoothed over and the planned reforms quietly withdrawn.

By Labour's annual conference in late September 1969, it looked as though the tide was turning. Chancellor Roy Jenkins sounded upbeat about a fall in unemployment, and he projected economic growth of up to 4 per cent. By the winter months, the long-standing Tory lead in the polls had all but vanished, while Ted Heath had failed to establish himself as a popular alternative prime minister.

In the early months of 1970, senior Conservatives began to speak openly about their fears that Wilson might soon call an election, one they were no longer sure of winning. On 18 May, the prime minister made his move, visiting the queen, who had flown back to London from her Sandringham estate in Norfolk. Just in time for the six o'clock news, it was confirmed that an election would be held a month later on 18 June.

Heath immediately declared himself ready for the fight, which looked like being a presidential contest between the two men. His task would not be easy – for the Conservatives to overturn a Labour majority close to 100, Heath would have to demonstrate not only that Wilson had failed, but that he would be better placed to succeed.

Parliament was dissolved on 29 May, and the prime minister was soon on the campaign trail, quickly visiting Yorkshire, London, East Anglia, Birmingham, Liverpool and Glasgow, all of which were baking in the hot spell. He was often accompanied by his wife, Mary, emphasising the contrast between Wilson the family man and Heath the bachelor.

On the back of what were now consistent polling leads most commentators felt that it was Wilson's election to lose, and that a consecutive third term would entrench Labour in power, spelling the end of Heath.

The Conservative manifesto, 'A Better Tomorrow' promised tax reductions, a smaller government, more competition and consumer choice, and as the unions had feared plans to limit strikes. In the foreword Heath directly attacked Wilson, saying the past six years had seen 'a cheap and trivial style of government' and that 'decisions have been dictated by a desire to catch tomorrow's headlines . . . government by gimmick has become the order of the day.'[3]

The prime minister's response was to suggest the Tory policies were the work of what he termed 'Selsdon Man', a reference to a Shadow Cabinet meeting at the Selsdon Park Hotel in Surrey earlier in the year. Though there was little evidence in the Conservative manifesto to support his claims, Wilson warned that to back Heath now would be to allow an individualist free market approach to take hold.

Labour's own manifesto – 'Now Britain's strong – let's make it great to live in!' was a defence of its achievements going back to 1964 on industry, jobs and the nationalisation of transport and investment in key industries. Promises were made of further progress, including in education, housing and health.

The backdrop to the campaigning was not the weather, but the finals of the football World Cup being held in Mexico, at which England hoped to retain the trophy they had won four years earlier.

The tournament began on 31 May, with the holders progressing to the quarter finals where they were knocked out on 14 June by West Germany, just four days before the election. The football not only provided a rare daily diet of live televised sport, but to a degree dampened interest in, and media coverage of, the election.

In the final week of the campaign, the polls were near unanimous in pointing to a Labour victory, though there were significant fluctuations and one company had Wilson 12 per cent in front, while another put the lead at just 2.5 per cent. There was little suggestion that Heath had any hope of being on course for Downing Street: a single poll the evening before the election showing a slight Tory lead was all but ignored.

Polling stations closed at 10 p.m. and attention quickly turned to the television stations. The BBC, while promising 'the flavour the feel and really the smell of election night in Britain', had come up with a novel idea to assist with the coverage.[4]

Instead of asking how people intended to vote they would be approached once they left the polling station. Having been identified as the most ordinary constituency in England, Gravesend in Kent was chosen for this experiment. It was a seat Labour had held in 1964 and again with a bigger majority two years later.

The result of that very first exit poll was a surprise. It was in line with the last of the pre-election surveys and put the Tories in the lead by 1 per cent. Extrapolated across the country this figure would be much higher, at almost 4.5 per cent, and enough to turf Labour from power.

The first result of the night came at 11 p.m. when Guildford declared, showing a 6 per cent swing to the Conservatives. In Wolverhampton's two constituencies the swing to the Tories was as high as 9 per cent. It was becoming clear, wholly unexpectedly, that Heath was set to triumph.

At his declaration in Bexley after 1 a.m., the clearly delighted Conservative leader made no mention of the national picture. Wilson was interviewed on Merseyside an hour later and refused to accept that his party had been beaten. In his view there was a long way to go and 'it could be a very close run thing.'[5]

He was mistaken. At mid-day on Friday, the prime minister was back in London preparing to tender his resignation. By 6.30 p.m., the queen had returned from a day out at the Ascot races, had seen Wilson and accepted that he could not go on as prime minister. Six years of Labour rule were, quite suddenly, at an end.

The Conservatives had triumphed with 330 seats in total, a majority of 31 over all other parties. Labour won 288 seats, a loss of 76, having taken 43 per cent of the popular vote, a 5 per cent drop from the previous election. The party suffered some wounding losses, seeing George Brown, Jennie Lee and Sir Dingle Foot, the solicitor-general, all defeated.

The newspapers were full of excitement at the birth of a new government but took a harsher tone with Wilson. London's *Evening Standard* reflected that Labour's leader had fought 'on a fundamentally complacent ticket, hoping that his skill with the media and his basic political savoir-faire would carry a decidedly bad record past the voters when they were not looking'.[6]

Wilson had been optimistic throughout, with Heath only claiming after victory to have known he was likely to win. In truth neither could have predicted the result given the drop in turnout – just 72 per cent of the eligible population voting, the lowest level since before the Second World War.

Public apathy hurt Labour, with the late swing to the Conservatives suggesting they had been able to both maximise their core vote and capture some of those who had gone elsewhere four years earlier.

Though hard to substantiate, some remained convinced that England's World Cup defeat played a part. The local government minister and avid Grimsby Town supporter, Tony Crosland, blamed the defeat on 'a mix of party complacency and the disgruntled Match of the Day millions', who had expected a Wilson triumph, but had kept their focus on the football.[7]

It had seemed before polling day that Labour's troubles were at an end. The party had gone into the election ahead, having been almost 30 points behind in late 1968, and there had been little indication during the campaign that Wilson was in difficulty, a lapse which would later cause anger and bewilderment in Labour circles.

By the late 1960s, the number of polling organisations and the frequency of polls had greatly increased. These were openly reported across media organisations and helped shape the political landscape both before and during the election. So why had the polls got things so badly wrong?

Labour's strength, especially as the governing party, may have been exaggerated by the polling techniques of the time. After the election, it was suggested that the public may have misled the pollsters, with voters shy of saying they would vote Conservative. Some of these were the 'Don't Know's'. There were wide variations in their numbers recorded in surveys, and the polling companies admitted to finding it hard to pin this group down.

Certainly, the electorate was more volatile and voting allegiances less secure than in the past. The main reason for this breakdown in entrenched political loyalties was probably economic. The Labour government had endured a tough battle since 1966 to put Britain back on its feet. Though wages were going up, they were doing so in response to rising inflation, with ordinary citizens seeing little or no real benefit. The British economy was also expanding at a slower rate than many other comparable industrial countries.

The problem for Wilson and his team was that they had presented themselves as sound fiscal managers, but the devaluation of the pound had fatally undermined this claim. By 1970, voters were all too aware of the impact of the economic uncertainty they were living through.

In the final days of the campaign the Conservatives saw an opening and, following a meeting at Heath's flat, decided to push hard on the themes of rising prices and increased living costs. Heath would present these difficulties as the price Britain was paying for Labour's devaluation.

Economic figures went against the government. It emerged that unemployment was at its highest rate in 30 years and, just days before polling, trade figures showed a £31 million deficit. Heath was able to exploit these new figures to imply there was even worse news looming ahead. Untarnished by office, the Tory leader naturally benefited from the public's loss of faith in Wilson.

In defeat critics accused the Labour leader of taking a low-key approach to the election, promising too little, and simply inviting the public to enjoy the summer sun while trusting all to him. It was a fatal misjudgement, as he found that voters had cooled towards him, with many deciding to stay at home.

Had he formed his third government, and lasted the full term, Wilson would have had a longer period in office than Churchill, Gladstone or Disraeli. Instead, it was a smiling Heath who entered Downing Street. The dividend for the new man, Wilson claimed, was that he would inherit 'the strongest economic position that any Prime Minister's taken over in living memory.'[8]

Though said without rancour, the reality, later confirmed by members of his inner circle, was that Wilson found what had been a wholly unexpected defeat both painful and deeply traumatic.

1970– General Election Result

Date of Election – 18 June

Overall Turnout – 72%

Labour

Candidates – 625

MPs – 288

Votes – 12,208,758

Percentage share of the vote – 43%

Result – Conservative victory

Highlight – Media focus on the 1970 football World Cup diverted news coverage away from politics and adversely impacted turnout and Labour's share of the vote.

Chapter 21

1974 (February) – Yesterday's Men?

'The issue which governs this crisis is not industrial dispute, it is inflation.'[1]

Harold Wilson

On 7 February 1974, Ted Heath appeared on national television to announce there would be a general election at the end of the month, even though he retained a working majority and Parliament had over a year to run.

The Conservative prime minister, facing a national strike by miners, sought to strengthen his hand by suggesting democracy was being subverted by a particularly powerful group of workers making unreasonable pay demands.

Heath was asking – who governs Britain? Was it the miners or the elected government? In doing so, he gave the impression of having lost control, though in truth since defeating Harold Wilson in the shock election result of 1970 Heath had rarely seemed fully in command of events.

His promise, on taking office, had been to reduce rising prices, increase productivity and bring down unemployment, all of which were ingrained into Britain's economic fabric during the years of decline in the 1960s and 1970s.

Under Wilson, sterling had been devalued, and there had been several rounds of deflationary measures and restraints placed on public spending and pay. Heath faced the same issues, but had different solutions, vowing to reject an incomes policy and instead letting the market decide wage settlements, while bringing in stricter controls on the unions, a policy which only served to increase industrial unrest.

At the core of many of these problems was a crippling rate of inflation. Under Labour in the two years from 1968, retail prices had been rising by 6 per cent annually, while under Heath the rate was heading towards 9 per cent in 1971. At the same time wages were rising, but without growth in the economy this was of little benefit. The novel combination of low growth and high inflation ushered a new word into the political lexicon – 'stagflation'.

The 'Nixon shock' in 1971, by which the US president effectively ended the system of fixed exchange rates which had pegged currencies to the value of gold and the US dollar, helped tip the UK economy into an extended recession. This was compounded by the 1973 oil embargo by the OPEC Arab states in response to Britain's support for Israel during the 'Yom Kippur War'.

This led to a reduction in the value of the pound, which made imports more expensive and further embedded rises in inflation as well as a spike in unemployment which, to Heath's great consternation, had topped one million in 1972 for the first time since the 1930s.

At the same time, the government's attempts to reduce the direct role of the state in the economy were running into difficulties. Rolls-Royce, the flagship British engineering company, fell into receivership with 80,000 jobs on the line and in Glasgow the Upper Clyde Shipbuilders yard was threatened with liquidation.

In each case Heath, in the full glare of national and international publicity, stepped in to save jobs and keep the businesses open. This and his U-turn in instigating a formal prices and incomes policy, led Labour MPs to mockingly welcome his conversion to socialism.

By mid-1973, Heath had won a major victory in steering Britain into the EEC and there were signs of economic improvement. Now, for the first time in two years, a poll even had the Tories ahead.

None of this diverted attention from the spike in oil prices, which rose from $3 per barrel to $12 by 1974. Action was needed to ensure Britain's domestic electricity production continued, and the best way of doing this was by producing more coal to keep the country's power stations running.

The National Union of Mineworkers, having won a 20 per cent pay rise following a 1972 strike, now became involved in a complicated wrangle with the government over pay. Aware there was a pressing need for more coal, they refused to work overtime unless properly paid for their efforts.

Negotiations soon broke down and Britain slipped into a state of emergency and a three-day working week, during which businesses had to limit their use of electricity. From the start of 1974, commercial enterprises could operate only on three consecutive days, shops often used candles, television broadcasting ended at 10.30 p.m. and it was even suggested people should brush their teeth in the dark.

Parliament sat in emergency session, and amid all this the miners held a ballot which overwhelmingly backed strikes. Inside the Conservative Party, the resolve that there would be no election until the autumn was beginning to crumble, as party strategists looked to move much faster.

Labour did not yet have the appearance of a government in waiting. The party had been frustrated in recent by-elections, failing to snatch Edinburgh North from the Tories, losing its deposit at Hove in November 1973, and on the same day seeing the SNP take its stronghold of Glasgow Govan.

The years since the defeat of 1970 had been hard for Wilson.

There was simmering resentment about losing to Heath, and though he remained leader, he no longer had the aura of hope he had possessed in 1964 when he first entered Downing Street. There was a sense that he had faded into the background, even finding time to write a personal account of his time at Number 10.

This was exemplified by the BBC documentary *Yesterday's Men*, a 1971 film featuring the former prime minister and several of his shadow ministers – Barbara Castle, Denis Healey, Roy Jenkins and others – talking about the adjustments to their lifestyles and deterioration of their incomes now they were no longer in government.

The broadcast provoked a fierce row, because Labour had not been told the true title of the film, nor about the accompanying satirical song which was played over images of Wilson gently golfing in the Scilly Isles: 'Humpty Dumpty he sat on a wall, giving the orders to men . . . Humpty Dumpty, he had a great fall now he's one of yesterday's men.'[2]

Wilson was also faced with the emergence of new power bases in the party, which gathered around a group of left-wing MPs led by Michael Foot and Tony Benn, as well as the TUC and trade union general secretaries. This worried Wilson, not only because it gave him less political space to work in, but he feared their policy ideas, such as the nationalisation of 25 of the country's top companies, would resonate badly with the public and ensure Labour was out of office for years.

His solution was to dilute open talk of nationalisation, replacing it with different language, such as pledges to create a National Enterprise Board and regional planning structures. With a deep split opening up over membership of the Common Market, Wilson told Castle – 'I know perfectly well what I am doing – my job is to keep the party united.'[3]

Labour, then, was far from ready to face the election of February 1974 when it came. Party bosses feared they would lose, and appealed to the miners not to push for a strike. They had good reason for their concern, with the polls regularly giving the Tories a lead of between 2 and 5 per cent.

Even at this stage, with Parliament still in session, events were taking place which would have a bearing on the election result.

In an extraordinary intervention, the hugely influential Conservative MP, Enoch Powell, wrote to his local party saying that Heath's decision to hold the election over the industrial situation was irresponsible. One of the nation's most popular and well-known politicians, he then advocated voting Labour as a means to ensure Britain left the EEC.

Heath then announced that the miners' wage claim would be examined by the Pay Board as quickly as possible, but with no deal in sight, the strike began on 10 February.

Wilson determined he would not let the industrial situation become the focus of the election. According to the Labour leader, the miners' dispute was a smokescreen, and the real reason voters were being sent to the polls was 'the disastrous failure of three and half years of Conservative government which has turned Britain from the path of prosperity to the road to ruin'.[4]

Labour set out its alternative in a quickly published manifesto, 'Let us work together – Labour's way out of the crisis'. This damned Heath's government as panic-stricken incompetents: 'our people face a series of interlocking crises. Prices are rocketing . . . more and more people are losing their jobs. Firms are going out of business. Housing costs are out of reach for so many families.'[5]

Labour also promised that a change of government would bring closure for the miners, and a re-examination of the terms under which the country had joined the Common Market. Labour aimed to 'bring about a fundamental and irreversible shift in the balance of power and wealth in favour of working people and their families', pledging greater economic equality, and the elimination of poverty.[6]

These were trumpeted as proudly socialist aims, but formed part of a wider strategy to bring about industrial peace. The unions would be asked to sign up to what Wilson called his 'Social Contract', prioritising co-operation rather than confrontation over wage restraints.

For the duration of the campaign the Labour leader was based at Transport House in Smith Square, a short distance from his home at Lord North Street. Mornings were taken up with a series of meetings and examination of internal polling data, during which election strategy for the coming days was planned out, often with Wilson present before he took the daily press conference.

As much as Heath had improved as a public performer since 1970, his confidence could not mask several blows his party suffered as the campaign wore on. Figures were released showing a stinging 20 per cent increase in prices on the previous year, then from the hearing of the Pay Board into the miners' case an extraordinary story emerged. Instead of being above the national average for manual workers in manufacturing industries, the miners were 8 per cent below the average.

The government had called the election on the basis that the miners were making unreasonable demands when all along it turned out they were being paid too little. It was a defining moment, with even Tory-supporting newspapers reflecting on what they saw as the government's ineptitude.

Lastly, three days before the election, dreadful trade figures were published – a deficit of £382 million, the highest ever recorded. Heath knew all too well the damage a far smaller deficit had done to Labour's hopes in 1970, and he tried to suggest the poor outlook showed he needed a stronger mandate. Labour's Roy Jenkins memorably hit back that 'he [Heath] presumably thinks a still worse result would have given him a still stronger claim.'[7]

Despite all this, the Conservatives retained a lead in the polls which fluctuated from 0.5 per cent to as high as 11 per cent. Labour registered a slight lead only in one poll late in the campaign. As voting began, the consensus was that it was Heath who would remain in government, Labour strategists now believed the best that could be achieved was for the Tories to become the largest party but falling short of a majority.

What the polls and strategists had missed was the impact of the rise of the Liberals under the charismatic Jeremy Thorpe. As leader, he had taken the unusual step of basing himself in his highly marginal seat of rural North Devon. His was an energetic and engaging campaign, and one which saw the Liberals soar higher than for many years, consistently polling over 20 per cent and at times reaching close to 30 per cent.

Fielding over 500 candidates, Thorpe was certain he was on the cusp of an historic breakthrough. While the Liberals were unlikely to form the next government, Thorpe knew he may have a role to play in a tight race, saying 'we are not seeking to obtain the balance of power. But if it happens, my answer is – I am prepared to work with any group of men and women who are going to get this country back on the rails.'[8]

Though there was no telling how many seats Thorpe could win, Heath had more to lose from the Liberal revival which would be unlikely to bite into Labour's industrial heartlands.

That was not to say that Wilson was confident of victory. On election night, 28 February, with the polls still open, the Labour leader told senior aides that once his result was declared on Merseyside he planned to slip away by plane, appearing to head for London, but in fact he would divert to a smaller airfield and from there go into hiding. This extraordinary idea sheds light on Wilson's desire not to be seen defeated again.

It seemed Wilson had good reason to be downcast. The early results were bleak with Guildford again the first to declare shortly after 11 p.m. Here and in Cheltenham, the Tories held their seats and Labour had been pushed into third place by the Liberal surge. That was not the whole story: both ITN and the BBC, now using the exit poll technique at several constituencies, pointed to a marginal swing to Labour.

This did not greatly raise Labour's hopes, but then the mood suddenly changed. The two Salford seats – both held by Labour – declared, showing more significant swings to Wilson's party. Then the three Wolverhampton seats swung heavily to Labour, by almost 17 per cent in Enoch Powell's own constituency. In the TV studios, a possible Labour majority of as much as 50 was suddenly being mooted.

When Heath's own declaration came, he gave a short speech thanking supporters for ensuring his return to the Commons, while the BBC anchorman, Alastair Burnet, reflected that the Tory leader had 'on his face, I think, the look of a man who does not expect to be Prime Minister again.'[9]

From this point Labour's upward trajectory continued, taking seats in different parts of the country including Luton East, Stockport North, Plymouth Devonport, Gateshead West and the swing seat of Gravesend.

Well after midnight Wilson appeared on television, looking composed in a pinstriped blue suit, partially hidden by billowing pipe smoke. Having declared himself rejuvenated by a few hours' sleep the Labour leader spoke openly about his hopes of ending the miners' dispute and getting the country back to a five-day working week.

The contrast with the Tory leader was marked, with Wilson giving a direct answer to the question of whether the election remained in the balance: 'I cannot see at this stage the Conservatives having an overall working majority, no. I think it is extremely difficult to forecast whether any party will have a majority or whether we shall have a small one.'[10]

This was prescient, given that by 9 a.m. on Friday morning it was obvious no party would achieve the 318 seats needed for a bare majority. The queen was about to touch down in London, having flown back from Australia to kiss hands with whomever was to be prime minister. She would be kept waiting for some time.

Heath went to the Palace to give the queen a report on the situation, while Labour kept a low profile, Wilson meeting the Shadow Cabinet and putting out a simple statement that the party was ready to serve. Things then grew worse for the Conservatives, with defeats among the last remaining few seats, notably at Bodmin where the Liberals won by nine votes and at Carmarthen where Labour triumphed by just three votes after several recounts.

The final picture showed Labour on 301 seats, four ahead of the Conservatives on 297. The Liberals, despite polling over six million votes, had just 14 MPs leaving an enraged Thorpe not quite holding the balance of power. The SNP took 7 seats, the Welsh nationalists Plaid Cymru had two, and 11 were won by the Ulster Unionists.

Not since Ramsay MacDonald in 1929 had the British electorate produced such a result. In this hung parliament, neither of the two main parties could control the Commons if working alone. Added to this was the complication that the Tories had actually won the most votes: 11.87 million (37.9 per cent of the total), which was 200,000 more than Labour on 11.65 million (37.2 per cent).

The answer to Heath's question about who was governing the country seemed to have been answered – 'not you!' The Tory leader now tried to broker an agreement with the Liberals, holding a meeting in Downing Street with Thorpe who had travelled up from Devon. This proved inconclusive, with the Liberal leader saying he had to consult his MPs.

Heath's next move was to offer the Conservative whip to some of the Ulster Unionists, but then on Monday 4 March the Liberals rejected his offer of a coalition, mainly over the demand they formally enter government and what they saw as the lack of meaningful proposals on electoral reform.

That evening, Heath went to the Palace to resign. Wilson, who had wisely lain in wait, was to become prime minister again. He had rebuilt Labour's position in the four years since losing office, and now returned his party to power in extraordinary circumstances.

A hugely experienced and streetwise politician, Wilson had been right to attack the Conservatives over their record, and right also to present himself and his party as the only way of turning around inflation, unemployment, the flagging economy and quelling industrial unrest.

In calling an unnecessary election, Heath had gambled he would defeat the miners, only to lose the Commons. Ultimately, the chaos of his years in power had undone him at the ballot box with an electorate in search of stability turning back to Labour and the familiar figure of Harold Wilson.

It is also true that the two-party system had fractured in February 1974 and though Labour lost half a million votes, it was the Tories who had been most damaged by the Liberals and the rise of different forms of nationalisms. The only good news for Heath was that talk of another election being required before long was already commonplace.

Pressed on all sides by the media almost right up against the black door of 10 Downing Street, Wilson was asked what it felt like being back, almost a decade after first taking office. His response was businesslike: 'we have got a job to do, we can only do that job as one people – and I'm going right in to start that job now. Thank you.'[11]

1974 – General Election (February) Result

Date of Election – Thursday 28 February

Overall Turnout – 78.8%

Labour

Candidates – 623

MPs – 301

Votes – 11,645,616

Percentage share of the vote – 37.2%

Result – Labour minority government

Highlight – Ted Heath calls a snap election asking, 'Who governs Britain?'

Chapter 22

1974 (October) – A Bumpy Ride

'The lights went on again. We brought the
heating back. We did what we said we would.'

Harold Wilson[1]

According to Harold Wilson, it took him just 50 hours to fix the problems which had long haunted Ted Heath in Downing Street. Having emerged as the largest party in February 1974, with four seats more than the Conservatives, the new Labour government immediately began to implement change.

After taking office on Monday 4 March, Wilson was able to move at speed using the plans outlined in his 'Social Contract'. In return for the unions agreeing to wage restraints, the government would repeal Heath's detested Industrial Relations Act and move to control inflation.

By lunchtime on Wednesday the coal dispute was formally over, with the miners winning a one-year settlement amounting to a 35 per cent pay increase. Naturally this also ended the restrictions of the three-day week which were lifted the following day.

While resolving the issues which had defined the political landscape in recent years, Wilson also found time to turn his attention to interior décor, returning pictures of Wellington, Nelson, Churchill and others to prominent spots in Downing Street. This was not mere whimsy; the intention was to signal a break with the former administration inside Number 10.

The new prime minister then turned his attention to preparing a Queen's Speech and constructing his Cabinet. 'So here we go for a bumpy ride' was how Barbara Castle, back in government as health and social services secretary, put it in her diary shortly after the election.[2]

As Castle indicated, the real difficulty would be governing without a majority. The good news for Labour was that this was not a new situation for Wilson, as during his first term in power between 1964 and 1966 he had held a majority of five seats or less.

Roy Jenkins now returned for a second stint at the Home Office, Denis Healey became chancellor and Jim Callaghan foreign secretary. Michael Foot came in at employment, Tony Benn went to industry, and Peter Shore, Tony Crosland and Shirley Williams also joined the government.

Wilson warned Heath, who remained as Tory leader, that there would be grave consequences at the ballot box for any party choosing to vote down Labour's programme. This was a marker that although Labour had not won a majority, as the biggest party they considered that the electorate had granted them the chance to govern and expected to have the space to do so, at least in the short term.

The Queen's Speech took place in the middle of the month, and though the sovereign spoke of efforts to renegotiate the UK's membership of the EEC, there was a far more pressing matter – Her Majesty telling both houses of Parliament: 'My Government will give the highest priority to overcoming the economic difficulties created by rising prices, the balance of payments deficit and the recent dislocation of production.'[3]

By this time the state of emergency had been lifted and Labour had frozen public and private sector rents and re-imposed the arms embargo on apartheid South Africa, reversing the policy of the previous government. Food prices would be kept down through subsidies, while the government promised more protections for consumers.

The announcements were intended to make it appear that the four years of Heath government had simply been an unproductive interlude, a sense amplified by Denis Healey's March Budget. In it, the top rate of income tax was increased from 75 per cent to 83 per cent, and corporation tax rose to 52 per cent. Pensions were increased, as were other social security benefits, in moves warmly welcomed by voters.

Still, Labour's high command knew they would struggle to get legislation through the Commons, and would have to go back to the country sooner rather than later. It already looked like this would take place in the autumn, with the timetable for a summer election being too tight.

Wilson's priority was to prove that he was getting to grips with the economy. Yet prices continued to rise, with inflation reaching 14 per cent and wages increasing by more than 15 per cent. At the same time, shares were declining in value more steeply than they had done after the Wall Street Crash of 1929.

Given that the impact of the Crash had led directly to the fall of the minority Labour government under Ramsay MacDonald in 1931, it is little wonder Wilson was concerned. The strain on the prime minister, physically as well as mentally was severe; at times there was a reliance on brandy, especially before important occasions in Parliament.

The fallout from minor scandals did not help, with Andrew Cunningham and T. Dan Smith, two major Labour figures from the North East, sent to prison on corruption charges. Another row broke out over land development and the use of Wilson's forged signature, and there was disquiet about the government seeing through a contract to build warships for use in Chile, where a right-wing military dictatorship had overthrown the government in 1973.

Compared to his time in power during the 1960s, the Labour leader kept a low profile and was happy enough to share the limelight with leading ministers. The Cabinet remained largely united, and as the months wore on hints of an improving economic picture emerged.

The number of days lost to strikes dropped dramatically, the balance of payments deficit fell, but then stubbornly rose again, while average earnings went up. Industrial output increased, though by frustratingly small margins and unemployment was brought down from just over half a million, before returning to almost the same figure by October.

The general impression was that Labour was starting to tame inflation, as Healey's summer mini-Budget – designed to reflate, or stimulate, the economy with VAT cuts and increases in food subsidies – took effect.

The Conservatives accused Labour of blatant electioneering, with Heath telling the public to 'beware of politicians bearing gifts – now as never before.'[4] Given that his party had a long history of such man-oeuvres, they had little grounds for complaint.

There were months of behind-the-scenes manoeuvring as the par-ties prepared for a general election. Meanwhile, a political balancing act played out: the Tories had to hold the government to account, but not throw it out of office too soon and risk a backlash from voters for doing so.

As expected, given the tight arithmetic, Labour suffered defeats in the Commons, several times during July alone. Yet the party retained a consistent poll lead over the Conservatives, as high as 13.5 per cent soon after taking office, but still at under 5 per cent by the autumn.

Heath, who had no great confidence about a quick return to power for his party, began discussing whether a better strategy would be to push for a national government, while the Liberals did likewise behind closed doors. Election talk continued throughout the summer, with most observers convinced that Labour was now set to win an outright majority, possibly even a landslide.

Wilson made speeches reminding voters of the ills of the three-day week under Heath, referring not only to the spike in unemployment that took place, but also to the lack of television in the evenings which had so annoyed the public. Meanwhile, Labour exploited its control of the levers of government, publishing a series of White Paper policy statements for future legislation.

As August slipped into September, the prime minister refused to play his hand, aiming to keep rivals guessing. After that, the pace gathered quickly. The Conservative manifesto was leaked to three national newspapers on 10 September, giving the Tories days of extra publicity.

In response, Labour released its manifesto on 16 September, but the election announcement – that the country would go to the polls on Thursday 10 October – came only two days later. Not since 1924, when the first Labour government was defeated, had a minority administration asked the people for an increased mandate, and not since 1910 had there been two elections in a single year.

Wilson took to the airwaves to say that he understood that, though an election was something few people wanted at a time of economic difficulties, the deadlock in Parliament had made it unavoidable. The prime minister went on to say the inflationary economic crisis was the most serious since the war. Then, moving deftly from pessimism to the promise of better times, he added 'we in Britain have it in us to win through and there is now evidence each week to show that the fightback has begun.'[5]

The party campaigned with the slogan 'Britain will win with Labour', this often appearing on a rosette motif, spearheaded by an advertising campaign which had a price tag of over £140,000 or £1.3 million today. There was one central message: Labour had the policies to see the country out of the present economic situation and into the years beyond.

The party stressed that the very future of the country was on the line: 'at the heart of this manifesto and our programme to save the nation lies the social contract between the Labour Government and the trade unions, an idea derided by our enemies, but certain to become widely accepted by those who genuinely believe in government by consent'.[6]

Edward Heath and his lieutenants began with a weak hand, but knew that many people viewed the unions as too powerful. It was also clear that something was breaking down in the traditional Labour vote, as fewer than half of all manual workers, and of all workers from homes with a trade union member, had voted Labour in February 1974.

The Tories adopted a cautious approach to the campaign, trying to amplify the congenial side of Heath – one which was normally only seen in private. He all but dropped walkabouts, where he would have direct and unplanned interactions with voters, instead using more formalised question and answer sessions.

Their hope was that in a tight race the Conservatives would be seen as stronger on economic competency, though opinion polls showed Labour in fact had more credibility on the economy.

Conservative strategists also pushed hard on national unity, issuing posters and leaflets carrying the message:

'Put Britain first
VOTE FOR NATIONAL UNITY
It's the only way to get a strong government that will
unite the country
Vote Conservative'[7]

It was a deliberate echo of the success the Tories had in the 1930s with the National Government. Heath and his team were suggesting to voters that they were acting in the national interest, being prepared to take the politics out of government if no single party could form an administration.

In reality, it was no more than a ploy to get the Conservatives back in the game, with the Liberals still unlikely to give them formal backing in a coalition or offer any kind of support.

The Liberals faced their own dilemma. Though they were in their best position for decades after polling over six million votes in the February election, this had not been translated into much more than a dozen seats. To really break the two-party dominance, their vote needed to rise by another 10 per cent at least.

The campaign itself was short, at just 22 days in length, with the added benefit for the incumbent party of its taking place in a period when no major economic figures were due to be released. All of this was Wilson's doing, the prime minister positioning Labour as a team of football players and portraying himself as a captain sorting out difficulties on the pitch while allowing the stars around him to show off their talents.

He was not willing to take part in the live televised debate suggested by the Liberal leader Jeremy Thorpe, and nor was Heath. Wilson was content to tour the country making the same basic stump speech, reminding people of the way things had been under the Conservatives, and arguing that Labour's plans for industrial peace were the only way forward.

This was not enough to stop Tory barbs about inflation and rising wages. The Conservatives and others openly suggested that the much-vaunted social contract was a ruse, something which was all very well and good in theory between Labour and the TUC, but totally unworkable in the face of an actual industrial dispute.

The official line from Conservative HQ on Smith Square was that statutory controls might be needed if voluntary arrangements to control wages did not work. The Tory case was hardly helped when, in the run-up to the election, the prominent MP Sir Keith Joseph called for control of the money supply to bring down inflation, while accepting that this would lead to job losses.

The most explosive moment of the campaign for Labour came over Britain's continued membership of the European Common Market. The party was pledging that within a year the electorate would have the final say on membership and the terms of entry.

Shirley Williams, the secretary of state for prices and consumer protection, was asked what she would do if there were a 'no' vote in a referendum. With Wilson eager to step in and help, Williams stated firmly that she would leave politics. Roy Jenkins then weighed in behind Williams, saying he would not stay in the Cabinet under such circumstances. Unsurprisingly, this was seized on as evidence of divisions at the top of the Labour Party.

The Tories thought they had stolen a march over Labour when Margaret Thatcher insisted, out of the blue, that a pledge to bring down mortgage rates would be implemented by Christmas. This gained favourable media coverage and concern for a few days in the Labour ranks before the party's own polling showed that the country felt Thatcher was making unaffordable promises.

From here, attention turned to Heath's offer of a national unity government and media questions about whether this was a serious proposition, given the lack of clarity about what it entailed.

Questions were raised both by journalists and MPs about whether Heath himself would stand down if he proved the major stumbling block in forming such an administration. The Conservative leader made no such promise, but his positioning still troubled Labour, and Wilson hit back, claiming that 'Coalition would mean Con policies, Con leadership by a Con party for a Con trick.'[8]

The other notable new dimension in the campaign was the rise of the SNP in Scotland. Having won seven seats in February that year, the nationalists aimed in October to become the second biggest party in Scotland. To counter this, with polls narrowing north of the border, Labour promised there would be a 51 per cent public stake in North Sea Oil.

Across the rest of Britain, polls showed Labour still ahead by between 5 to 10 per cent. This fuelled a widely held expectation that Wilson was heading back to Downing Street armed with a majority. Such was the confidence in this result, that by the time voting began a million pounds worth of bets had been staked on the outcome, with one punter placing a £25,000 wager on a Labour victory.

Once voting had ended on election night an exit poll by the Harris organisation suggested that his money was not just safe, but that the bet would deliver a handsome return. Wilson was projected to be deep into landslide territory, a full 180 seats ahead of the Tories.

The pattern of February was repeated, with the same handful of seats declaring early. The first came shortly after 11 p.m. at Guildford and then Cheltenham, both Conservative holds. Then came the two Salford seats, the first Labour holds – and with slight swings to Wilson's party.

There were gains too, most notably at Lincoln where an explosion of cheering greeted the news that a young Margaret Jackson (later Beckett) had ousted the pro-European Dick Taverne, who had stood as an independent after being deselected by his local Labour party.

With 50 results declared, the mood began to change. TV pundits examining the national swing now veered away from any suggestion of the large Labour win predicted by the exit poll. Instead, the settled view was that Wilson would lead the biggest party and was likely to emerge with a majority in the Commons barely above half a dozen seats, and 20 at the most.

Certainly, no one was now talking in terms of the Tories winning outright. Edward du Cann, the Chair of the 1922 Committee, expressed his disappointment to the BBC that the Conservatives had not won. This was followed by the appearance at his own count of a very solemn Heath, his subdued demeanour telling the story of the night.

At Wilson's own declaration at Huyton there was no hint of triumphalism, but when interviewed shortly after, he admitted Labour could have an overall majority and fully expected to be able to implement his party's manifesto.

The trouble was that as the night wore on, the electoral picture remained largely static. Only two dozen seats changed hands, and Labour failed to capture a single one of the 145 being declared the next day.

When the final picture emerged Labour was not only the largest party – taking 319 seats, and making 19 gains – but it had made it to the promised land of majority rule. There was a snag though. The party's majority was only 3 seats, well short of recent expectations.

It appeared as though the result left things still on a knife-edge, with Labour little better off than at the outset of the campaign. In reality, Wilson's party was 43 seats in front of the Conservatives, giving Labour ample space in which to govern. The remaining seats were split between the smaller parties, with the Liberals on 13 and the SNP taking their representation up to 11 MPs.

Across the country there had been a fairly even swing from Conservative to Labour of 2.2 per cent. Had it been just a little higher, especially in Tory-held marginals, it would have made all the difference. Also, turnout was down 6 per cent from the 78 per cent high in February, all of which underlined the absolute necessity of getting supporters to the polling stations. Wilson understood this point all too well of course, with Labour having lost in 1970 in part because of voter apathy.

Curiously, he had now conjured victory with just over 39 per cent of the vote, having been removed from power four years earlier having won 43 per cent. Wilson was now the greatest election winner in Labour's history, having been in office longer than Clement Attlee, and with four election wins to his name.

He had cannily positioned his party as the only option to take Britain forward and leave behind the mess and chaos of the Tory years from 1970 to February 1974. In doing so, he had the assurance of the Social Contract agreement with the unions, signposting a clear move towards lasting industrial peace.

Having left office only months earlier Heath and the Conservatives struggled to convey a hopeful message to voters, their call for national unity being both flaccid and imprecise. In contrast, Labour benefited from being the recently installed incumbents, who were seen to be getting on with the job of governing the country.

Wilson had also been right to play up the experience of his team, many of whom already understood the rigours of government. Though he was not campaigning with the zest of the 1960s, Wilson had the advantage of facing an opponent in Heath who was all but shying away from looking voters in the eyes on streets up and down the country.

Having defeated Heath for the third time, Wilson and his Labour Cabinet now faced the looming challenges of inflation, unemployment and the cost of living. As the prime minister put it on election night 'I think it's going to be a hell of a job.'

'I don't want to forecast but I think it's going to be very, very hard slogging for a couple of years and I have not disguised that from the people in this election or in the last election.'[9] The journey on that rocky road, which had been predicted by Barbara Castle, was really only just beginning.

1974 – General Election (October) Result

Date of Election – 10 October

Overall Turnout – 72.8%

Labour

Candidates – 623

MPs – 319

Votes – 11,457,079

Percentage share of the vote – 39.2%

Result – Labour government

Highlight – This was the last of four consecutive battles between Harold Wilson and Ted Heath for Downing Street.

Chapter 23

1979 – Sea Change

'The most right-wing Conservative Government
and Leader for fifty years; the first woman
Prime Minister. I cannot absorb it all.'

Tony Benn[1]

The road to the general election of 1979 was an arduous one for Labour. It led ultimately to a nerve-shredding no confidence vote which forced the government to the country. Parliament had seen nothing like it since the fall of Ramsay MacDonald's first administration more than half a century before.

In the turmoil of the late 1970s, Labour's election victory of 1974 had faded into the distance along with the main players of that era. Ted Heath was gone by early 1975, sensationally replaced by Margaret Thatcher, the first female leader of any mainstream British party. Labour's Barbara Castle was quick to spot the danger, describing Thatcher as 'clearly the best man among them . . . she will have us fighting for our political lives.'[2]

Labour's prime minister had also stepped down: Harold Wilson shocked the nation by abruptly announcing his departure in the spring of 1976. In part, he felt the new Conservative leader was the problem, believing that after a decade battling Heath, he would have to start all over again with a new, younger, opponent.

Wilson was only 60, but he had been in Parliament for over three decades and on the front bench nearly all of that time. He was by then Labour's greatest election winner and the longest-serving peacetime prime minister in the twentieth century. He made way for an older man. At 64, Jim Callaghan had vast experience, having been chancellor, foreign secretary and home secretary.

Callaghan knew his inheritance all too well, having seen first-hand the difficulties faced by Wilson in his final term since 1974. There was a growing sense that Britain was falling into a steep decline. The performance of the economy, and in particular the spiralling rate of inflation continued to be the most pressing issue.

In summer 1975 inflation touched 25 per cent a year, the highest rate in Europe, all but shredding Wilson's 'Social Contract' which called on trade unions to exercise voluntary wage restraint. Railway workers, dockers and hospital staff all went on strike for better pay.

A formal policy was introduced limiting wage rises to no more than the equivalent of £6 a week, an increase of about 10 per cent. Official figures at the end of 1975 reported a 7 per cent fall in the standard of living in Britain, though by this stage inflation had begun to fall and the balance of payments figures were the best for some time. The reasons, though, had as much to do with the discovery of North Sea oil, with the first oil pumped ashore in June 1975, as with the government's deflationary measures.

The other major shift was Europe and the confirmation of Britain's EEC membership. Labour had promised a referendum on the issue, and although Wilson led the campaign to remain in the EEC, he understood how divisive this was across his party, and Labour MPs were given the freedom to campaign as they saw fit.

Many on the Labour left, most prominently Tony Benn, thought Europe was likely to damage British democracy and threaten jobs, while other big Labour figures were enthusiastic: the 'Yes' campaign was supported by Callaghan, Healey and Roy Jenkins, the holders of the three great offices of state.

At the referendum, which took place in June 1975, the country voted by 67 to 33 per cent to remain in the Community. After long years of Labour division, the matter seemed finally settled, highlighting Wilson's skill in managing his party.

However, at the same time there was growing discord over the perceived inaction on Scottish devolution. In early 1976, two MPs – Jim Sillars and John Robertson – broke away to form the left-leaning Scottish Labour Party over what they felt to be a lack of commitment to deliver a powerful assembly in Edinburgh.

There was a furious reaction, with the Scottish secretary Willie Ross, telling Sillars 'there is a special place in hell for the likes of you.'[3] Their defection tipped the party into a minority government position at a particularly difficult moment, just weeks before Wilson's retirement.

As Callaghan took office, he had to contend with further issues. In September unemployment passed the one and a half million mark, a figure which shocked politicians on all sides. At Labour's Conference in September, Callaghan gave a speech which called into question the entire thrust of Labour's approach since 1945. The prime minister told gloomy delegates listening in silence: 'we used to think that you could spend your way out of a recession and increase employment by cutting taxes and boosting Government spending.'

'I tell you in all candour that that option no longer exists, and that in so far as it ever did exist, it only worked on each occasion since the war by injecting a bigger dose of inflation into the economy, followed by a higher level of unemployment as the next step.'[4]

This was a Labour leader speaking to activists in a way his predecessor might have found unpalatable. Callaghan knew that Britain was seeing slower economic growth than other comparable countries.

Output in France and Germany had risen 9 and 10 per cent respectively the previous year; at home it edged up only a shade over 1 per cent.

As the weeks wore on, pressure grew on the pound, which had been falling since spring 1976, and it sank to an all-time low of $1.56 in October. As the pound continued to struggle, the government asked the International Monetary Fund (IMF) for a loan of almost $4 billion – the biggest in the history of the organisation – to stabilise the British economy.

In return, the government had to accept heavy cuts in public spending as well as in the budget deficit reductions, terms which were agreed by Denis Healey as chancellor, but were deeply controversial among his Labour Cabinet colleagues, some of whom invoked the financial crisis of 1931 which had led to the fall of the second MacDonald government.

Following the IMF agreement, the economic picture improved in 1977, and in the end the full loan was not needed. Yet the crisis had added to the sense that Britain was ailing, and the public were understandably unwilling to accept a long-term negative impact on living standards. As a result, opinion polls now showed the Conservatives consistently ahead of the government.

In March 1977, Callaghan entered into a formal agreement with the Liberals to shore up the government on key votes. This 'Lib-Lab' pact was renewed in July and lasted another full year until the summer of 1978. By that time, Labour had drawn neck and neck with the Tories in opinion polls amid indications that Callaghan was preparing for an election.

With living standards on the up and inflation falling, October 1978 seemed the most likely time to go to the country. However, faced with this decision – and as opposition parties were writing their manifestos – Callaghan suddenly decided against it.

The annual Trades Union Congress in Brighton was primed to hear the announcement directly from the prime minister, but instead, on 5 September, he rather curiously sang them lines from an old music hall song about a jilted bride.

'All at once, he sent me round a note, here's the very note, this is what he wrote, cannot get away to marry you today, my wife won't let me.' As delegates applauded, Callaghan made sure they understood, saying 'now let me make clear, I have promised nobody I shall be at the altar in October, nobody at all.'[5]

Callaghan's fear was that Labour was still only able to achieve a hung Parliament, while the economic predictions for 1979 were tantalisingly good, suggesting that waiting a few months longer was the best option. It was to prove a tragic mistake.

In late 1978, and into the new year, industrial action began to snowball in what would be the hardest winter since the early 1960s. Thousands of Ford workers went on strike demanding pay increases significantly above the 5 per cent government guidelines. Several weeks later bosses at the American car giant agreed to a 17 per cent rise for employees.

In what came to be known in the press as the 'winter of discontent', the Callaghan administration then suffered a domino effect of wage demands from both public and private sectors, leaving the government's pay policy in tatters. The media had a field day reporting rubbish piling up in the streets, the dead left unburied, hospitals able to deal only with emergencies, and the army being put on standby to help deliver oil.

In the midst of this, the prime minister returned from high-level international talks in tropical Guadeloupe. Appearing relaxed, Callaghan batted away a question about chaos at home by suggesting all was well. The next day *The Sun* newspaper ran the headline 'Crisis?

What Crisis?'; though the prime minister had never uttered those words, they were used relentlessly against him.

On 22 January, in freezing conditions, 1.5 million workers took part in a 'National Day of Action', the biggest single walkout since the General Strike of 1926. Tony Benn sounded a warning note in his diary, writing that 'the press is just full of crises, anarchy, chaos, disruption – bitterly hostile to the trade union movement. I have never seen anything like it in my life.'[6]

The Conservatives now pounced, perfectly aware that Labour's great strength, its links with the unions, was fast becoming a weakness. Margaret Thatcher used a broadcast in which, talking directly to camera, she suggested that 'what we face is a threat to our whole way of life'.[7] Within days, the Tories soared to a 20-point opinion poll lead.

On 1 March, voters in Scotland and Wales went to the polls to decide on the plans for devolved assemblies which had been passed by the Scotland Act the previous year.

In Wales devolution was rejected, while in Scotland there was 52 per cent support. This, however, was insufficient because the legislation which enabled the referendum required 40 per cent of the total Scottish electorate to vote in favour for it to pass, a caveat which had been driven through the Commons by Labour backbenchers.

Devolution was effectively dead in the water. The SNP, with 11 MPs, were furious and put down a motion of no confidence in the government. With Liberal support, this then became a Tory motion, one which was debated on Wednesday 28 March.

It was very unclear whether the government would survive. The SNP remained resolute that they would vote against Labour, but Callaghan also refused appeals from ministers to offer the Scottish nationalists something. The prime minister did get support from

Plaid Cymru and a handful of others. Yet crucially, there were likely abstentions from two Irish nationalists.

Tonight, the BBC current affairs programme, captured the drama live. Shortly after 10.20 p.m., a roar went up from the Opposition benches before the formal announcement of the result. The Labour government had fallen, having been defeated on the motion 311 to 310.

Immediately, Callaghan was on his feet calmly saying that his party would 'take our case to the country'. Then it was the turn of Thatcher, who called for an election 'at the very earliest opportunity'.[8] With that, the Commons moved quickly on to its next business, though there was a coda to this dramatic moment, as some Labour MPs sang the 'Red Flag' to keep their spirits up.

Harold Wilson, the man who had led Labour to such success over the previous 15 years, and who thought the loose grouping of opposition parties would never work together to damage Labour, reflected 'if for a time it was rotten garbage that threatened the Labour Government, it was devolution which forced it to the country'.[9]

With the announcement of 3 May as the election date, the campaign began almost immediately. Unlike the other parties, Labour did not yet have a manifesto prepared, and the document had to be thrashed out between Callaghan and senior figures in early April with limited involvement from other quarters such as the NEC and the unions.

It emerged with the title 'The Labour Way is the Better Way', and promised to 'keep a curb on inflation and prices', give 'a high priority to working for a return to full employment' and deal with the unions through negotiation in what was termed 'a major extension of industrial democracy'.[10]

While some of this was natural Labour territory, other parts were very obviously intended to head off Tory attacks. Expecting that Thatcher would promise to reduce direct taxation, lower inflation and reform the unions, Labour made similar pitches alongside commitments to 'enlarge people's freedom'.

The Conservatives' own document was straightforward in its language and had the rather utilitarian title 'The 1979 Conservative Party General Election Manifesto'. In this, Thatcher made her pitch: 'For me, the heart of politics is not political theory, it is people and how they want to live their lives'.[11]

Though starting with a poll lead of around 15 per cent – at the time the largest held by any opposition party seeking power in British election history – the Conservatives had no way of knowing how a female leader would play with the electorate when it came to choosing a prime minister.

Callaghan, with his sunny persona, remained more popular than both his party and the Conservative leader. Nevertheless, Thatcher became a growing point of fascination as the five-week campaign progressed.

It was the first election for more than a century to be fought in April. The weather was generally good, and voting was set to take place on the same day as local council elections in much of England and Wales. The bookies had Thatcher at 4 to 1 on to triumph, but the Tory machine continued to stress that complacency was the enemy.

Labour had hoped that a relatively long campaign with Thatcher as the focus would help them. They hoped that her health and her voice might not take the strain, and that the longer she was exposed to scrutiny, the greater the likelihood of a major gaffe.

In 1978 Thatcher and her party had greatly upped their communications professionalism by bringing in Saatchi & Saatchi to manage advertising and broadcasting. A young agency with a reputation for being aggressive, they devised the memorable poster campaign using the slogan 'Labour Isn't Working'. This depicted a long queue waiting for unemployment benefits. Such creative tactics made their mark politically.

The problem for Callaghan was that in response, Labour stuck with tried and tested methods, employing Edward Booth-Clibborn, the Chair of a creative arts charity. He brought in sympathetic advertising and marketing people, but the strategy lacked the focus and surefootedness the Conservatives brought to their communications.

In an election more dominated by the media than ever before, the idea was to make Thatcher seem appealing to those who had not voted for her party in the 1974 elections, while at the same time heightening dissatisfaction with Labour.

Though Callaghan was a much more experienced campaigner, it was Thatcher who excelled in front of journalists. Variously, she was seen waving her shopping basket, sampling tea and even cuddling a calf. By contrast, Callaghan hated photocalls, seeing them as gimmicks.

Each day, Labour would hold an early campaign meeting with the PM directing matters more closely than under Wilson. After the morning press conferences, the main players would disperse to the 80 key marginals and Callaghan would be back in Downing Street around 10 p.m. and in bed around midnight.

On paper, Labour was in a good position to remain in power, only needing to gain a handful of seats, while the Tories had to take over 50 to achieve a majority.

Sadly, the Party was not in great shape for the battle given there were fewer than 80 full-time agents working across the constituencies. The polling data also did not give a clear picture about where gains might come from. Despite outward appearances, Callaghan was not confident.

The prime minister was also facing a smoothly operating Tory machine, which not only attacked Labour policies but also used the old framing that behind respectable figures lurked left-wing bogey-men. Labour's response was to offer Shirley Williams to the media as a reassuring counter to Mrs Thatcher. Healey, Roy Hattersley and Peter Shore were also all highly visible.

Michael Foot and Tony Benn were less frequently seen and there was a row when Benn said that a vote for Labour would be one against the Common Market in its current form.

The intervention of the former prime minister, Harold Wilson, was more problematic. He told the *Daily Mail* that his wife might vote Conservative because she was keen to see a woman as prime minister. To make matters worse, the *Sunday Express* then suggested that Sir Harold's long-serving political secretary, Marcia Williams, was also toying with voting for Thatcher.

With the strain telling, Callaghan walked out of an ITN interview but was later persuaded to return for a second session, though this did not stop the matter getting into the press.

At least he did not suffer from poor economic figures coming out before polling in the way Wilson had in the past. In mid-April, the Retail Price Index showed inflation had remained just below the 10 per cent mark. A week later it was revealed that unemployment was falling.

Callaghan was seen as dignified and statesmanlike by the press, though perhaps not sparkling. The prime minister warned against the dangers of electing the Tories, speaking on the themes of unemployment, jobs, prices and taxation. Were Thatcher to govern, how many jobs would be lost, where was the money to pay for tax cuts, how would prices be kept down?

As the campaign closed, Labour showed some advance; the Tory lead was now an average of 5 per cent. The electorate seemed undecided, with pollsters recording that many people were switching their voting intentions back and forth.

In his final broadcast, Callaghan looked ahead across the decade to come, pledging that Labour in the 1980s would still focus on ending poverty, building homes and caring for those who most needed assistance.

The national newspapers greeted millions of voters at breakfast time with headlines mainly favouring Mrs Thatcher. The *Express* simply said 'Give The Girl a Chance', while for *The Sun* it was 'the first day of the rest of our lives' calling on voters to 'vote Tory this time'. The *Daily Mirror*, as ever, gave full backing to Callaghan crying 'Forward with the People' – 'vote Labour today'.

After this it was left to the broadcasters to supply the drama as the votes were counted. The BBC highlighted what it called a 'Prediction – pre result' before any constituency had declared. Devastatingly for Labour, the Tories were expected to comfortably reach the 318 seats needed to form a majority, but be short of a landslide.

Glasgow Central was the first constituency to declare and though a solid Labour seat it carried an indication of how things would unfold. Labour's vote had gone up, but the Conservatives had managed to edge out the SNP and come second.

Attention then turned to Cheltenham and Guildford which were both comfortably held by the Tories with swings from Labour of almost 5 per cent, indicating the tide was turning decisively towards Mrs Thatcher. This was reinforced by a greatly increased Conservative majority in the East London marginal of Upminster.

Jim Callaghan had little to say as he arrived for his count in Cardiff, while a beaming Thatcher on her way to her declaration in Finchley pronounced herself cautiously optimistic. By the time she reached Tory Central Office, there were cheering supporters both inside and outside the building. A few yards away, Labour's Transport House was all but in mourning.

In the end, the Conservatives won 339 seats, making 62 gains while Labour lost 50 overall, and saw Shirley Williams defeated along with seven junior government ministers. This provided Mrs Thatcher with a 44-seat majority.

It was achieved on a national swing of just over 5 per cent, the largest since the war. Sadly for Labour, it was also the third election in a row in which the party had failed to reach 40 per cent of voters, suggesting a long-term decline.

At 2.30 p.m. on Friday 4 May, the day after the election, Jim Callaghan came out of Downing Street for the last time as prime minister. Dressed in a dark suit and deep red tie, smiling and waving to well-wishers he was driven to Buckingham Palace to resign as prime minister.

An hour later, Mrs Thatcher arrived at Number 10. Crowded by uniformed police and journalists' microphones, Britain's first female prime minister chose to utter a prayer attributed to St Francis of Assisi.

'Where there is discord, may we bring harmony. Where there is error may we bring truth. Where there is doubt, may we bring faith. Where there is despair may we bring hope', she said.[12]

The election was a moment of climax after the chaos and turbulence of the 1970s. It ended a period of Labour dominance which, with only a short interlude under Ted Heath, stretched back to 1964, an era which was characterised by extreme economic difficulty. An exasperated public had eventually lost trust in the dominant governing party.

There was a feeling, one pushed by the Tories, but shared even by some Labour voters, that the trade unions had grown too powerful and were a destabilising force in public life. Thatcher, aided by allies in the media, was able to present union reforms in terms designed to look reasonable.

For Labour, in contrast, the 'winter of discontent' torpedoed Callaghan's hopes that the economy would continue to improve and yield him a benefit at the ballot box. There would be no fair wind for a 1979 election, and being forced to go to the polls on the back of a confidence vote was seen as a sign of weakness. With prices having doubled, and unemployment at its worst level in 40 years the public craved the stability which, it was felt, would only arrive with a change of government.

Walking across Parliament Square during the campaign, Callaghan told Bernard Donoughue, head of the Number 10 policy unit, that he believed the election would be lost regardless of what he said or did. In the prime minister's view, a sea change was taking place in British politics.

As Donoughue explained in an interview for this book, Callaghan saw a generational shift taking place. 'The post war settlement of the Labour government, of welfare Britain and all of that, was accepted and established for about 40 or 50 years.'

'We were then moving into a different world and there was no doubt Jim and Harold were part of the post war settlement and when that came to an end they came to an end.'

He had not discussed it with Callaghan, but Donoughue does not think it would have made any difference to call the election the previous autumn. 'I feel there was a sort of understandable personal element to this,' he said. 'Jim knew he might lose in '78, I think he might well have lost and he didn't want to lose. I felt he would rather have another six or nine months in office.'

In Donoughue's view once the election was underway, the contrast between the two parties was obvious, the Tories hungry for office and Labour exhausted – just as it had been in 1951. 'There was a general feeling among us that we hadn't done a bad job between 1974 to '78.

In '79, it all fell apart; we hadn't done a bad job, but we didn't have anything new to offer', is how he puts it.

He also admits that Labour could have done more to target Thatcher's policies and Thatcher the candidate – all of which had been perfectly framed by the media and marketing men. The problem was the prime minister was resistant to this. As Donoughue explains – 'I wrote a speech for [Callaghan] . . . because I thought the campaign was really about Thatcher.'

'I could see her virtues, but I also saw her desperate shortcomings as a right-wing Tory and a fairly unimaginative one . . . I gave him the speech and he handed it back to me and said "I'm sorry Bernard, I'm sure you are right about Mrs Thatcher but she's the next Prime Minister and I'm not going to be, as the previous Prime Minister, attacking her."'

Donoughue is frank about Callaghan's mindset at the time, explaining how 'Jim really thought she was the right person for the job. That's why he said [there would be] a sea change with Thatcher', adding that 'in his way Jim thought it was the right thing for the country, he didn't think we had anything more to offer and he thought she did.'

In the end Labour lost, Donoughue believes, because they 'had just run out of ideas and run out of a way forward. The trade unions were desperately unpopular and (there was) nothing we could do about that. We had just run out of steam, and there we are.'[13]

1979 – General Election Result

Date of Election – 3 May

Overall Turnout – 76%

Labour

Candidates – 623

MPs – 269

Votes – 11,532,148

Percentage share of the vote – 36.9%

Result – Conservative government

Turnout 1979 – 76.0%

Highlight – Margaret Thatcher becomes Britain's first woman prime minister.

Chapter 24

1983 – The New Hope

'Stand down Margaret'[1]

The Beat

At the outset of the 1983 general election Labour urged the public to end the unfolding disaster of Thatcherism, saying 'our task will be to heal these wounds and rekindle among the British people a new sense of unity and common purpose'.[2]

The four years since Jim Callaghan had been swept from office had left the country divided. Although the Conservative government had come under often intense pressure over its policies, voters would go to the polls with Labour facing a serious threat from former colleagues and the two main parties more ideologically opposed than at any time in the previous 40 years.

Though the Tories still had a healthy majority, and Parliament had a year left to run, Margaret Thatcher sought to capitalise on a newfound popularity and to exploit turmoil among her political opponents.

The scene was set for an explosive election which had its roots in places as diverse as Limehouse, Toxteth and Port Stanley in the South Atlantic.

All this began for Labour in the autumn of 1979 when the Party's annual conference voted in favour of local constituency parties having the power to deselect their sitting Member of Parliament. It was a victory for the left – followed a year later by an agreement that future leadership elections would be decided not just by MPs, but also by ordinary members and trade unions.

Amid all this, and while the old system remained in place, in October 1980 Callaghan stood down in the hope that Denis Healey would become his successor. However, in a close race, MPs eventually turned to a romantic figure from the left in the shape of Michael Foot.

Known as a distinguished journalist, intellectual and skilled parliamentarian, they hoped he could unite the party in a way that the bullish Healey could not. In victory, the 67-year-old Foot said the main issues facing the country were unemployment and the scrapping of nuclear weapons.

Three months later, in January 1981, a special conference at Wembley Arena ratified the decision to allow other parts of the movement to have a say in electing the leader. There would be a weighted formula for this – 40 per cent of the vote to trade unions, and 30 per cent respectively to local parties and MPs.

To some MPs on the right of the party, this extension of democracy was deeply troubling. In their eyes, the Labour Party was moving ever further leftwards, promising unilateral nuclear disarmament and departure from the European Economic Community. Former Cabinet ministers David Owen, Shirley Williams and Bill Rodgers felt Labour was being infiltrated by far-left elements and embarking on a course which was electorally doomed.

The day after the Wembley gathering, the three were joined by the former Labour chancellor Roy Jenkins, who had been serving as president of the European Commission. Now, the so-called 'Gang of Four' issued what came to be known as the Limehouse Declaration.

Named after the area of London where they met, the opening paragraph made clear their intention – 'The calamitous outcome of the Labour Party Wembley conference demands a new start in British politics. A handful of trade union leaders can now dictate the choice of a future Prime Minister'.[3]

This represented the formation of a 'Council for Social Democracy', which soon became the Social Democratic Party, or SDP, armed with the support of 13 other former Labour MPs and one from the Tory ranks, plus a number of peers.

It was the most significant split in the Labour Party for half a century, and most media commentators looked favourably on the development, with many believing Thatcher would be a one-term prime minister of little distinction.

By June, the SDP had formed an electoral pact with the Liberals and before long Jenkins and Williams had returned to Parliament in high-profile by-election victories at Glasgow Hillhead and Crosby. Under the arrangement the Alliance, as it became known, fought local elections in 1982 and 1983, making significant gains in both years.

At the same time, Labour remained mired in factional in-fighting, with Tony Benn just failing to oust Healey from the deputy leadership at another acrimonious party conference. Healey later reflected that winning 'by a hair of my eyebrow', (his were famously bushy), prevented further haemorrhaging of Labour MPs to the SDP.[4]

For a party hoping there would be a quick return to power, such public bloodletting served simply to obscure serious Conservative short-comings in government.

The Tory troubles stemmed from the promises made in the victory of 1979 and their dogged determination to move to a new economic model, changing the fundamental basis upon which Britain was run.

Thatcher sought to tame what she believed to be high levels of government spending, borrowing and taxation, in her view the mark of Labour governments. To allow the free market full rein, she contended that high interest rates were the necessary means of slaying the old dragon of inflation.

In this, she followed the prominent right-wing economist, Milton Friedman, who said there needed to be strict control of the amount of money in circulation, a theory known as monetarism. There had been hints of this type of thinking among Labour under Callaghan, but in a much more restrained way, and with the aim of keeping the economy balanced and people in jobs.

The price for monetarism was colossal, with unemployment surging past 2.5 million by the time inner-city riots exploded across major English cities in the spring of 1981. These began in Brixton in London and spread over the summer to Leeds, Manchester, Birmingham, Merseyside and beyond.

In March the same year, 364 prominent economists wrote to *The Times* rejecting monetarism on the grounds that 'present policies will deepen the depression, erode the industrial base of our economy and threaten its social and political stability'.[5]

This was an unprecedented level of criticism from eminent professionals. The backdrop to it had been Geoffrey Howe's 1981 Budget, which contained measures that seemed to ignore the deep recession and adhere only to the desire to control inflation. Labour said it had been a Budget designed to put millions more on the dole, and it sparked the defection of a Tory MP to the SDP.

Mrs Thatcher had already made it plain she would not be moved, telling her party a few months earlier 'you turn if you want to. The Lady's not for turning.'[6] Those who questioned her methods came to be derided as 'wets', but it was beyond doubt that the government was struggling in the polls at the beginning of 1982.

Conservative support had fallen greatly since 1979 and at times Labour had a significant lead, though not a sustained one. By the end of

1981, fewer than 20 per cent of those asked in surveys approved of the government's record in office. The numbers dissatisfied with Thatcher herself were consistently in the 60 per cent plus bracket, but agonisingly for Labour, the public felt similarly negatively about Foot.

By April 1982, all that had changed, thanks to an unforeseen military conflict thousands of miles from home, ignited when Argentina invaded the Falkland Islands, a tiny British archipelago in the South Atlantic.

At the outset of the Falklands crisis Parliament sat at the weekend for the first time since Suez in 1956. Labour urged further diplomacy but backed the use of force if necessary. Days later, a huge task force sailed from Portsmouth accompanied by flag-waving well-wishers and patriotic media coverage. This was Britannia reborn as a power in the world, a military rather than an economic one.

The conflict cost 255 British lives and around 650 dead on the Argentine side before the capital, Port Stanley, was recaptured in June. The immediate effect was to give Thatcher a new authority – now she was truly the Iron Lady.

By May 1982, the Tories had the support of half the electorate and Thatcher was her party's prize asset. Questions inevitably began to emerge about the timing of the next election, with some MPs pressing for an October poll.

Labour, meanwhile, was focused on its own divisions, with growing tensions not only over policy, but also the influence of the far-left group, Militant. Then, in March 1983, the party narrowly held the seat of Darlington in a by-election, a result which ended any prospect of the Labour leader being replaced with Healey, whom the Tories feared far more than they did Foot.

A month later, on the back of what seemed to be an emerging economic upturn, Tory agents across the country told Thatcher their preference was for a June poll. Labour's performance in the local elections on 5 May was the deciding factor. While Foot saw Labour gain only a handful of seats, the Tories had over a hundred new councillors. Four days later Thatcher told voters they would have a further say in a general election on 9 June.

The signs were ominous from the outset for Foot and Labour. The first opinion poll showed they were on just 31 per cent, 15 points behind Thatcher's party, with the Alliance on 21 per cent attracting away many traditional Labour supporters.

Mrs Thatcher attempted to define the campaign in a news interview by claiming that the election was not a matter of political convenience, but was taking place in the national interest, leaning into the patriotic feeling following the victory in the Falklands.

Michael Foot was having none of it, saying that the government seemed to be rushing to the ballot box after a 'helter-skelter, hugger mugger, discreditable decision which I am sure the country will recognise.'[7]

Parliament was dissolved with just four days notice and thoughts then turned to the question of candidates. At speed, Labour undertook 80 or so selections, around a dozen of which were in what were viewed as winnable seats. There was also consideration of the manifesto, the campaign platform which would frame the party's bid for power.

Policy documents had been circulating since 1980, and in March 1983 a paper, 'The New Hope for Britain', won the backing of shadow ministers and the National Executive Committee. In essence it became a draft manifesto and was then adopted formally with the same title.

The Shadow Cabinet discussed it on 10 May, and the NEC met the following day at Labour's Walworth Road headquarters. In the event, the manifesto was agreed after little more than an hour's discussion, the shortest meeting of its kind in Labour's history. It produced a lengthy document, running to almost 40 pages, calling on voters to 'think positive think Labour'.[8]

The manifesto was avowedly left wing in outlook, with policies seeking greater taxation of the rich, withdrawal from the EEC and abolition of the House of Lords. Unemployment was to be reduced below one million within five years and there would be a return to nationalised industries.

It was an attempt to draw the country back into the realms of the post-war consensus but it also told the story of a party ill at ease with itself. This was no more obvious than in the fudge on nuclear weapons: 'We must use unilateral steps taken by Britain to secure multilateral solutions on the international level. Unilateralism and multilateralism must go hand in hand if either is to succeed.'[9]

The shadow environment secretary, Gerald Kaufman, dubbed the manifesto 'the longest suicide note in history', an instantly memorable phrase which stuck.[10] Others suggested that those who did not share Foot's political outlook would be perfectly happy to blame a left-wing manifesto should Labour be defeated.

Many candidates refused to accept the programme and instead fought highly individualised constituency battles. The Conservatives jumped on the manifesto, buying 3,000 copies at a cost of 60p a time directly from Labour, and using them to highlight what they portrayed as Foot's extremism.

The manifesto's contents provided Thatcher with ample attack lines against the cost of Labour's plans. The chancellor, Geoffrey Howe, claimed the proposals to undo the previous four years of Tory rule would carry a price tag of more than £34 billion a year. The Alliance joined the assault with similar lines calculated to undermine Labour.

Labour began each day at Walworth Road with an early morning meeting digesting the latest polling before a gathering of the campaign committee. The main protagonists – most often Foot, Healey and Roy Hattersley – then had to transfer the two miles to Transport House in central London to face the media.

By contrast, the Conservative operation was leaner and concentrated not only on what was already in the newspapers but identified the probable themes of the day. Thatcher often took the lead and decided on strategy. The government also had the distinct advantage of being the last to go before the press.

The Conservatives positioned themselves as a party giving the nation back its confidence and self-respect, suggesting that the choice was between continuing down their path or going backwards under Labour. Foot, on the other hand, questioned whether anyone would have voted Tory in 1979 had they known the high levels of unemployment and the economic upheavals to come.

This was a distinct feature of the campaign for Labour. While the Tories, with their slick communications, pushed messages about the future of the country, Foot tended to look backwards, often by several decades.

On one occasion, the Labour leader attacked Lord Hailsham, the lord chancellor, for his appeasement stance pre-1939. 'The old boy has plainly lost his marbles. Poor old, dear old Worzel Gummidge. He is ranting. He is hysterical,' was the biting response from Hailsham, a caricature which delighted Labour's opponents.[11]

There was a further colourful turn when the focus moved from British television characters to Hollywood. The actress, Shirley MacLaine, revealed that she had had an affair with an unnamed Labour MP whom she nicknamed 'Gerry', beginning a guessing game across the press.

For the main protagonists, there was little time for light-hearted thoughts. Ferried by saloon car, Michael Foot carried out dozens of constituency visits during what was a hectic schedule with only Sundays off. Often there were cheering crowds and standing ovations in response to his almost always upbeat speeches.

At times, though, there was a lack of polish. Foot visited the Tory stronghold of Banbury, spending four hours in the town. First, he went to a hospital ward for geriatric patients, but many were too infirm to acknowledge him, and then he moved on to an unemployment centre, where the press could not follow, negating the publicity aspect of the visit.

By contrast, Mrs Thatcher regally travelled the country by plane or in her battle bus, risking only limited interactions with the public – her team preferring a series of fully ticketed events which avoided the threat of heckling.

With the polls refusing to shift in the party's direction, the Labour campaign gathered in an air of crisis. Party strategists took matters into their own hands, pivoting to present the front bench as a team, with Healey pushed ever more to the fore.

Yet Labour also did well with a series of hitherto concealed or ignored documents, the most potent of which indicated there were plans to dismantle the National Health Service. Other papers suggested unemployment was much higher than the figure needed to control inflation, and that the jobless figures were likely to rise towards a jaw-dropping six million.

The Conservatives were quick to rebut these serious charges, helped by the publication of figures showing inflation falling (down to 4 per cent), the lowest level in 15 years. On a technicality, the unemployment rate also dropped by over 100,000, though the overall figure still showed more than three million out of work.

While ministers used these figures as evidence that their monetarist strategy was working, Labour remained under attack from pro-Conservative newspapers. *The Daily Mail* gave prominence to a story that a planned major investment by the Nissan car company, creating thousands of jobs, would not happen should Foot win and take Britain out of the EEC.

In the final days before polling, Labour enraged the government over the war with Argentina when first Healey went on the attack saying 'this Prime Minister who glories in slaughter has taken advantage of the superb professionalism of our forces in the Falkland Islands.'[12] Days later, the shadow education spokesman, Neil Kinnock, said it had been a pity soldiers had to die to prove the Tory leader had guts.

In a sense, these Labour attacks were understandable and inevitable. Thatcher really was glorying in military victory, and she had pressed ahead with the war when others in her Cabinet had baulked.

On the final day of campaigning, military helicopters flew the media and the prime minister to the Isle of Wight, where the prime minister was photographed arms outstretched in front of a giant union flag painted on the doors of an aircraft hangar.

As it had been in 1979, she was embracing the power of modern communications and messaging. Foot was a different animal – he had spent almost half a century speaking without notes, only to find himself unable to grasp the art of the news soundbite.

On the morning of the election, he emerged from his constituency home in Tredegar to walk his dog, Dizzy, who had become an unlikely star of the campaign. Standing arm in arm with his wife, the Labour leader conveyed an urgent message to the British public 'use your vote, it's very precious. Use it to get a decent government.'[13]

Any hope that this would transpire was extinguished shortly after the polls closed at 10 p.m. The ITN news network pointed to a sizable Conservative victory, and this was soon backed up with similar figures from the BBC.

The first proper results came in after 11 p.m., and these were equally ominous; the Tories held Torbay, Cheltenham and Guildford, with Labour losing deposits in each constituency. Shortly after midnight, it was clear Mrs Thatcher would remain in power with a greatly increased majority, something senior Labour figures were not seeking to dispute on the airwaves.

Their pessimism was justified. Labour had just 209 MPs, a loss of 60 seats on the previous election and by some distance the lowest the party had managed in the post-war era. The numbers voting Labour had fallen by more than three million and several prominent figures lost their seats, most notably Tony Benn and Joan Lestor.

Thatcher's triumph saw the Conservatives back in power with 397 MPs, a landslide which provided a Commons majority close to 150. This had been achieved with little over 42 per cent of the vote, on a national turnout which had fallen to 72 per cent of the electorate.

Labour had managed less than 30 per cent of the vote, albeit enough to secure second place ahead of the Alliance, which won a quarter of national vote. However, this returned just 23 MPs, infuriating Jenkins and David Steel.

Undoubtedly it had been a disastrous election for Labour and even the routing of most of those who had crossed the floor to join the SDP could offer little consolation. In the eyes of an electorate now less wedded to class or party loyalty, Labour had appeared too divided to govern and had repeatedly been painted as too dangerous to be allowed to do so, especially over defence.

The manifesto, with its great sweep of pledges, was also blamed, though Foot pointed out that what was being offered to the electorate was simply the fruits of a decade worth of policy-making.

Curiously, Labour's pitch was similar in key elements to that of the Alliance which also prioritised reducing unemployment, increases to child benefit, pensions and a major council-house building programme. All of this was deemed credible, while simultaneously the narrative took hold that Labour's promises failed to stack up.

At the same time, the Tories executed the most media-driven campaign British politics had known. Building on their successes in 1979, strategists maximised publicity for the leadership, with TV a key strand and an outlay of over £2 million on advertising alone.

Image was everything, with lengthy consideration of even seemingly minor details such as the shade of blue curtains used at the manifesto launch. All this suited an era in which the pace of the news cycle was quickening, something defined by the advent of breakfast television, with ministers and shadow ministers making appearances on the morning sofa giving interviews.

For Foot the outcome was the result of 'a deeply reactionary and offensive campaign fought by our opponents'. something which made 'all the more scandalous and unforgivable the treachery of those who helped to enable the Tories to win the election, defectors from our own ranks.'[14]

Though they had taken only a few seats, the SDP had a significant impact on Labour as part of the Alliance, meaning this time the third party took 12 per cent more of the vote than in the previous election. While it is very hard to say what proportion of these voters backed Labour in 1979, it is undoubtedly the case that the SDP sold itself as the Labour party with nuclear bombs and without the unions.

While the Falklands changed perceptions of the personality of the prime minister, the split in the anti-Tory vote (in effect the Labour vote), gave Thatcher the political space she needed to create a clear path to victory.

The prime minister had been able to cast a spell which made it look as though she had the sensible solutions Britain required. While

Labour fought over tactics, policy and direction, Thatcher was able to appear reasonable, despite her methods being well outside what had been considered the political mainstream.

The scale of defeat was doubly traumatic for Labour. Not only had it been delivered in large part at the hands of those who had turned their backs on the party, but Thatcher now had the means to shape the 1980s as she saw fit.

Within hours she was getting stuck into a Cabinet reshuffle, rather chillingly telling the BBC's Robin Day: 'I'm not a good butcher but have had to learn to carve the joint . . . I have not been extreme in the last four years, I am not an extreme person. We shall not be extreme now.'[15]

Labour had begun the election by proclaiming new hope, only to be left in despair. On television, a grave-looking Neil Kinnock considered the task ahead, saying 'the battle is to win the next election because I think the British people, or sections of the British people, yesterday voted to live on their knees. And we have got to lift them off that.'[16]

1983 – General Election Result

Date of Election – 9 June

Overall Turnout – 72.7%

Labour

Candidates – 633

MPs – 209

Votes – 8,456,934

Percentage share of the vote – 27.6%

Result – Conservative landslide

Highlight – Future party leaders, Tony Blair, Gordon Brown, Paddy Ashdown, Charles Kennedy and Michael Howard were all elected for the first time.

Chapter 25

1987 – The Dream Ticket

This election will decide whether our country
is to be a United Kingdom or a divided kingdom[1]

Labour Manifesto

On the morning of 12 June 1987, Anne Diamond was perched on the TV-am breakfast sofa showing the front pages of the newspapers to the nation. A little too perkily for anyone of a Labour persuasion, the television presenter went through each in turn.

'Maggie's Hat Trick', 'Maggie the Third', 'SuperMag wins her hat-trick', 'Thatcher's Historic Victory'.[2] The headlines told what was becoming a familiar tale of woe for Labour in the era of Margaret Thatcher. Then, cutting to a reporter standing next to the black door of 10 Downing Street in the morning sunshine, it appeared for all the world as though Britain was a happy and contented place, rather than a country which had lived through some wildly turbulent years since the previous election.

Labour had made strenuous efforts to remould itself in the hope of regaining power. It was a monumental task, with the Conservative leader dominating at home and abroad, deploying a brand of popular Conservatism which had been accepted by considerable sections of the British electorate.

The Thatcher credo was a smaller state, greater individual responsibility, increased home ownership and the privatisation of formerly nationalised industries. Hand in hand with these went share ownership, aggression towards trade unions and a decisive turn away from the pursuit of full employment.

Carried out by a confident government, this programme amounted to huge shifts in British life. The prime minister held a 144-seat majority and she was on record saying her aim was to destroy socialism – it was nothing less than a counter-revolution against the reforms of the Labour governments of 1945 to 1951.

The 1983 defeat floored Labour, with the party receiving its lowest share of the vote since the Great War and the fewest number of seats in half a century. Quickly, it tried to move on with a new leadership team replacing Michael Foot and Denis Healey later the same year.

Neil Kinnock, the shadow education spokesperson from the soft-left of the Party, was elected leader, winning a clear mandate across the electoral college. Roy Hattersley became deputy leader, having been defeated for the top job. This partnership was quickly dubbed the 'dream ticket', with supporters enthused by Kinnock's energy.

At 41 years of age, Kinnock was the youngest leader in the party's history, rousing delegates at the annual conference in Brighton when he beseeched them to 'remember how you felt on that dreadful morning of the 10 June. Just remember how you felt then and think to yourselves: "June the 9 1983, never, ever again will we experience that."'[3]

He went on to predict the government would bring industrial tragedy to the country and that the British people would make the Conservatives pay for doing so. The complication was that this relied not only on Labour winning new voters, and bringing many others back into the fold, but doing so in an era which remained one of genuine three-party politics.

Throughout the Parliament the Alliance, with a new SDP leader in the guise of David Owen, was often as high as 20 per cent in the polls and at times drew level with both Labour and the Conservatives. There was a growing realisation that Labour, which was almost absent in terms of MPs across the south of England, needed to widen its appeal to the haves as well as the have-nots.

Internal reorganisation saw the new leadership quickly establish the Campaign Strategy Committee, largely bypassing the ruling NEC to oversee polling, campaigning and communications. It was the prelude to further changes with a new general secretary, and in 1985 the appointment of Peter Mandelson as director for campaigns and communications.

These innovations were taking place within Labour while major industrial and social upheavals were at the forefront of the news. The most significant was a strike by the National Union of Mineworkers aimed at halting a rolling programme of pit closures which was devastating communities in the North of England, Wales and Scotland.

Thatcher, who had witnessed first-hand the strength of the NUM in helping to bring down the Heath government in February 1974, had long planned for just such a dispute, stockpiling coal in readiness. Having decided at a special conference against holding a national ballot of members, in March 1984, the miners' union was plunged into a year-long strike.

It was an era-defining dispute marked by numerous violent confrontations between striking and non-striking miners, as well as with the police. In June, officers from across England, many on horseback and wielding truncheons, charged pickets at the Orgreave coking plant in South Yorkshire.

Over 120 people were injured, some seriously, and there were multiple arrests on what in many cases were later proven to be trumped-up charges. The violence shocked journalists and the queen, on seeing the television news, was reported to have been appalled, saying 'oh, that's awful. Oh, we shouldn't do that.'[4]

Kinnock, the son of a Welsh miner with thousands of pitmen in his own constituency, supported the miners' case, but took the view that Arthur Scargill, the leader of the NUM, should hold a ballot so that the strike had legitimacy in the eyes of the public.

It was a landmark dispute which pulled communities apart and left families starving. Days short of the strike's first anniversary, on 3 March 1985, the NUM agreed to return to work. The BBC interrupted its daytime television schedule with a newsflash, such was the importance of the announcement. A clearly crestfallen Scargill said that though the strike was over, the fight would go on to retain pits and jobs.

The elections to the European Parliament, in June 1984, saw Labour take 15 seats from the Tories in what was seen as an important test for the new leadership. Not only did the Party gain almost 40 per cent of the vote, but the Alliance performed badly and was left without a single MEP.

In October the same year, the IRA detonated a 20lb bomb at the Grand Hotel in Brighton, targeting the Cabinet and prime minister as they slept. Five people were killed, and many others wounded in the explosion which ripped the front off the building. Mrs Thatcher survived, but only by good fortune, and she continued with her Conference arrangements the next day.

That determination could also be seen in the drive to undo nationalisation in sections of industry. Privatisation was a radical agenda designed to shrink the influence of the state and the unions, while at the same time reconfiguring the economy and creating a nation of shareholders.

The first major utility to go was British Telecom in the winter of 1984. Backed by a huge advertising campaign, applications flooded in and almost £4 billion was raised. Labour complained that the Tories had deliberately set the sale price at half the market value, but the party made no commitment to renationalisation.

Interviewed for this book, Neil Kinnock explained that this was a matter of priorities rather than an acceptance of the Conservative agenda. Labour's outlook was to consider the money coming in from the planned or already executed privatisations.

As Kinnock saw it 'we had to say – if we have £20 billion, £60 billion, £100 billion what do we spend it on? We spend it on old age pensions, schools, childcare and not paying shareholders.'[5] He does though suggest that had Labour come to power it might have been possible to use money earmarked for subsidies to buy shares in the newly privatised industries and retake control, thus reversing Thatcherism.

Kinnock is a politician from the shop floor who dealt in practicalities, and that meant, above all else, Labour in government. At the party Conference in 1985 he set out his stall, taking on the far-left Militant tendency, or what the newspapers had come to call the 'loony left'.

In a powerful speech which had the air of a sermon, he first painted a stark picture of Labour looking inward instead of tackling the crisis of unemployment and poverty. Knowing his remarks would be replayed in millions of homes that evening, he turned his fire on the Militant leaders of Liverpool City Council.

They had recently set an illegal budget after resisting government cuts which would have sharply increased rents and halted regeneration plans. In Kinnock's view they were the peddlers of an approach which was 'out-dated, mis-placed, irrelevant to the real needs', ending with what he called 'the grotesque chaos of a Labour council hiring taxis to scuttle round a city handing out redundancy notices to its own workers'.[6]

It was a defining moment which delighted his friends and dismayed his enemies in the hall and far beyond. In fact, he had hoped to make a speech on this theme a year earlier but had felt unable to do so while the miners' strike was taking place.

Now the clock was ticking towards the next election, and even at this stage the Party was already making plans for that contest. Unsure of when it might be called, a campaign management team was set up to sort out any difficulties before they arose, rather than in the heat of battle.

Labour was wise to do so, as the government found itself destabilised by unexpected events, the most prominent of which was an explosive row over how to rescue Westland Helicopters, a British aerospace company. Michael Heseltine suddenly resigned as defence secretary in January 1986, prompting a debate in Parliament, questions about the prime minister's integrity and the eventual resignation of Leon Brittan as trade and industry secretary.

The theme of a divided Britain was underscored later the same year with the 'Big Bang' in London's financial district. Pushed by Thatcher and her ministers, the City was deregulated and computerised, catapulting the square mile to the forefront of the world's financial markets.

By January 1987, the most pressing question in politics had become the date of the next election. Labour was by now almost level in the polls, but in February and March voting preferences shifted back towards the Tories. Labour also lost the Greenwich by-election to the SDP, a seat which they had held since 1945.

This gave a clear signal to Thatcher that the Alliance remained a threat to Kinnock's hopes at the ballot box. Then in March, Nigel Lawson announced major tax cuts in the Budget, including a 2p reduction in income tax. Labour's response was clear: this was a pre-election giveaway, a bribe to the electorate.

Though preparations were well underway at Conservative Central Office, the result of the local elections on 8 May confirmed to Thatcher that she had every incentive to go to the country without delay. The Tories gained 75 seats while Labour lost close to 250. Three days later, the announcement came that a general election would be held on 11 June.

This coincided with economic indicators the government could use to its advantage. The balance of payments was healthy and though inflation was rising a fraction, it remained at just over 4 per cent. Unemployment was also falling, down by almost 40,000 in April, although overall the jobless total remained huge, dropping only just below three million in May.

A confident Thatcher told the BBC at the start of campaigning that she did not believe this would be her last election as leader. She also suggested a measure of fee-paying could be introduced into state education and hinted at a review of the NHS. Much of this made her ministers nervous, believing voters might conclude that the Tories arrogantly thought the election was already won.

For Labour things began daily at 7 a.m. with Bryan Gould and Peter Mandelson, the two election co-ordinators, meeting at the Party's HQ in South London to examine polling and media coverage. A press conference then followed, before the campaign was taken out into the country.

Kinnock led throughout, with supporting roles for Bryan Gould, Roy Hattersley and others, in what was a slick campaign. It was more tightly organised than past efforts and this looked to be paying dividends, with data indicating that Kinnock's was the personality voters most warmed to.

The flipside was that Thatcher was still seen as the strongest possible leader. As a counter, the Labour campaign planners decided the best strategy was to play to their positives and push their leader forward in what amounted to a near presidential campaign.

Kinnock became the focus of media conferences and political broadcasts. Even before the election, his advisers had been convinced that he needed to be seen on television, prompting the making of a short film, dubbed 'Kinnock the Movie' by Hugh Hudson, the director of the box office smash-hit *Chariots of Fire*.

Unlike in 1983, the Labour manifesto 'Britain will win with Labour', did not propose pulling out of the EEC or abolition of the House of Lords. Some on the left pushed for withdrawal from NATO and closing US bases in Britain, but these policies were resisted. Instead, the manifesto proposed a major accelerated reform programme concentrating on unemployment and poverty, spending on health, housing and education and the rebuilding of Britain's manufacturing base.

The Conservatives looked for weaknesses in Labour's approach and made much of Militant's influence, while casting doubt on the party's competence on the economy. They also sought to portray Labour as weak on nuclear defence.

In a television interview on 24 May, Kinnock suggested to David Frost that Britain would be safe without nuclear arms because conventional troops would be enough to stop the country being overrun by any invading force. This was mocked as a 'Dad's Army' strategy by the popular press and the Tories then produced a poster of a soldier, hands aloft in surrender, with the accompanying text 'Labour's Policy On Arms'. It was a damaging moment.

With a week to go until polling everything suddenly seemed up for grabs. An opinion poll for the *Daily Telegraph*, carried on the major TV news bulletins, showed the Conservative lead down to just 4 points, with BBC *Newsnight* similarly predicting that a hung parliament was likely.

Labour's response was to say their own polls showed they were closing fast on the Tories. The tension showed at the Conservative press conference on what came to be known as 'wobbly Thursday' (4 June), with Thatcher taking almost six minutes to answer a question on whether Britain was divided.

With £6 billion wiped off the value of shares by a nervous stock market suddenly jittery about a Labour victory, Thatcher imposed her will on events. The prime minister sanctioned the spending of another £2 million in a single week, pushing the core Tory message out across the newspapers that 'Britain is great again. Don't let Labour wreck it'.[7]

At his final rally in Cardiff, Kinnock told activists they had won the arguments, and the final days of Thatcherism were close at hand. In truth, hope was fading that such a feat could be achieved.

As voting closed at 10 p.m. on election night, ITV's Alastair Burnet was handed an envelope, containing the top secret exit poll result. Data from 100 constituencies, where voters were asked after leaving the polling station who they had backed, was used to predict the outright winner.

Carefully, Burnet read the contents: 'we are forecasting now, on the exit poll, a Conservative majority of 68. Now if that is true it means Mrs Thatcher is back in Downing Street for another five years.'[8] The BBC had a different take, predicting a majority of just 26 – in line with forecasts that Labour had been closing fast in the final days.

The two exit polls were confusing. On the one hand, it was highly likely Labour had been defeated, but it was also possible that they might still stop Thatcher winning outright. As John Smith, the shadow trade and industry secretary, put it: 'as far as I can see this election is still wide open. We might get to a situation where Mrs Thatcher doesn't have an overall majority.'[9]

This early optimism was understandable, but proved to be misplaced once the first results rolled in. At Torbay, the government's vote share rose by 1 per cent and sparked an immediate revision upwards of the expected Tory majority. When Guildford declared shortly after 11 p.m. with no fall in the Conservative vote and then Basildon was held with an increased majority, a trend was established.

This would continue in the coming hours until, shortly before 3 a.m., it became mathematically certain Mrs Thatcher had triumphed. The eventual majority over all other parties would stand at 102, down considerably from four years earlier, but still a landslide. For the first time since Lord Liverpool, 170 years earlier, a prime minister had won three elections on the spin.

The deeper detail painted a picture of a fractured electorate, with the varying swing to Labour across the country telling the story. This was almost non-existent in the south of England but stood at over 3.5 per cent in the North and higher still in Scotland.

Thatcher's Party took five seats off Labour in the South and lost only one. They lost four in Wales, while Labour made seven gains in the North. In Scotland the result was even more pronounced – the Tories losing 11 seats, down to a mere 10, with Labour on 50.

Kinnock's Party finished with 229 seats, a limited advance from the 209 they had won four years earlier, with most of their gains coming at the expense of the Conservatives. The Alliance could manage only 22 seats (with 23 per cent of the vote), a crushing blow to any hope they had of supplanting Labour. On top of that, they had lost Roy Jenkins, defeated by Labour in Glasgow.

For Thatcher there was again an obvious electoral benefit from the three-party era. The Conservatives won with just over 42 per cent of the vote, while Labour and the Alliance together accounted for over 50 per cent of the ballots cast. In simple terms, more people were still voting against Thatcher than for her, and in the main they were voting Labour.

The *People* newspaper, which backed Labour, reflected that 'the anti-Thatcher vote in Thursday's election exceeded that of her supporters. The haves triumphed over the have-nots.'[10]

Not that this troubled *The Sun* which declared: 'YOU wanted more money in your pay packet to spend as you choose and you voted for Maggie . . . YOU wanted strong defence based on the nuclear deterrent . . . YOU wanted freedom to choose the best education, the best health care and best home for your family'.

The country, or significant parts of it, felt that in Thatcher they had a prime minister with a purpose, and in her policies a clear direction of travel. These had bedded in across the years, from selling off millions of council homes to the continued privatisation of and individual share ownership in state-owned corporations.

By 1987, not just British Telecom, but British Aerospace, Cable and Wireless, British Gas, British Airways, the Trustee Savings Bank, Rolls-Royce and more had been sold off. Those able to take part in what was seen as aspirational Britain either felt individually better off or bought into the idea that they were.

Even though Labour was both more united and professional than in the recent past, even though they had a dynamic young leader who understood presentation and image, it was not enough. Essentially, the gap from the 1983 nadir was too great to bridge.

Kinnock offered a strongly defined moral counterpoint to Thatcher, and a vision of a different country but, like Foot before him, he also had to endure vicious press attacks on his personality. These had one aim: to damage his credibility as an alternative prime minister.

Interestingly, he does not consider the influence of the media to be terribly significant in terms of winning votes. Rather it was the issues he had to deal with in the years between elections which made the difference: the high-profile battle with Militant but also continually having to make the case that people should not turn to the SDP.

As he puts it: 'some people have accepted it, though happily not too many, that it was their presence and their breakaway and their audacity that enabled me to make the change in the Labour Party. No, it didn't, it slowed it down by about three bloody years.'

'I not only had to deal with the substance of the arguments being made by the Bennites, I had to press back against the more popular claim that this [his reforming agenda] was SDP mark II. It wasn't, it was Labour Party mark I.' Kinnock believes the main motivation behind the SDP was 'political hubris', a demand from some who led the breakaway always to be at the top of politics.

The miners' strike, he argues, also had a big impact on Labour's chances of victory. 'The most important fact it had was to take virtually two years out of our change agenda and momentum.' Not only that, he contends, there was an effect before, during and after the dispute because: 'the Labour movement did nothing, thought about nothing, collected for nothing, marched for nothing, drafted for nothing other than the miners' strike.'

The coverage of the violence between pickets and police was used by Conservatives in the election and as Kinnock points out, 'all they had to do was show some film of Orgreave and that prompted in Britain, not just in the middle classes but working-class people as well, disgust that some bloody demagogue would exercise the national interest.'

'And the fact that it was the miners, a trade union affiliated to the Labour Party and here's Kinnock who's got everything but pneumoconiosis and scars, so you can't vote Labour even if you believe in their policies because they are going to bring us this.'[11]

Essentially, Labour's leader was still in the process of building the party's electoral potential at this stage, with its main opponents pulling the needle of the political compass in new directions and many voters still wary of Labour.

In the eyes of many whose votes it wished to capture, negative perceptions remained about the party's credibility on the economy, as well as other issues, in particular defence in an era still dominated by the Cold War.

Kinnock readily admits he had never expected to win in 1987 and always thought it would take more than a single election to return to power. The hope had been to capture over 40 seats, but only 20 were gained, though it was a close-run thing in a further two dozen constituencies.

Labour lost in 1987, he reflects, because 'the hill was so steep . . . and for impressionable people they (the government) could talk about the good days to come. That had its effect, and here was the background of the miners' strike, us still a unilateralist party, edging towards a rational policy on Europe, but Thatcher was still riding the wave.'[12]

Although it was commonly accepted that Labour had won the battle of the campaigns – and with it much respect – Mrs Thatcher now looked set to push her brand of extreme Toryism into the next decade.

1987 – General Election Result

Date of Election – 11 June

Overall Turnout 1987 – 75.3%

Labour

Candidates – 633

MPs – 229

Votes – 10,029,778

Percentage share of the vote – 30.8%

Result – Conservative landslide

Highlight – Mrs Thatcher wins an historic third term with a majority of just over 100 seats.

Chapter 26

1992 – Well All Right!

'the cold blue landscape of winter
suddenly alive with bright red roses'[1]

Winter Ending by Adrian Henri.
(Labour Manifesto)

With unemployment soaring, interest rates above 10 per cent and house prices tumbling in a stubborn recession, it seemed Labour and Neil Kinnock were on the cusp of taking office after 13 years in the wilderness.

To many observers 1992 bore the hallmarks of being a change election – not that change had been in short supply in the period since Labour's defeat in 1987.

Facing a Conservative Party which had dominated the 1980s, and having seen off a serious threat from the breakaway SDP led by former Labour heavyweights, Kinnock now leaned heavily into a modernising agenda. The aim was to attract the skilled working classes and others back to his party. This was the language of priorities – and the priority was to win.

There was optimism that victory could be achieved, which partly stemmed from the findings of the polling companies that repeatedly showed voters not only valued a society with an active state and decent public services, but also that they remained lukewarm about free market solutions.

Many of those who had voted Tory under Margaret Thatcher seemed to have done so because her governments had made them better off, or at least made them feel they were gaining financially. In short, an element of Conservative support was only as solid as the economy was strong.

After the third defeat to Thatcher, the Labour leadership sought the means to guide Labour into the 1990s and back into government. A wide-ranging policy review began soon after the Conservative's 1987 landslide victory.

Modernisers sought to cast aside what they believed to be barriers to a wider pool of voters backing Labour. There would be no return of privatised utilities to public hands, no withdrawal from the European Community, higher taxes for the wealthiest were no longer prioritised and the unilateralist stance on nuclear disarmament was scrapped. On the economy there was a move to a 'supply-side' model in which greater competition would see the state regulate rather than run industries.

Much of this was implemented at the 1988 conference, but only after Tony Benn had challenged Kinnock for the leadership in a bid to halt the changes. As Benn saw it: 'we could be seen as a purely opportunistic party that is prepared to say anything to get into office and is ready to sacrifice good policies when the opinion polls swing against us.'[2]

It was a forlorn venture on Benn's part. Kinnock took close to 90 per cent of the vote and delegates endorsed the policy review by another large margin. If not quite a mirror reflection, this was an echo of the way in which the Conservatives had accepted the Attlee-led reforms after the Second World War to stay in touch with the electorate.

By early 1989 Labour had been behind the Tories in the polls for more than two years, though there were also worrying signs for the government, which lost more than a dozen seats to Labour at the European Elections. For Kinnock this was a boost; it was the first time his party had beaten the Conservatives in a nationwide vote since the general election of October 1974.

At the beginning of 1990, with that long-held Conservative poll lead having vanished, the mood grew still darker on the government benches over reverses in by-elections which foretold of impending catastrophe at the ballot box for those wearing blue rosettes.

The Conservatives lost seven seats across the Parliament from 1987 – four to Labour and three to the Liberal Democrats, the party which had been formed out of the old SDP/Liberal Alliance.

The most significant of these contests was at Eastbourne in the autumn of 1990. The sitting Conservative MP, Ian Gow, had been murdered by an IRA car bomb. Despite shock at Gow's death, the Liberal Democrats were able to score a stunning victory, comfortably wiping out a 16,000 Conservative majority.

Senior Tories knew this was not a matter of local difficulties. Voters were restless over rising interest rates and paying their mortgages and worried about the dark clouds of recession.

There had already been major violence in English cities over Thatcher's flagship policy, the Community Charge or Poll Tax, which imposed a flat-rate charge on every adult regardless of their living situation or ability to pay. Many Conservatives feared that what had happened in the by-election on the sleepy South coast could be repeated all over the country in a general election.

Events quickly unfolded. Geoffrey Howe, who had been chancellor, foreign secretary and finally deputy PM, left the government with a sensational resignation speech. His decision was not directly about the

Poll Tax, though he was critical of the prime minister's unwillingness to listen to senior colleagues.

Howe felt he could no longer tolerate disagreements over closer political and economic union with Europe. His searing conclusion was that 'the time has come for others to consider their own response to the tragic conflict of loyalties with which I have myself wrestled for perhaps too long.'[3]

Thatcher, the election-winning superstar, was abruptly and dramatically forced from office little more than two weeks after Howe's speech in November 1990. Having narrowly failed to fully see off a leadership challenge from Michael Heseltine, her senior ministers told her she could not go on.

This she accepted sorrowfully, saying 'I have concluded that the unity of the Party and the prospects of victory in a general election would be better served if I stood down.'[4] To her enraged supporters it had been nothing short of a political assassination.

'On the night that she went I thought – our greatest electoral asset has gone through the door', is how Neil Kinnock remembers Thatcher's downfall. 'I stood on the desk in my office and said to a very excited packed room – "drink and be merry tonight because tomorrow we have got a very different battle."'

Against whom this would be was the consideration for Kinnock. 'I thought, which pleased me very much, that we would be fighting Michael Heseltine, simply because he was such a divisive figure in the Tory Party. As an individual he would not have been easy, because Heseltine is a fully professional politician. But because he was a fighter and would punch you back, he was punchable.'

Instead, Kinnock's opponent would be John Major, the chancellor, who had risen quickly, and was a most unusual Conservative. Brought up in a working-class home in Brixton, his father had been a trapeze artist for a time. As Kinnock explains: 'John Major never occurred to anybody that night, to anybody, maybe even including Major. Four or five days later everything had shifted.'

'I said to my people – "now then are we going to have him as son of Thatcher, because that's his background, or are we going to say they had made a very deliberate switch from Thatcher because that's the only chance they have got of conning the people?". And we never decided which way we were going, not properly, not fully.'[5]

Major spoke of building a country at ease with itself, highlighting his desire to allow everyone the chance to fulfil their potential. This was a significant turn away from the harsher elements of the Thatcherite doctrine.

Having moved to a new leader and received a bounce in the polls, the government began building towards an election. The newspapers were full of talk that Major wanted to move out of his predecessor's shadow by securing a personal mandate.

Yet significant obstacles remained. Major's calculation was that the poll tax had not been neutered as an issue (even though the new Council Tax had been announced in March), and while inflation was falling unemployment was still on the rise.

Local election results in May 1991 saw Labour and the Lib Dems inflict huge losses on the government, the Conservatives losing more than 900 seats. 'The Tories will not want a general election now, but our country desperately needs one,' was the judgement of Jack Cunningham, Labour's election campaign manager.[6]

Yet the issue of when to go to the country bubbled under the surface and was prominent once again after the summer recess. Then, on the back of further poor by-election results, the Tories finally quashed growing speculation of a November poll. They chose the day before Kinnock's set-piece speech to the Labour Conference in Brighton to inform the media. Kinnock responded by telling delegates that the Tories had first lost a leader and now lost their nerve.

Even at this point in the autumn of 1991, with an election having to be held by the following summer, Major still had a few more cards to play. The Maastricht Treaty was agreed in December, binding the European Community closer together. To the surprise of many, Major secured the UK's opt out from provisions on what was known as the 'Social Chapter' – a suite of rights for workers. Labour supported the treaty, but felt the concessions were a disaster.

Then, almost as soon as the new year had been ushered in, the Tories fired the starting gun on the pre-election campaign, Major telling activists that low taxation was key to the election, and the party warning of what it called 'Labour's Tax Bombshell'.

Since the latter part of 1991, Kinnock had been urging the shadow chancellor, John Smith, to produce his 'Shadow Budget'. Kinnock maintains that Smith repeatedly refused to unveil this, hoping instead to demolish the government's strategy once the Tories had revealed their hand.

The chancellor, Norman Lamont, made his move on 10 March with what he called 'A budget for the recovery'. A new 20 per cent income tax band was introduced on the first £2,000 of taxable income, and personal tax allowances were raised in line with inflation.

Labour sniped that this was both unaffordable, given the state of the nation's finances, and a crude attempt to boost Tory popularity on the cusp of a general election. The next day, Major emerged smiling into Downing Street to announce that an election would indeed take place, on 9 April.

The battle over taxation would take centre stage in the campaign, and the first act in this drama was the unveiling of Smith's much-anticipated plans. This he did with a confident authority in front of an invited audience and press pack before posing for pictures with his team at the Treasury.

The shadow chancellor promised that anyone who earned less than £22,000 – around £55,000 today – would gain from Labour's measures. He reckoned this would mean about 80 per cent of taxpayers.

Tory-supporting newspapers painted all this as an attack on the rich (and therefore anyone who aspired to have more money), as well as a squeeze on the middle classes and pensions. Yet Labour's poll lead grew in the following days.

In a sense this was not surprising: the ground had been prepared long in advance, with many speeches and remarks by senior Labour figures in which the role of markets was given prominence and socialism was rarely if ever mentioned.

It was unclear whether it would be enough to take Labour back into office, which would require a post-war record swing of over 8 per cent. Major and the Conservatives knew their task – and it was simple – to instil doubt in the minds of those thinking that it was time for a change of government.

Labour based itself largely in offices at 4 Millbank where, then as now, many news outlets were housed. Adopting the well-worn pattern of past elections, the day would begin early with a briefing of key personnel. Journalists then jostled in for the press conference before jostling out again half an hour later to make their way round the corner to Tory HQ in Smith Square.

At these gatherings, the Conservatives focused on tax as an issue and wider claims that Smith's plans would cost the public £35 billion. By this stage, they were running a nationwide poster campaign – 'Labour's Double Whammy', featuring two large red boxing gloves.

Each glove carried a message – '1. More Taxes' '2. Higher Prices'. It was, inevitably, the work of the Saatchi & Saatchi agency, and an attempt to deflect from the fact that Britain was going through the deepest recession in Europe, and the longest since the war.

Labour did not lack ammunition to counter Tory claims on tax. The Party's manifesto, titled 'It's Time to Get Britain Working Again' contained concrete proposals to turn the country's economy around. The theme was national recovery, throughout the many spheres of economic and political life, with more money promised for education, an additional £1 billion for the NHS in the first year, and investments in house building and public transport. It was a joined-up plan based around steady economic growth and cuts to unemployment.

Taxation would be made fairer, with more raised for child benefit and pensions and the basic rate left unchanged at 25 per cent. Britain, the manifesto declared, had to be a major player in Europe and there would be no renationalisation of industries sold off by Thatcher and no reform of trade union laws.

The Conservative manifesto was a continuity document with little in the way of new ideas beyond some privatisation in British Rail and the coal industry. The Liberal Democrats had a good front man in Paddy Ashdown, but were fighting on the same ground as Kinnock's modernised Labour.

Throughout the election, events were coloured by the opinion polls simply because these were so plentiful, a total of 50 were undertaken during the campaign. The data suggested things were on a knife-edge, with Labour either ahead or neck and neck in all but a handful of cases.

This helped to amplify the sense that a change of government was possible, and to some degree shaped the decision-making of the parties on a day-to-day basis. The most obvious example of this was Major's decision to try to inject more life into the Tory campaign.

Less than two weeks before polling he abandoned formal events in which he took questions from an audience and instead began to use a megaphone to speak to voters in the streets atop what party officials described as a soapbox.

The media warmed to this, not least because it created the air of a bygone era. Getting their teeth into the story, journalists asked if Kinnock was about to follow suit, but Labour dismissed this as gimmickry and a sign of desperation from the Tories.

Labour had been bruised by what came to be known as the 'War of Jennifer's Ear' (a sideways reference to an eighteenth-century military conflict with a similar title). It all focused on claims made in a Labour election broadcast about delays in treating a five-year-old girl on the NHS for glue ear, making comparisons with the speedy treatment available to those able to afford such care in the private sector.

The point Labour were trying to make was about waiting lists and their plans to increase the budget of the NHS to European levels. All this was lost amid claim and counter claim from relatives, and between the parties, over the veracity of the story. For a full three days the issue dominated the election, losing Labour valuable time in which to campaign on health, one of the party's strongest suits.

Then, one week from polling, Labour held an evening rally in Sheffield in front of more than 10,000 supporters. For British politics the scale of the event was huge, resembling more the razzmatazz of party conventions in the United States.

Due to the busy campaign schedule, Kinnock had arrived by helicopter, while the Shadow Cabinet, dubbed the 'Cabinet in Waiting', were cheered through the crowd and onto the stage. When it was his turn to speak, Kinnock called out several times – 'well all right' to which the audience roared back in kind.

Looking back, he describes the atmosphere as 'tumultuous', comparing it to the molten heat of the Bessemer process used in steelmaking. 'When I walked into that hall in Sheffield it was exactly like that,' he says. This huge surge of excitement being fuelled by the notion that Labour was within touching distance of government.

'On the night it was a series of balls ups,' Kinnock admits. 'My instructions, and they were very specific instructions, were absolutely contradicted. I said, we all come onto the stage from backstage together, nobody uses the term "the next Secretary of State", "the next Prime Minister". And all that was contradicted.'[7]

The deputy leader, Roy Hattersley, had introduced his boss as the man who would soon be in No. 10. When contrasted with the simplicity of Major's soapbox campaign, the events in Sheffield began to be seen as triumphalist. This was potentially damaging in a tight election race in which the media and voters were looking closely at the man who would potentially be prime minister.

The final days of electioneering prompted still more predictions of a hung parliament, and saw Paddy Ashdown suggest that agreement to work with the Conservatives in any coalition arrangement might be hard to come by.

Labour seemed more inclined to at least examine the key Lib Dem demand of moving to a proportional voting system. Major then turned to the idea of constitutional change as a threat, suggesting the future of the United Kingdom itself was unclear, with Labour proposing the immediate establishment of a Scottish Parliament.

On polling day itself Labour were confronted with an astonishingly hostile headline in *The Sun* newspaper – 'If Kinnock wins today will the last person to leave Britain please turn out the lights.'[8] Alongside this, Kinnock's face had been squeezed inside a lightbulb. Serious political coverage it was not: the intention was simply to scare people into voting Conservative.

'Neither then nor now did it make any difference to me', Kinnock says. 'That kind of stuff on election day, I doubt if it's worth a thousand votes. It's what goes before, every single day, the cartoons, the headlines, the opinion pieces, all that. I can't say I laughed at it, but I just shrugged my shoulders really. I was much more impressed that the *Financial Times*, for the first time in history, recommended a Labour vote.'[9]

As the clock ticked down towards the end of voting, Tory Central Office privately believed that enough had been done to make them the biggest party, and perhaps even retain a majority. At the same time, Labour thought the Conservatives would fall short of the seats needed for an outright win, and Kinnock was therefore likely to be PM. Some ministers evidently agreed, having already cleared their government desks.

Hopes were further raised when the broadcasters revealed the exit polls just after ten o'clock. 'Our view is it's going to be a hung parliament. This election is too close to call,' said David Dimbleby for the BBC. 'We are saying it could be – from the Conservatives short by 10 of an overall majority, to Labour the largest party and short by 13 of an overall majority.'[10]

The most likely outcome was the Tories short by 25 seats. The cameras cut to Kinnock and his wife Glenys looking tense while watching the coverage at a constituency gathering.

Just over an hour later, Labour held the first seat to be declared – Sunderland South – with a swing of just over 2 per cent. Of greater significance was the key marginal of Basildon in Essex, where the Tories held on, dashing Labour's hopes locally while raising questions about the national result. Immediately the experts in the TV studios began to suggest that a majority for John Major could be on the cards.

As the night wore on, the apparent advantage swung in a topsy-turvy fashion. Labour next gained Pendle and Hyndburn, while the fall of the Tory seats of Cheltenham and Bath to the Lib Dems put things back in 'too early to tell' territory. Things again looked less rosy for

Labour when the target of Battersea stayed blue, with the Conservatives increasing their majority.

By 2 a.m., with more than half the results in, the prediction was that the Tories would be the biggest party and were on course for an outright majority in the Commons. Even at this stage Kinnock refused to throw in the towel, suggesting at his own count that the battle was still ongoing, but adding a telling rider that he was prepared to serve his country in any capacity required.

It was not until the early afternoon of Friday, the day after polling, that the 326th seat fell to the Tories and a bare majority was secured. Major had won a famous victory, his party's fourth in a row, and had done so with the most votes ever secured by any party in a British election, over 14 million.

The final picture showed a majority of 21 seats, the Conservatives winning 43 per cent of the vote compared to Labour's 34 per cent. For Kinnock and his party, the dejection was acute. Not only had victory seemed possible, but they had been unable to unseat opponents who had been in office for 13 years and were now overseeing the longest recession since the 1930s.

Was there an overarching reason for this? 'Yeah, me', says Kinnock straightforwardly. 'This isn't self-deprecation it's a political reality, I'd been there too long. The problem was there was no one else at that stage who could have run the Labour Party and improved on our prospects.'

He thinks John Smith would have struggled to control all the elements in the party, and it was too early for Gordon Brown, 'though if I had been hit by a bus my dying words would have been "Gordon" because at that time he would certainly have been the most capable guy.'[11]

He also admits to having had a growing feeling during the campaign that Labour would not make it over the finishing line, though not miss by much. 'In the first week of the campaign I thought we were in with a chance of a hung parliament, and I thought there was a chance we would be the government. By the end of the first week my reservations grew and by the last week I knew we were not going to make it,' he says, reflecting that voters were courteous, but both he and his wife Glenys could sense reservation.

This speaks less to *The Sun*'s claims that its polling day headline had been key to Tory victory, and more to the reflections found elsewhere in the press that many voters still did not trust Labour to protect their personal finances. They feared a rise in taxes when they had already been hit hard by recession. They craved economic stability and bought into the idea this could be delivered by Major. In this respect, Major was only too happy to paint Labour as weak on the economy, arguing that a Kinnock-led government would be costly to voters.

A largely hostile media carried these messages daily and did so with little reference to Kinnock's considerable efforts to modernise Labour. In the collective public memory, the divisions and disorganisation in the party of the 1980s remained fresh enough to matter.

Those on the left of the party told another story, that Labour's defeat was down to the lack of any real socialist programme. The feeling here was that the modernisation agenda, such as moving away from nationalisation, had stripped the party of its distinctive voice.

It's also often overlooked that Labour had been tipped to win because the Tories had been in deep turmoil in the years leading up to the election. Once shorn of Thatcher, this mattered far less. Major looked, sounded and seemed like a significant change.

As Kinnock puts it: 'I knew that by choosing Major they provided us with much more of a challenge than they would have if they had chosen Heseltine and much, much, more of a challenge than Thatcher did. If she had hung on, we would have won the election, I have absolutely no doubt about that.'

Labour's campaign had not been as smooth as it was in 1987, but it is unlikely that events such as the Sheffield rally were significant enough to tip the scales. However, there does seem to be some evidence of a swing to the Conservatives late in the campaign.

It may also be that the polls were so out of step with the result because turnout was historically high, at just under 78 per cent, the highest since February 1974. Labour in fact won the most votes ever for an opposition party. All the same, the result was desperately disappointing and in the immediate aftermath many wondered whether Labour's failure meant it could ever win again.

There was little room at this point for deeper reflection which may have concluded that having sought to overturn a majority of 86 at dissolution, significant progress had been made. The Tory landslide years were over and a cushion of 21 seats would not necessarily make things easy for the government.

It soon became painfully apparent just how close Labour had come to victory. As Kinnock explained, the polling guru Bob Worcester telephoned him days after the election to commiserate. 'He asked whether I knew by how much we'd lost the election. I said "Bob, it's tattooed on the inside of my eyelids, we lost by 21 seats." "Yeah, yeah," he said, "you actually lost by 1,420 votes, that's the total of the bottom eleven Conservative majorities."'[12]

The Conservatives were not as dominant as they appeared and were being assisted by a winner-takes-all constituency system, though that was of no comfort to Labour in 1992. The burning question remained – what had the party to do to win further support from the public and return to power?

1992– General Election Result

Date of Election – 9 April

Overall Turnout 1992 – 77.7 %

Labour

Candidates – 634

MPs – 271

Votes – 11,560,484

Percentage share of the vote – 34.4%

Result – Conservative government

Highlight – *The Sun* newspaper claims it was the reason for John Major's largely unexpected Conservative victory.

Chapter 27

1997 – A New Dawn

'Things can only get better'

D:Ream[1]

'We always said that if we had the courage to change we could do it, and we did it.'[2] These were the words of Tony Blair to ecstatic supporters in the early hours of 2 May 1997 after Labour had won the greatest general election landslide in its history.

After 18 years in the cold, the party was back with a majority which all but buried the Conservatives. It was a victory the scale of which the new prime minister himself struggled to comprehend. In truth, the signs had been there for some time; yet having seen the sun go down on their hopes at each of the four previous elections, Labour had adamantly refused to take their triumph for granted.

The outcome was a majority of 179 over all other parties, a monumental figure compared to John Major's 21-seat margin five years earlier. The long march towards this moment had begun days after that bitter 1992 defeat, when Neil Kinnock formally resigned the leadership.

Having steered his party for nine years, through two election defeats, he departed with a heartfelt reflection – 'my sorrow is that millions, particularly those who do not have the strength to defend themselves, will suffer because of the election of another Conservative government.'[3]

Kinnock would remain in post until a new leader had been chosen, but the message was clear – Labour had not gone far enough towards convincing the electorate they should be allowed to govern once again.

The task of moving the party onto that terrain would not immediately fall to Tony Blair, who at the time was shadow employment secretary. John Smith, a shining star of the Parliamentary Party known for his skill and wit in debate, won the crown.

A Scottish lawyer in his early fifties, Smith exuded respectability and had experience of government having served in Jim Callaghan's Cabinet. Being four years older than his predecessor he was not, however, a fresh face.

Smith won the leadership handsomely across the electoral college of constituency parties, unions and MPs. His only rival was Bryan Gould, from the party's soft left, who won just 10 per cent of the vote, while Margaret Beckett became deputy leader.

Gould, a journalist and academic, soon departed front-line politics. As a strong advocate for the power of the state in shaping people's lives, he warned that Labour would win but, he feared, do little in office.

Gould's analysis spoke directly to the difficulties of making further wholesale changes to Labour's approach. The leadership and senior figures around Smith – Blair and Gordon Brown, the shadow chancellor, in particular – were convinced this was the only route to electoral success.

Instinctively Smith's politics were redistributive, but he was also fully aware of the need to bomb-proof policy against Tory attacks, especially the charge of being a tax-and-spend party. He had been bruised by the 1992 Shadow Budget debacle which was widely felt to have damaged Labour's chances in what was a tight election.

The most significant move towards modernising the party came in 1993 at the annual conference in Brighton. With his leadership on the line, Smith's plans to introduce a one-member one-vote system, so reducing the power of the unions, were pushed through by a whisker. The Labour leader pulled no punches with delegates about why reform was needed, saying 'the changes I propose are vital – absolutely central – to our own strategy for winning power'.[4]

Smith was in his element as leader, taunting the Tories in Parliament. Repeatedly, he savaged the government over its poor economic performance. One moment Major and his chancellor, Norman Lamont, were unflatteringly compared to Laurel and Hardy and the next the prime minister was 'the man with the non-Midas touch', overseeing a country 'where the Grand National does not start and hotels fall into the sea.'[5]

Growing ever more assured in the role, and often referred to as a future prime minister, fate then took a decisive and tragic hand. John Smith died suddenly as a result of two heart attacks on 12 May 1994. He was 55 and had led his party for just under two years. It was a moment of shock for the country and in the Commons MPs openly wept at his passing.

Labour had by now built up a strong lead, consistently running 15 or more points ahead of the Conservatives in the opinion polls. When Smith replaced Kinnock, the two main parties had been neck-and-neck, at close to 40 per cent. That picture changed dramatically on 16 September 1992, a day which went down in infamy as 'Black Wednesday'.

It was then that Britain crashed out of the European Exchange Rate Mechanism, a system of fixed, linked exchange rates within the European Community. The level at which sterling joined the ERM was set too high, and the British economy was viewed as weak by international investors. As a result, the currency began to be sold in waves across the international market, leaving the Major government to scramble to prop it up. Billions of pounds in foreign currency reserves were squandered in a single day, while interest rates were hiked from 10 per cent to 12 per cent and then to an eye-watering 15 per cent.

Labour charged that the Conservatives had betrayed the British people by piling more agony onto an already deep recession. It was political dynamite which exploded Tory claims to be competent managers of the economy.

The reputation of the Conservative Party had been shredded, and Major himself weakened, by this day of disaster. The slim majority the prime minister had won in 1992 would become a millstone as the Parliament wore on.

Major ended up mired in misfortune, at one stage tabling a parliamentary confidence vote in his own administration and referring to members of his own Cabinet as 'bastards'. It was an era defined by 'Tory sleaze', with a succession of resignations from the government over personal and financial scandals.

The sense of crisis pervading the Tories could be seen in the results of the local elections in May 1993, when the party lost almost 500 seats. This was followed by defeat to the Lib Dems in a by-election at Eastleigh, where a 17,000 majority was easily overturned, and the Conservatives fell to third place behind Labour.

By August 1994, Labour's lead in the polls stood at over 33 per cent, according to Gallup. A new leader was now in place, as Tony Blair had won the race to succeed John Smith. Blair was the very model of a young London lawyer and seemed well placed to widen Labour's appeal across southern England.

He had emerged as the front-runner soon after Smith's death, the only question being whether Gordon Brown – long seen as the heir apparent by both Smith and Kinnock, among others – would also run.

A fortnight after Smith's death, amid mounting speculation, the two men met at Granita, a popular restaurant near Blair's Islington home.

There they struck a deal by which Brown would step aside but be given control of economic and social policy in the event of a Labour election victory. Competing claims subsequently emerged that the other strand of the agreement was that Blair would make way for his friend during Labour's second term in office.

Blair moved quickly to set the tone for his leadership, describing Labour as a 'one nation' party – language long associated with the Conservatives – and winning agreement to amend Clause IV of Labour's constitution, so dropping the historic commitment to common ownership of the means of production.

He had succeeded where Gaitskell had failed, confirming to the party's left that socialism was being pushed firmly aside in the quest for victory. 'Let no one say radical politics is dead. Today a new Labour Party is being born', was Blair's response.[6]

This idea of a new party would later be crystallised into the name 'New Labour'. Commentators saw the Clause IV moment as decisive, a display of bold leadership in the style of Margaret Thatcher, whom Blair admired and openly praised.

Realising he had near complete control of a party desperate to get the Tories out of office, Blair ran a highly centralised leadership. Only he and Brown were responsible for policy decisions, the Shadow Cabinet being simply informed, rather than having any significant input.

This also led to what was known as the 'tight marking' of the government – not allowing any light between Labour and Conservative frontbenchers. Labour would not offer up much in the way of new policies so as not to create potential avenues of attack for opponents.

The central idea behind all of this, including the acceptance of much of existing government policy, was about reassuring voters. This also reflected the way Labour was being funded, not only through the unions alone, but increasingly by large private donations.

Blair and his team had little time for dissenting voices and strove to maintain party discipline. In a bid to professionalise the party, over 200 staff were employed at Millbank Tower in a shift towards near permanent campaigning.

The media operation included what was termed a Rapid Response and Rebuttal Unit, designed to quickly kill off negative media coverage and supported by a computerised database – Excalibur EFS (Electronic Filing System).

'All of this was very important,' according to Joy Johnson, a senior BBC political journalist who was brought in by Labour as Director of Media in early 1995. 'It was all set up before me, but I think I gave it a bit of an edge. They just had to be able to kill a story, having rebuttal was the right thing to do.'

Labour also implemented an on call 24-hour media operation, with a news briefing to candidates before the breakfast meeting each day. Johnson's remit was to oversee the media aspects of elections and campaigning and her background in journalism meant she could see the potential of Millbank Tower.

'It was like a newsroom,' Johnson says in an interview for this book, 'with the editing suites all around which could be used for offices and then you had steps down to where they had their press conferences. So it was very like a newsroom or a studio.'

She admits that when she started in her role, she did not find a party acting as though it was on the cusp of victory. 'No it wasn't like that, the Labour Party is always very professional. It was very much let's keep going, take nothing for granted, no complacency.'[7]

Johnson departed after a year and Peter Mandelson, who had been influential under Kinnock, took charge. Alastair Campbell, a former tabloid journalist who was Blair's press liaison was also playing a prominent role, as did the political strategist, Philip Gould.

Campbell was keen to win favourable coverage from a traditionally hostile media which was already becoming more receptive as Labour moved away from its socialist past.

With still more scandals enveloping the government, Labour also hoped to pick up endorsements from newspapers when the election eventually came. To this end, Blair flew to Australia in the summer of 1995 to address Rupert Murdoch – the owner of *The Sun* – and his executives.

The popularity of the party was reflected in its coffers, with tens of thousands of new members coming on board in the years after Blair took over. Membership tipped well over the 400,000 mark, helping create a war chest of around £13 million.

On the economic front, inflation, interest rates and unemployment all began to fall, indicating that an incoming Labour government would inherit growth. Conversely the Tories would wait as long as possible before going to the country in the hope of capitalising on the recovery.

By the end of 1996, Labour had huge polling leads and even led on the question of who was least likely to put up taxes. In January 1997, Brown had ruled out introducing a 50p top rate of income tax, adding there would be no rise in the standard rate.

Blair was pictured next to posters promising no tax rises for five years. Brown went further still. There would be no blank cheques for the public sector and no increases to national insurance payments, all of which aimed to neutralise the issue of taxation, a traditional weak spot for the party. Added to this were tougher messages on crime and scepticism about the European single currency.

As the weeks wore on into 1997, it became evident that the date of the election would be 1 May, with local elections already slated for that day across much of England. This was confirmed on 17 March by Major after the traditional audience with the sovereign. The longest peacetime Parliament for 80 years was closing.

Tony Blair got Labour's response in first, even before the official announcement, describing the election as a choice 'between a Conservative Party that is an utterly disorganised shambles, that has provided very incompetent government but has been weakly led, and a Labour Party that is genuinely New Labour.'[8]

Audaciously, despite them having been in office for 18 years, Major sought to portray the Conservatives as the party which offered change. Rather than the traditional three to four weeks of campaigning, he set out a six-week timetable, believing that the longer Blair was put under the full scrutinising glare of a general election, the greater the chance he would be exposed.

Having been over the course successfully before, the Tory prime minister appeared confident, even though the polls remained dire. This was backed up by the bookmakers, some of whom had Labour at 8-1 on to romp home.

In the opening days of the campaign there were a protracted series of discussions over television debates between the party leaders. For a time, this seemed likely to happen, but in the end no deal could be struck which was acceptable to Labour, the Tories and the Liberal Democrats alike.

Labour's morning press conferences began with music, the hit single from the pop group D:Ream – 'Things Can Only Get Better' – being played as the politicians emerged. Blair was the star, but Gordon Brown took the chair. Then, while Blair was out on his battle bus, regular strategy meetings continued, taking place at 11 a.m., 3 p.m. and 7 p.m.

The sense from journalists watching closely was that Blair grew in confidence as the campaign wore on, becoming better at speaking off the cuff. Meanwhile, Major tried to repeat his soapbox trick from 1992, but soon abandoned this amid security worries and voter hostility.

For Major, the spectre of sleaze continued to stalk his party. In the safe Tory seat of Tatton, the sitting Tory MP Neil Hamilton refused to budge as a candidate while waiting for the outcome of a report into the row over 'cash for questions' (the accusation that Hamilton, and several other MPs, had accepted money from lobbyists in exchange for tabling questions in the Commons). The respected BBC war correspondent, Martin Bell, stood against him as an anti-corruption candidate, while both Labour and the Lib Dems withdrew from the race.

For the most part, Blair was treated with reverence by the public and press, as the man soon likely to occupy 10 Downing Street. However, one bizarre encounter with a DJ from Preston's Red Rose station left the Labour leader exasperated; he was asked whether he picked his nose, ironed his underpants and would be willing to sleep with a supermodel. Major, meanwhile, was unable to name each of the chart-topping Spice Girls.

The manifestos provided more substance. Labour's was revealed at the beginning of April with the title 'New Labour, Because Britain Deserves Better' and featured a portrait of Blair himself on the cover.

His vision of what was termed a 'new politics' had an increase on education spending at its core: there were promises to get 'stable economic growth', 'rebuild the NHS', 'get 250,000 young unemployed off benefit and into work', 'build strong families and strong communities', and a pledge to hold a referendum on any moves towards the single currency.[9]

It was a set of policies which southern England could hardly quibble with, though it was left to the Liberal Democrats, calling for a 1p increase on the basic rate of tax, to advocate for the type of redistribution traditionally associated with Labour.

Europe was another key battleground, with the Referendum Party fielding over 500 candidates and calling for an in/out national vote on Britain's EU membership. With a series of highly visible adverts on the high street – paid for by Sir James Goldsmith, the party's multi-millionaire founder – this was vexatious for Major, as many of his own MPs were against a single currency and made no secret of it.

As the campaign drew to a close, Blair was being told by advisers that they expected to win handsomely. Labour's booking of the Royal Festival Hall on London's south bank for a large victory rally was leaked to the media, and the *Daily Telegraph* reported that Major had refused to sign off a last-minute multi-million-pound publicity blitz, believing his successor could better use the funds.

Polling day itself was a bright warm affair for many, though with reports that voters were not rushing to the ballot box in anything like record numbers. When the first result was declared – the safe Labour seat of Sunderland South – it showed an 11 per cent swing, putting Labour on course for a resounding victory. Blair at this stage remained outwardly cautious, coyly telling reporters on the way to his own count 'let's just wait and see, shall we'.[10]

The first Labour gain came shortly after midnight – the leafy seat of Birmingham Edgbaston turning red for the first time. Thereafter, the gains came thick and fast, the Tories losing every seat they had held in Scotland and Wales and many more across swathes of England. Martin Bell defeated Neil Hamilton in Tatton, and the Lib Dems won 46 seats, taking many of them from Major's party in the South West.

The national swing to Labour was 10 per cent, a figure not approached since the great post-war triumph of 1945. Government ministers were defeated in record numbers, most spectacularly the arch-Thatcherite Michael Portillo, a moment which summed up this night of disaster for the party that had so long dominated British politics.

At 2.30 a.m., Major revealed that an hour earlier he had telephoned Mr Blair and congratulated him on his victory. The Conservatives, he said, had been 'comprehensively defeated' and the Labour Party was enjoying 'an extremely successful evening'.[11] In a graceful speech, he wished the Labour leader every success as prime minister.

Having held his own seat comfortably, Blair flew to London by private jet, accompanied by his wife Cherie. From Stansted Airport, he went to greet the crowds gathered on the banks of the Thames, who had been chanting along to 'Things Can Only Get Better', which was playing on repeat.

As the first shades of light began to emerge, Blair appeared and told the crowd and millions still watching at home: 'a new dawn has broken, has it not. And it is wonderful.'[12] It was an ecstatic scene, and a political recovery on a scale which could not have been imagined in the darkness of 1992.

For many Britons, in that moment, it did not matter what 'New Labour' offered, only that the long nightmare was over; the Tories had been pushed into opposition for the first time since 1979.

Across the parliament these had been years of near unending difficulties for the Conservatives, with Major on the defensive throughout. Having hoped to make electoral capital out of the economic recovery which had taken hold, his party's reputation was sullied by the Black Wednesday debacle. From this point on the Tories were seriously hobbled.

With a small majority whittled away to vanishing point, the government, while fighting numerous allegations of misdeeds or 'sleaze', also had to contend with growing divisions over Europe which had intensified in the years after Britain had fallen out of the ERM.

It could be argued that Major had lost the election as soon as the effects of Black Wednesday were felt, and indeed from then on the polls were consistently in John Smith's favour. Yet this would be to ignore the fact that the Tories had nearly four years in which to win back the trust of the people, and they failed to do so.

Blair and his disciplined team understood all of this, took nothing for granted and went much further than Kinnock had done to reassure sections of the electorate that it was safe to vote Labour.

The return of trade union power was now highly unlikely, public ownership was a thing of the past, the free market had been embraced, tax rises were out of the question and Labour had even made a clear commitment to stick to Tory spending plans.

These positions, contortions which to those on the party's left bent Labour out of shape, generally met little serious resistance. The year 1997 was an essential victory for Labour after the previous four losses. However, Clare Short, who served in Blair's Cabinet as international development secretary, strongly feels that Labour was set to win long before he took over. In an interview for this book, she pointed out that under John Smith 'all the polling showed that Labour was going to win with the kind of majority of about fifty and were ahead on economic management.'

'Now the whole story that has been told over and over again is that it was not until Tony took over and they revamped everything and dropped lots of the commitments, and had the little (pledge) card, that changed everything.'

'So we were all set to win and John dies and, tragically for the Labour Party and indeed the country Tony takes over. There's no doubt he has the glitz and I'm sure the majority got bigger, but it is not true that it was because of the glitz and him that we won, we were going to win anyway.'

'It's famously said that oppositions don't win elections, governments lose them,' Short says, reflecting that the Conservatives were a mess by 1992 and continued to fall apart, with Labour the beneficiaries. 'Everyone was so sick of the government and all the mess. The opposition sanitised itself, or made itself more attractive, but the government's lost it – and that was 1997.'

'On the other hand, there are people who are still MPs who say they can remember 1997 and when you were knocking on doors people say – yes we want to vote Labour, it wasn't just about people wanting to get rid of the government.'[13]

To the true modernising believers, the 'Blairites', as they would universally be known, the changes were not only necessary to win, but reflected how they saw Labour's place in the world at the end of the twentieth century.

Their vision was one of reform and renewal, asking the public to see Labour in a new light, portraying this almost as a means of salvation for the country as well as their party. New Labour had grasped the nettle and the unflinchingly professional operation built around the leadership, in campaigning, media and more, ensured the Tories were not only defeated, but routed.

To Peter Mandelson, voters had not only turned their backs on the Conservatives but actively sought a new direction. Having been returned as MP for Hartlepool he said of the electorate: 'they like what we stand for, they like our courage, they like our confidence, they like our conviction and they'd like us to govern for the many not just the few.'[14]

His point was amply demonstrated when Blair arrived with his wife at the gates of Downing Street on Friday lunchtime in bright sunshine. Having been escorted by motorcycle outriders through the London traffic and into Whitehall, the new prime minister suddenly emerged from his car to greet the well-wishers who thronged the street.

Past the black security gates party members and workers awaited, many waving miniature Union Jacks. It was a joyous scene quite removed from the norm of British politics and illustrated the sense of expectation people now felt about the incoming government.

With almost 420 MPs Labour cared little that just 71 per cent of the electorate – the lowest since the 1930s – had taken part. In his moment of triumph, Blair reflected on the troubled past stretching back to 1979, before looking towards the future.

'For eighteen years – eighteen long years,' he said 'my party has been in opposition. It could only say, it could not do. Today – we are charged with the deep responsibility of government. Today, enough of talking. It is time now to do.'[15]

1997– General Election Result

Date of Election – 1 May

Overall Turnout– 71.4%

Labour

Candidates – 639

MPs – 418

Votes – 13,518,167

Percentage share of the vote – 43.2%

Result – Labour landslide

Highlight – Aged 43, Tony Blair becomes the youngest prime minister since Lord Liverpool in 1812.

Chapter 28

2001 – The Quiet Landslide

'The 2001 election was an odd, disjointed affair.
The outcome was never in doubt.'

Tony Blair[1]

Labour had stormed to power in 1997 with the country desperate for change, but promising not to shake things up too much. The party's task by 2001 was to show to voters that they had delivered and would keep doing so with all the hopes for a new century stretching into the distance.

Led by Tony Blair, this was a government free of the kind of problems which had dogged Labour administrations of the past. The economy was growing, and the party had more MPs in Parliament than it had ever known.

Yet given how much they had yearned for power in the long years of opposition, Labour was quick to give it away. Four days after coming to office the chancellor, Gordon Brown, announced that the Bank of England was to become independent of political control.

Brown claimed the move would end cycles of boom and bust, yet politically it also meant a Labour government was unchained from any fallout from the setting of monetary policy and interest rates.

Brown's first Budget set out a £5 billion windfall tax on the privatised utilities, with half of this going into schools. At the same time, corporation tax was cut and the chancellor confirmed his intention to stick to Tory spending plans.

Then, two weeks before the people of Scotland and Wales voted in favour of a devolved parliament and assembly in Edinburgh and Cardiff respectively, the world was shocked by the death of Diana, Princess of Wales, in a car crash in Paris.

For Labour, the challenge of dealing with unexpected and momentous events in government became a reality. With his family outside a church in his constituency, Blair found words of tribute which captured the moment. 'She was the People's Princess and that is how she will stay, how she will remain in our hearts and our memories for ever.'[2]

This gave the prime minister an almost presidential air, and in the days which followed the government did much to mediate in what became a crisis for the Royal Family over their less-than-emotional response to the passing of the princess.

When normal politics resumed, the party was forced to return a £1 million donation from the Formula 1 motor racing chief, Bernie Ecclestone, in a row over the exemption of the sport from a tobacco sponsorship ban.

The local elections of May 1998 – in which the Tories gained over 250 councillors – came just as Labour broke new political ground. The signing of the Good Friday Agreement was a moment of huge significance and success for Blair, bringing peace to Northern Ireland which had seen so much bloodshed in the previous three decades.

In December, Peter Mandelson, the trade and industry secretary, had to resign over a large undisclosed loan from the paymaster general, Geoffrey Robinson, who also stood down. Mandelson would then return to the government as Northern Ireland secretary, before being forced to resign once more in 2001 over allegations he exerted influence over a passport application by an Indian billionaire.

Amid these scandals Blair and Brown managed to usher in the introduction of a national minimum wage. This had been a Labour pledge for decades and was strongly opposed by big business and the Conservatives alike. In practice, it proved to be both popular and hugely successful.

Other notable events saw the euro introduced by 11 member states of the European Union at the start of 1999. The question of whether Britain would go into the eurozone would remain a live issue through to the election and well beyond. The same year, Britain came to the aid of Kosovo Albanians in a military campaign which ousted Serb forces from the region of former Yugoslavia. Blair, without UN Security Council backing, played an instrumental part, viewing the matter as a humanitarian intervention against the tyranny of Belgrade.

There were growing problems on the domestic front, with more than 60 Labour MPs rebelling over Blair's new welfare measures which cut entitlement to invalidity benefit, while Peter Kilfoyle left the government, to become 'a critical friend on the backbenches'.[3] Labour also made headlines with efforts to stop Ken Livingstone becoming the party's candidate for mayor of London, only for the leftwinger to then win as an independent in May 2000.

The government was also hit by two major crises. The first, in September 2000, saw a blockade of fuel depots and petrol stations by farmers and truckers. Furious over the rising global price of oil and the fuel duty hikes, their actions led quickly to food shortages, panic buying and the closure of schools.

Labour suddenly slumped in the polls with *The Daily Telegraph* reporting 'a close aide to William Hague' – the new Conservative leader – saying 'people just do not believe what Tony Blair tells them. They have been telling us for months that he is arrogant and out of touch.'[4]

In truth this was a brief blip. The government soon got fuel supplies moving again, though the matter of a fair deal for farmers lingered on.

The widespread outbreak of foot and mouth disease in February 2001 provided a still greater test.

The highly infectious condition, which mainly affects cattle, pigs and sheep, plunged British agriculture into crisis and caused a downturn in tourism. As a mass slaughter of millions of animals across the country got underway, Labour ministers came under fire for a perceived slowness in grasping the situation.

Blair eventually took charge himself, having been shocked at the scale of the problem. Cases continued to rise as the weeks rolled past through March, scuppering Labour's plans for a general election at the beginning of May.

Local elections, due to take place that month, were postponed until Thursday 7 June. Nothing was said publicly about a general election, but this did little to dampen expectations that the two polls would be held simultaneously.

With all parties primed for weeks awaiting the formal announcement, Blair and his advisors chose a girls' school in south London to confirm the general election would indeed take place on 7 June. The setting was meant to underscore Labour's commitment to education, but for many onlookers – including the head of the school – it felt uncomfortably partisan and lacked the sobriety of the usual statement in Downing Street.

Regardless, Labour went into the campaign with a 20-point polling lead over the Conservatives. Blair and Brown, close to a dual premiership at times, were far and away the dominant political force in the land.

Brown had been steering Labour's campaigns strategy committee from 11 Downing Street for months, and by early 2001 a draft daily grid was in place, with campaign messages worked up. The key figures, alongside Brown and Blair, were familiar: Peter Mandelson,

Alastair Campbell, Philip Gould, with the addition of the Brown pro-tégé, Douglas Alexander MP.

Nothing was taken for granted: Labour hoped to replay the campaign of four years earlier. Everything seemed to be in place, with improvements in public services and ongoing economic stability. Brown placed his solid, prudent and successful management of the economy at the centre of Labour's offer.

For Jim Callaghan, Harold Wilson and other past leaders, all of this would have been a dream scenario. Inflation stood at 2 per cent, interest rates were historically low and unemployment was down at levels not seen since the late 1970s.

Mark Seddon was speechwriter for the former UN secretary general, Ban Ki-moon, and having edited the influential left-wing *Tribune* magazine, he worked closely with Gordon Brown. In 2001, he was a member of Labour's National Executive and a Parliamentary candidate.

Interviewed for this book, Seddon makes the point that though Labour was trying to repeat the trick of winning a landslide, there were differences with the picture in 1997.

'Of course, the first time round they simply didn't believe it was going to happen. By the time 2001 came along they did think they were going to win, and they were right,' he said.

'I suppose what people would say is the 2001 election didn't have to be exciting. What you had was a fairly united party and people were on the whole quite content and were prepared to give it another go.'

Seddon also thinks the main political figures the electorate had come to know so well were an advantage. 'The frontbench team that Labour had, both as a Shadow Cabinet and then Cabinet, was extraordinarily talented. [Donald] Dewar, [David] Blunkett, [John] Prescott, Clare Short, Robin Cook. It was a very impressive lineup.'

'Then there was all the glitz and the PR and this young guy, Tony Blair,' he adds, making the point that Labour had a leader who was a step change from the past. 'Blair wasn't what a lot of people were told they should expect from the Labour Party. And Tony Blair made his best efforts to tell people he wasn't of the tribe, he came to this he wasn't born into it, all that sort of stuff.'[5]

Much of this is a reflection on just how Blair and his supporters had so successfully altered Labour and its image, though that did not mean things always went according to plan. For the machine-driven operation which Labour oversaw at the time, 16 May 2001 was a disaster.

The day began in Birmingham with the launch of the party's manifesto, 'Ambitions for Britain'. This set out plans for thousands more teachers, doctors, nurses and police, alongside a pledge not to raise income taxes. There would also be greater scope for private contractors, especially in health and education, a core Blair belief. From here the prime minister went to visit a new cardiac unit at a local hospital.

On arrival, he was accosted by Sharon Storer, the partner of a cancer patient, who harangued him about the state of NHS services. This was a deeply uncomfortable encounter in the full glare of the media, with Storer saying 'all you do is walk around and make yourself known, but you don't do anything to help anybody.'[6]

Around the same time that day in Blackpool the home secretary, Jack Straw, faced jeering and slow handclapping at the Police Federation's annual gathering. Straw had been attempting to defend the government's record on law and order at a time when officers were leaving the force and morale was low.

To cap it all, the deputy prime minister, John Prescott, ended up in a street brawl in north Wales after being struck at close range with an egg. Prescott, showing lightning reactions, aimed a left jab into the face of Craig Evans, who was part of a larger group demonstrating about what they felt to be a lack of support for farmers and farm workers.

The incident was directly connected to ongoing stresses in rural areas related to the foot and mouth outbreak, but was also an echo of the fuel blockades. The Prescott punch exploded across the media, leaving ministers genuinely perplexed as to how to respond to an unprecedented situation.

Blair, who admits his jaw dropped when told of Prescott's fracas, was among many who worried about the possible effect on the election. In the end, the media took a balanced view, with newspapers broadly supportive of Prescott's position that he had been acting in self-defence.

Blair himself found the campaign downbeat and only after speaking by phone to the former US president, Bill Clinton, did his mindset change. Clinton's advice had been to fight with all the urgency of an election which was on a knife-edge.

On paper, things seemed far from close. Labour had the natural advantage of incumbency, consistent polling leads, and their main opponents remained divided, most notably over Europe. Dozens of Tory candidates broke from the official policy of not joining the euro in the lifetime of the next parliament. Instead, they advocated not joining at all, in line with the forcibly expressed views of the former prime minister, Lady Thatcher.

Requiring a swing of over 7 per cent just to deprive Labour of a majority the Conservatives settled on a core vote strategy. This meant reaching at least 35 per cent on polling day, a figure which, if the turnout was low, might well be enough to achieve a decent result.

Central to the Conservative offer was a promise of £8 billion worth of tax cuts, while matching Labour's projected spending on the NHS, schools and the police. Notably too, there was a pledge to knock 6p per litre off fuel duty.

While Thatcher was a problem for Hague over Europe, she happily informed supporters he was the man to lead the country. Putting the boot into Blair, she told a rally that 'today's Labour Party has no discernible principles at all. It is rootless, empty and artificial.'[7]

Regardless, New Labour's top brass were determined to look forward, rather than back to the 1980s. Brown was clear that the campaign could not be a referendum on the period since 1997 but had to focus on what Labour planned to do for the country in the years to come.

Blair talked openly about public service reform, taking a lead among the nations of Europe, and placing community at the heart of politics, an obvious contrast with the Thatcher era. For the second election running, *The Sun* newspaper backed Labour. Even more remarkably, and in a major break with tradition, *The Times* also endorsed Blair's party as did the *Financial Times*.

There was a gift for Labour in mid-May when it emerged that the shadow chief secretary to the Treasury, Oliver Letwin, had let slip plans for a £20 billion cut in public spending if the Tories were to win the election. This triggered a media hunt for the Tory MP, with 'Wanted!' posters issued, and one Labour MP even dressing up as Sherlock Holmes in a bid to find the hapless Letwin.

From here until polling day Labour, at Brown's insistence, never stopped making the point that the government had achieved economic stability, and the Conservatives were determined to undo this. Labour ran messages about 'Tory cuts' (the Y becoming a giant pair of scissors) and 'Tories' £16 billion cuts will hit hospitals'.[8]

With growing concerns about a low turnout, Blair used the weekend before polling to caution the electorate against the threat of an upset result should Labour supporters fail to go to the polls. To underline the point, posters emerged of Thatcher's generously sculpted hairstyle superimposed onto Hague's face.

Then, as polls were about to open Blair urged people to make their vote count, while Brown said 'our message to the British people is if you entrust us with a second term, we will work for you.'[9]

Once the last votes were cast and ballot boxes sealed and embarked on their journey to counting centres, broadcasters took to the air to announce with great fanfare the result of the exit poll: Tony Blair was on course for his second successive landslide.

Long before midnight, the pattern had emerged. There was only a small swing to the Conservatives, and other opposition parties. Hague would have to wait until after 2 a.m. for the first sliver of good news, a gain in Romford which was then followed by a smattering of others as the hours ticked past.

Labour made just two gains and lost half a dozen seats overall, but the most telling figure was a national turnout of just 59 per cent. This was down a full 12 per cent since the previous election and was comfortably the lowest since the 'coupon election' of 1918, confirming apathy, when the result was seen as almost preordained and the Tories were regarded as not yet fit for office.

Blair and his Party had emerged virtually unscathed, with a majority of 166. To celebrate, a rally took place early on Friday by the banks of the Thames, outside Labour's Millbank HQ, where hundreds of happy supporters greeted the prime minister and other senior figures.

Gone was the great outpouring of emotion which heralded the 1997 earthquake, replaced now by something more akin to contentment at this quiet landslide. It had been achieved 101 years on from Labour's first general election when, under the banner of the LRC, the infant party had won just two seats.

As Blair pointed out, it was also the first time that Labour had twice in a row won clear majorities on which to base full terms in office. As the prime minister put it: 'our mandate is to carry on the work we have started. The policies and the foundations we have laid over these past few years give us the ability now to complete the task that we set ourselves.'[10]

Shortly afterwards, William Hague made a short statement confirming that he was standing down as Conservative leader. Far from there being a quiet pro-Tory mood in the country, which he had suggested before polling, his party had again been swept aside.

Through the years 1997 to 2001, Labour was supremely confident, utterly dominating British politics and doing so armed with a sense of purpose. In part the existing electoral maths – the large mandate won in 1997 – accounted for this swagger, making defeat unlikely.

On top of that the economy had been well managed, and people felt relatively secure and upbeat about their future. Blair and Brown came to be trusted, voters feeling they were unlikely to waste their money.

This allowed Labour to make a careful case for improvements to services such as health and education. By contrast, the electorate did not believe the Conservatives could, as they proposed, reduce taxation and improve the public realm at the same time.

In truth, the Tory pitch to the nation was not taken as seriously as that party would have wished, and again this was Labour's doing. The Conservatives were still in the process of regrouping after being removed from office with such a heavy defeat four years earlier. Tony Blair had also grown into the role of prime minister and led a largely united party. Set against Blair, many voters just did not view Hague as a credible alternative PM.

Though Blair and his colleagues had been through some scrapes, they had seen relatively little support ebb away in the years since coming to power. The British people were content to stick with what they had and give Labour more time to continue the work of turning the country around and move still further away from the chaos and division of the John Major years.

For Mark Seddon, it was always likely that New Labour in 2001 would seek to build a narrative about needing more time to fully make its mark. 'That first Labour term, much of the big policy initiatives were inherited from John Smith, whether it be the minimum wage or devolution or what have you,' he said.

'All of that, did it really set people on fire? It probably didn't actually. It's not really meat and potatoes stuff. That might have been a contributing factor to that very, very low turnout, along with the fact that people thought "oh they are going to win anyway". Inevitably, you were going to see some voters drift away.'

'Clearly Tony Blair had succeeded only where [Clement] Attlee and Harold Wilson had before. Though you read the stats and all the claims that were made about Blair winning the most elections – it was Harold Wilson who did that. Nonetheless you can't take away from it, Blair was a very, very effective election winner.'[11]

2001 General Election Result

Date of Election – 7 June

Overall Turnout – 59.4%

Labour

Candidates – 640

MPs – 412

Votes – 10,724,953

Percentage share of the vote – 41%

Result – Labour landslide

Highlight – Voter apathy leads to the lowest turnout in over 80 years.

Chapter 29

2005 – We Can Unite Again

'He has not lost power, but he has
lost unconstrained power'

Andrew Marr on Tony Blair[1]

'We understand that a plane has crashed into the World Trade Center we don't know anything more than that.'[2] With those words from CBS News, the United States began to learn of the 9/11 terrorist attacks on New York, Washington DC and the Pentagon.

The horrors of that clear September day in 2001 killed almost 3,000 people, causing widespread fear and anger in America and sending shockwaves across the world.

From these al-Qaeda suicide hijackings to Labour's performance in the 2005 election, it is possible to trace a direct line, one which runs through the resulting wars in Afghanistan and Iraq. And though Tony Blair could not have foreseen it when signing up to President George W. Bush's military campaigns, this was a turning point for New Labour and his own political career.

Until this point, it had largely been a glittering time in office for Labour and its leader. The scale of the second landslide, in 2001, had surprised even Blair and in the years which followed Labour oversaw a buoyant economy, with the Conservative Party still experiencing its own difficulties.

The attacks of 11 September came just three months after Labour had won its second successive term in office. What Bush called the War on Terror, which then followed, had a profound impact on the party and the course of British politics. From this point on, foreign and defence policy became a major focus, sapping much of the government's energy.

On the day of the attacks themselves Blair, who had been at the Trades Union Congress in Brighton, immediately pledged strong British support for America, calling for the international community to face down terrorism.

Attention almost immediately turned to Afghanistan, where it was known al-Qaeda and the Islamist group's leader, Osama bin Laden, were based. The United States invaded, with British military support, seeking to remove Afghanistan's Taliban regime which had been sheltering al-Qaeda. The justification given to the United Nations was self-defence, and by Christmas the Taliban had been toppled, though in time it would re-emerge to wage a prolonged guerilla counter-offensive.

In January 2002, Bush declared Iran, Iraq and North Korea to be a growing danger. His rationale was that these countries were seeking to gain, or already possessed, what came to be widely known as weapons of mass destruction.

These countries did not have any direct link to the 9/11 attacks, but soon senior American figures spoke of removing Saddam Hussein in Iraq. By September, with the case built over months that Baghdad had chemical, biological or nuclear weapons, Bush was urging speedy action.

At home Blair, presented an intelligence dossier on Iraq to Parliament. The media jumped on the claim that the country had weapons which could hit Britain within 45 minutes. Though Iraq would publish a lengthy denial, by early 2003 the government had added a second dossier to reinforce its case.

With the move to war underway, a million people poured through London in the biggest peace march in British history, part of a tapestry of protest in hundreds of cities around the world.

Blair seemed unmoved that his government was now pitted against large sections of the electorate. 'I ask the marchers to understand this: I do not seek unpopularity as a badge of honour,' he said. 'But sometimes it is the price of leadership and the cost of conviction.'[3]

In February 2003, 121 Labour MPs voted against their own government, saying the case for military intervention had not been proven. Left-wingers, including the Father of the House, Tam Dalyell, were furious that the prime minister had not even been present for the vote.

On 17 March, Robin Cook, the leader of the Commons and former foreign secretary, resigned from the Cabinet. In a masterful speech, he appealed 'for this House to stop the commitment of troops in a war that has neither international agreement nor domestic support.'[4]

The following day, MPs gave the green light for invasion and within 48 hours the bombing of Baghdad had begun. Less than three weeks later, American troops had stormed into the Iraqi capital and Bush would soon declare that his country's mission in Iraq had been accomplished.

It was not the case: in the coming years Iraqi resistance would continue with suicide attacks and urban fighting, all of which took place amid claims of abuse and torture, most notoriously by US forces at the Abu Ghraib prison. When it was revealed that a handful of British soldiers had been involved, an appalled Blair apologised to the Iraqi people.

The situation in Iraq toxified the Blair brand, even in the eyes of his supporters. A close ally, Lord David Puttnam, told a TV interviewer in May 2004 that 'the prime minister is synonymous with Iraq, and Iraq will only deliver bad news. If I were him, I would go before the summer recess.'[5]

The mounting toll of British casualties anguished the public – clashes with insurgents and roadside bombs were the main causes of death as troops tried to install democracy. By the end of 2005 almost 100 UK servicemen and women had died, while this figure was dwarfed by estimates of civilian Iraqi deaths.

While Iraq, and to a degree Afghanistan, dominated events in this period, the Blair government also had troublesome issues to contend with elsewhere.

In 2002, there was a clear break with what had been the orthodoxy since 1997 when Gordon Brown increased national insurance to pay for the NHS. While this caused little fallout, it did allow the Conservatives to suggest the chancellor had broken a promise to the British people not to raise contributions.

Then in 2004, Labour proposed hiking university tuition fee charges to as much as £3,000 per year for students in England and Wales. Backbenchers were bitterly angry, and the measure only just squeaked through the Commons after intense lobbying by ministers. It was not only the principle of top-up fees which had caused the difficulties; the whole idea ran counter to an explicit commitment in the 2001 manifesto that Labour would not do this, playing into a growing narrative about trust in the government.

The next day, Lord Hutton delivered his verdict on the circumstances of the death of the Iraq weapons inspector, Dr David Kelly. He had been found dead after giving evidence to a Commons committee and having been named as the source used in a controversial BBC radio broadcast which claimed Blair had deliberately misled Parliament over Iraqi weapons.

Hutton exonerated the government, leading to resignations at the top of the BBC. Had he not done so, and had Blair lost the tuition fees vote, then the prime minister would probably have departed. By this stage voters could be forgiven for considering that New Labour's gloss had worn rather thin.

The saving grace was that throughout this period the British economy remained highly stable. Inflation was the lowest in Europe, and in 2004 Brown revealed that the UK was enjoying its longest period of growth since the industrial revolution. As a result, money flowed into the public services.

Labour faced ineffective opposition. The Conservative leader, Iain Duncan Smith, had failed to convince his party that he was the man to lead them out of the wilderness. Still trailing badly in the polls, he was replaced by the former home secretary, Michael Howard. The appointment did little to trouble Labour, who immediately pointed to Mr Howard's previous support for the poll tax and opposition to the minimum wage.

There was one significant, gnawing, handicap for Labour throughout much of this time, however: the growing tensions between Tony Blair and Gordon Brown. The source of the estrangement between the two men, who had worked so closely since coming into Parliament together 20 years earlier, was the question of the leadership.

This went back to the time of John Smith's death a decade earlier. Brown had expected that by the middle of the second Labour term he would have become prime minister. According to the journalist Robert Peston, the chancellor had rounded on Blair in 2004 over what he saw as broken promises, saying 'there is nothing that you could say to me now that I could ever believe'.[6]

Blair rejected this claim when it emerged early in 2005, addressing the matter in a speech and making it clear he planned to fight the next election on a New Labour manifesto. Using buzzwords he had long relied on – ambition, aspiration, prosperity, opportunity – Blair's address fired the starting gun on the long campaign into the election proper.

There was a novel effort to rebuild Blair's battered reputation. The prime minister appeared on television programmes to face hostile questions from the public. Dubbed the 'masochism strategy', it aimed to show Blair listening, humble, good natured and authentic.

Blair's senior aides – Alastair Campbell and Philip Gould in particular – also saw the electoral dangers of the detachment between the two men at the top of the party. It would be much harder for Labour to maximise their ace card – economic stability and increased public spending – if the chancellor was not front and centre of the campaign.

More than that, there was a real fear that Blair campaigning without Brown would cost the party votes in many key seats. To that end, agreement was eventually reached that Brown would play a central role in the election and be seen to do so alongside the leader.

On 16 March, Brown's Budget offered assistance to pensioners and families, outlining his and Labour's achievements. The promise to voters was of continued efforts to build a strong economy and a fair society, based on opportunity and security for everyone.

This was a boost to Labour going into the Easter recess through to early April. During this period, with final preparations being made for the campaign, the former Labour prime minister, Jim Callaghan, passed away at the age of 92. When MPs returned to London on 4 April another death – that of Pope John Paul II – delayed Blair's announcement of the election by 24 hours.

With opposition leaders already out on the campaign trail, the prime minister confirmed polling day would be 5 May. Blair positioned this as a chance to build on his achievements of the past eight years, promising more stability and investment to come.

Michael Howard lost no time in taking the gloves off. The Tory leader said his party was the alternative to what he called 'the smirking politics of Mr Blair', who was, he added, 'already secretly grinning' about another five years in office.[7] It was an attack Labour had been expecting and it signalled a dirty fight ahead.

Already, the sense was that Blair was a more vulnerable leader than in 2001, especially on the question of trust, and that the Tories, with Howard calling the shots, were willing to go on the offensive. However, it would be a relatively short campaign: once Parliament broke up on 11 April there was less than four weeks to polling.

The Liberal Democrats, armed with their anti-Iraq war stance and a popular leader in Charles Kennedy, expected to do well, while Labour knew that every vote would be important. No one was thinking any longer of landslides: the aim was simply to win.

To that end, the polls were in Labour's favour, consistently giving Blair a lead of between 2 and 6 points, suggesting that despite Iraq he would still secure an historic consecutive third term for his party. Though nothing like the leads Labour had held going into the two previous elections, the upper end of these estimates would still deliver a comfortable majority.

The Conservatives, meanwhile, were hoping that if there was to be a low turnout and they could maximise their core vote, they could do far better than predicted. It was exactly what Labour guarded against, using posters with the warning cry – 'if one in 10 Labour voters don't vote, the Tories win'.[8]

Advertising had already been a battleground in the months leading to the election. In January 2005, Labour ran into difficulties over claims of anti-Semitism when a picture of Howard and Oliver Letwin (both of whom are Jewish) was superimposed onto flying pigs.

The party had also accused the Tories of being liars, and in the campaign proper the Conservatives retaliated in kind, claiming that Blair had been prepared to lie over the case for war, and would likewise be prepared to lie to win an election.

In a major broadcast interview, Howard then explicitly accused Blair of failing to tell the truth about the reasons for going to war. To some this seemed rather an odd claim, given the Tory leader had been a strong supporter of military efforts to remove the Iraqi dictator.

Labour's focus remained squarely on what had been achieved in office and the aspiration to do more – the manifesto being titled 'Britain forward not back'. It was a wholeheartedly New Labour document: there were promises of investment in schools and healthcare, a rise in the minimum wage, and all without income tax hikes. Again, as at every election since 1987, the words socialism or socialist did not appear.

With Brown at his side, the Labour leader took pains to point out that a strong economy was at the heart of these plans. Notably, too, Blair repeated the pledge set out in the preface to the document – that this would be his last election as leader. Brown was not named as a preferred successor, but there was little need to make the point overtly.

Though Cherie Blair often travelled with her husband, Brown was his most prominent campaign colleague. This show of unity denied journalists a further opportunity to write about tensions between the two men and proved that Labour could work as a team. One of the most memorable images was the sight of Blair presenting a 99 ice cream, complete with flake, to a laughing Brown while out speaking to voters.

The other issue which the Conservatives sought to highlight was immigration, and by extension asylum. They ran a poster campaign – 'it's not racist to impose limits on immigration' – with the much mocked slogan below it: 'are you thinking what we're thinking?'[9]

Howard believed immigration to be running out of control and had identified this as a Labour weak spot. On 22 April in Dover, Blair took this issue head on with a passionate speech in which he praised the contribution of migrants to the UK.

The prime minister accused the Conservatives of wishing to withdraw from the UN Refugee Convention and ridiculed as a 'fantasy island' plan the idea that those arriving on British shores would be sent to overseas processing centres.[10]

On 28 April, Downing Street published in full the legal advice by the attorney general, Lord Goldsmith, on the legality of going to war in Iraq. This showed Blair had been told that a second UN resolution was the safest course of action – something the government knew would not be forthcoming – only for Goldsmith's final advice to raise no such concerns.

It was the issue which dominated a BBC *Question Time* Special at the end of the election campaign. Blair faced the audience once Kennedy and then Howard had departed, the Tory leader having repeated his claim that the PM had lied.

Blair was asked several times about the legal advice and Iraq more widely. Each time he was able to make a spirited defence, while admitting mistakes had been made. In retrospect, he reflected, it would have been better to publish the raw intelligence leading to Britain's involvement.

In the days remaining until the election, the Lib Dems focused almost exclusively on Iraq, remaining eager to withdraw British troops. Labour responded with warnings that a vote for Kennedy's party could let Howard into Downing Street through the back door.

With polling day on the horizon, a 24-year-old Guardsman, Anthony Wakefield, became the latest British soldier to be killed in Iraq, his widow blaming Blair personally for his death. The comments were widely reported across the media, but importantly, the Labour leader knew he retained wide support from editors.

This point was proved when both *The Times* and *The Sun* again came out for Labour, the latter going with a football-themed front page showing Blair and Brown together with the headline 'COME ON YOU REDS'.[11]

For Labour there was relief that the polling trends seemed to be borne out by the exit poll, which appeared as ever with great fanfare once voting had ended. Based on questioning 20,000 people leaving the polling stations, and commissioned jointly for ITV and the BBC, this predicted Labour had won a 66-seat majority.

An important caveat was quickly added – viewers were told it was hard to know exactly what had happened in marginal seats and the size of Labour's majority could go up or down. The reason for the caution was the suggestion that the two major electoral issues – Iraq and immigration – might cause voters to react in different ways.

Some who were angry at Labour over the Iraq war were likely to vote Lib Dem, while those more concerned about immigration might cleave to the Tories. Reporters based at Labour HQ at first suggested there was some anxiety about the overall result, but such jitters soon faded.

The early declarations showed, in fact, that in safe seats the swings away from Labour were greater than in the marginals and it was all over by 4.30 a.m., when Labour secured its 324th seat, enough for a majority.

At his own count in Sedgefield, the prime minister saw his vote fall by 6 per cent. The main beneficiary was the independent candidate, Reg Keys, whose son had been killed in Iraq. Keys won 10 per cent of the vote and almost finished in third place.

His powerful speech was a lament for his late son and all those who had died. 'There are lessons to be learned and I hope in my heart that one day the Prime Minister will be able to say sorry, that one day he will say sorry to the families of the bereaved,' Keys said, with Blair watching on.[12]

The Labour leader, in a downbeat acceptance speech, nodded to the achievement of securing a third term, while accepting the wider context. To some heckling voices he reflected 'I know too that Iraq has been a divisive issue in this country, but I hope now that we can unite again and look to the future, there and here.'[13]

The present was clear enough – Labour finished with 355 seats and the Conservatives on just 198. It was a good election for the Lib Dems: with 62 seats (up 10), they now had MPs in many British cities.

Privately, Blair was despondent not to have won again by a three-figure margin, but a majority close to 70 seats was still a fine achievement. Certainly, past leaders – Callaghan, Foot and Kinnock – would have been delighted with those figures.

It was also true that victory had been accomplished with just 35.2 per cent of the vote, the lowest for a single party majority in British electoral history up to that point. Though turnout was slightly up, at 61 per cent, it remained historically low. Since 1997, Labour had lost almost four million votes. Some of those went to other parties, but in many other cases people simply stayed at home.

The next morning the Labour leader swept up Downing Street in his Jaguar to be greeted by banks of reporters and film crews. Gone were the flag-waving crowds, gone too were the handshakes and the smiles of yesteryear. Speaking haltingly, Blair reflected on the time which had passed since 1997, saying that it was an honour to able to serve again, that he had listened and learned over people's feelings on Iraq.

As he posed for photos in front of the black door of Number 10, journalists shouted questions, asking if it would be possible to execute a programme for government with a reduced majority. The political reality was that there remained plenty of room to push legislation through Parliament.

Those at the top of the party had played things well in 2005, spotting that economic stability was still the absolute trump card and wisely deploying Brown to highlight this lasting success. Even though Blair had become an unpopular figure, or at least a politician the public were angry with, none of that ire or discord mattered as much as sound national finances and living standards.

In an interview for this book Alastair Campbell, one of the most prominent Downing Street figures under New Labour, admitted: 'Tony Blair's critics like to say his entire Premiership is defined by Iraq. I would argue that the government he led for a decade has one of the broadest and most consequential legacies of any in my lifetime.'

Campbell's contention is that New Labour delivered on commitments set out in the party's earliest days – particularly on fair wages and a Scottish Assembly. As he pointed out, 'the Blair government delivered them, along with a wider programme of devolution. The Good Friday Agreement, which helped bring peace to Northern Ireland, is in the top rank of Prime Ministerial achievements.'

'Bank of England independence was a historic change and a key reason for the stability and growth which followed. Tax credits helped bring down poverty. Investment and reform in public services helped drive up standards, so that when Labour left office NHS satisfaction ratings were the highest ever.'

'Then there was Lords reform. Freedom of Information (even if he [Blair] had doubts about it!). Banning fox hunting (ditto). The Human Rights Act. Legalisation of same-sex civil partnerships. There were other reforms which sadly haven't endured which should have, such as the Sure Start programme', he added.[14]

It is a substantial record, but having won for the third time running commentators made the point that Blair was fighting his last election and wondered openly when his premiership would conclude.

2005 General Election Result

Date of Election – 5 May

Overall Turnout 2005 – 61.4%

Labour

Candidates – 627

MPs – 355

Votes – 9,552,436

Percentage share of the vote – 35.2%

Result – Labour government

Highlight – The 'Blair Must Go Party' and 'Iraq War. Not In My Name' were among the 315 parties registered with the Electoral Commission at this election.

Chapter 30

2010 – A Privilege to Serve

'That is that. The end'

Tony Blair[1]

Having spent 13 years in office, the Labour government ran out of road in the most dramatic election in decades. It was an ill-deserved outcome given the government had been instrumental in thwarting a major financial catastrophe at home and abroad.

By 2010, Tony Blair's 'Iraq election' victory five years earlier was little more than a distant memory and having signalled he would depart before Britain next elected a government, the prime minister honoured his pledge and stood down in June 2007.

Blair had occupied 10 Downing Street for just over a decade, the longest stint as prime minister of any Labour leader. He was afforded a standing ovation across the Commons during his final appearance in Parliament.

The runaway favourite to succeed him was Gordon Brown, who had been chancellor since 1997 and long coveted the leadership. Though others tested the water, only John McDonnell from the left of the party mounted a campaign, and he was unable to reach the threshold required to run.

Brown as a consequence became leader and PM-elect without an election either in his party or the country beyond. On taking the helm, he told reporters he would prioritise education, health and restore trust in politics, saying 'I will try my utmost. This is my promise to all of the people of Britain. And now let the work of change begin.'[2]

Labour immediately returned to a lead in the polls but Brown had little time to enjoy any honeymoon, with his first weeks in post beset with numerous crises. First, he won praise with a sober call for unity after a failed terrorist bomb plot in London and an attack at Glasgow airport by the same Islamic extremists.

Then, with much of England experiencing by far the worst flooding in half a century, Brown quickly pledged millions of pounds in relief. In August, he abandoned a family holiday to deal with an outbreak of foot and mouth disease.

There was also a political dilemma. Some aides believed an early general election would give Brown a personal mandate to make the changes he so desired. The intention was to capitalise on the poll gains made following Blair's departure and catch the Conservatives off guard. Brown himself had been thinking more in terms of an election in 2008, but from August 2007 speculation was allowed to grow that Labour were preparing for a snap poll.

Labour set up a media centre, booked billboard sites for posters, and made other tentative preparations including drawing up the outlines of a manifesto. There even followed a 'Not Flash, just Gordon' poster campaign highlighting the virtues of the new prime minister.

No decision had been taken by the time Brown delivered his leader's speech at Labour's annual conference. Speculation rumbled on into October when, with the polls narrowing after the Tories revealed popular plans on inheritance tax and stamp duty, Brown decided against pressing ahead.

The decision not only cost Labour over £1 million in now worthless preparatory work, but caused significant political damage. Though the prime minister tried to explain that he wanted more time to showcase his policies to the British people, the Labour leader was now cast as a ditherer and 'Bottler Brown' by his opponents.

It was a crucial moment which allowed the youthful new Conservative leader David Cameron – elected in December 2005 – space to begin reshaping the narrative around the prime minister, someone who until this point had enjoyed a reputation as a colossal political figure.

Yet all these political calculations were made redundant by the crisis of enormous severity which soon emerged to threaten the global economy, placing Brown at the centre of urgent efforts to find a solution.

In September 2007, with Labour and much of the Westminster village ruminating on whether there would be an autumn election, savers at Northern Rock triggered the first run on a British bank in well over a century.

Banks had already begun to curb their lending to each other drastically after concerns grew about bad debts in the United States mortgage market. Northern Rock – the fifth largest mortgage lender in the UK – asked the Bank of England for support because funds from other banks were suddenly drying up.

Savers were soon queuing at branches to get their money out, and though the Treasury stabilised the situation, this was just the beginning. With trust in the state of numerous financial institutions on both sides of the Atlantic having evaporated, a massive crash was triggered. In the UK, Northern Rock, Royal Bank of Scotland, Lloyds TSB and HBOS were all partly or wholly nationalised.

The idea of a Labour prime minister taking banks into public ownership would normally have been greeted with outrage in financial circles. Instead, it was hailed as a masterstroke on the part of Brown and his chancellor, Alistair Darling.

In October 2008, Brown gave the green light to a £500 billion rescue package for the banks and urged other countries to follow suit to preserve the world's financial system. By saving financial institutions, the prime minister was at the same time preserving people's homes, jobs and savings – literally ensuring the cash machines kept working.

It was a long and arduous process, requiring a second bailout in 2009. At every step Brown was at the heart of things, with world leaders, including President Obama, often seeking his advice on how best to proceed.

At home, the fallout from the prolonged crisis was becoming obvious by the start of 2009. Unemployment rose past two million, economic output was falling, and Britain tumbled into recession. Much-loved high street names, most prominently Woolworths, went out of business. Having been saved by the Labour government, many banks now played a much more cautious game, lending less frequently.

From this point on, the huge debt burden caused by the crash and the subsequent bailing out of the banks would become a cornerstone of the political agenda. Carefully, the Conservatives began to turn Labour's great success of saving a world economy in meltdown against them.

The central message the Tories trotted out was that Brown had taken Britain into recession when the country had a huge structural deficit – that public spending was far higher than revenues. Time and again, David Cameron blamed Brown and Darling, using phrases such as 'they didn't fix the roof when the sun was shining,' accusing the government of failing to plan for the bad times.[3]

This idea took hold, regardless of the fact that the recession was caused by the bursting of the US housing bubble. The political reality was that Labour was in power and therefore open to attack.

In May 2009, another crisis erupted when the *Daily Telegraph* published details of MPs' expenses. The revelations unfolded over several weeks, with many claims revolving around second home allowances, renovations and tax arrangements. Some deeply angered the public, including that of a Tory MP who claimed back more than £1,500 for an ornamental floating duck island.

The Commons Speaker, Michael Martin, was forced from his post in May 2009, blamed for a lack of leadership and overseeing a rotten system. Gordon Brown apologised on behalf of all MPs, but the pledge he had previously given, of bringing trust back to politics, now seemed risible.

A month later, the communities secretary, Hazel Blears, abruptly resigned her Cabinet post after a meeting with Brown. Aides sensed a growing plot from some Blairites to unseat him, fears which were well founded.

As council and European election polls closed the very next day, James Purnell, the pensions secretary, also resigned, telling Brown to 'stand aside and give Labour a fighting chance of winning the next election.'[4] Immediately, Brown faced a very real threat, for had respected figures such as Alan Johnson and David Miliband followed, he would most likely have been forced out.

In the end, it turned out that Purnell had acted as a lone wolf, but the results of the elections were of no comfort. Labour lost almost 300 council seats and were pushed into third place by UKIP – the United Kingdom Independence Party – in the European poll.

In the months which followed there was an attempted relaunch of the government. Styled as 'Building Britain's Future', this outlined policies designed to move from recession to growth while restoring trust in the political system. It did not herald an immediate change in fortunes, as the Tories gained Norwich North in a by-election in July with a large swing.

Then, at the end of September 2009, just hours after Brown had given a fighting speech to the party's annual conference in Brighton *The Sun* newspaper, which then had a daily circulation of three million, announced it was switching its support back to the Tories.

In effect, this was the starting gun on a long campaign into the election. In late December, it was revealed that Brown, Cameron and the Lib Dem leader Nick Clegg would go head-to-head across three live television debates in front of a studio audience.

With millions more watching at home Labour believed this would be a chance to shift the narrative around Brown, and that up against other leaders his experience and command of detail would shine through.

The election year of 2010 opened with a Conservative onslaught almost as soon as the festive holidays had concluded. The Tory theme was 'Year for Change'. Labour responded with a dossier focusing on Conservative plans, which caused Cameron difficulties, especially over his proposals for drastic spending cuts.

Just when he had succeeded in landing a blow on the Tories, Brown was hobbled by another assault on his leadership. This time two former Cabinet ministers, Patricia Hewitt and Geoff Hoon, called for a leadership election to unite the party. Their move backfired, causing anger among colleagues, and the plot quickly faded.

In the weeks which followed, the Tory poll lead fell and kept falling. Labour also enjoyed the good economic news that the country was out of recession and unemployment was consistently dropping.

In late March, Alistair Darling used his Budget to announce further support for the banks and suspended stamp duty on homes sold for under £250,000 – stealing a popular Tory policy. His main thrust, though, was to warn of the risk of falling back into recession if Britain were to ditch Labour.

Setting the stage for the election to come, he urged the public to stick with 'a government which has been right about the recession, right about the recovery, and is right about supporting the people and business of this country to build a prosperous future.'[5]

Labour then used a poster to mock Cameron as the unreconstructed, abrasive TV detective from the hit show *Ashes to Ashes*. The message was again one of caution – 'Don't let him take Britain back to the 1980s'.[6]

The shadow boxing and speculation was at last put to an end when Gordon Brown and his entire Cabinet stood in Downing Street on Tuesday 6 April to announce that the general election would take place exactly a month later. The Labour leader spoke of his ordinary roots, in contrast to the Eton-educated Cameron, and promised to go round the country making his case that Britain was on the road to recovery under Labour.

Almost immediately, there followed a dash by the party leaders to visit numerous marginal constituencies. The Tories were buoyed by the opinion polls, as for the first time since 1992 they went into the election ahead, though only with a single-digit lead.

Labour had hoped to focus the first week of campaigning on plans for the economic recovery but ended up in a prolonged sparring bout with the Tories over the planned 1 per cent rise in National Insurance. When the shadow chancellor, George Osborne, suggested a Conservative government would undo this, Labour attacked, accusing him of planning reckless cuts in public spending to pay for the Tory proposal.

On 12 April, Labour unveiled their manifesto, 'A Future Fair For All', the cover depicting a family in silhouette looking out across rich green fields warmed by rays from the rising sun.

The content seemed to have been carried across the Blair and Brown years – promising there would be no increases in income tax, or extension of VAT in many areas. There would be a new right to see a GP at evenings and weekends and a pilot scheme to give all primary-school children free school meals. There was a pledge to halve the budget deficit within four years, plus a levy on banks.

It was a rich package of measures designed to show energetic purpose – a counter to the Tory message of change. The Conservative launch, the following day, was studded with musical reminders of this theme, such as 'Changes' by David Bowie. Cameron's party also had an innovative wheeze – calling their manifesto 'Invitation to join the government of Britain'.

He also called on people to become part of 'The Big Society', a through-the-looking-glass kind of socialism where people (without the help of the state) were encouraged to play a bigger role in their communities.

The Big Society was much mocked, mainly for being a rather woolly concept, and attention soon turned to the first of the televised live debates between party leaders, a new development in British political history. This was held in Manchester on 15 April.

It was soon obvious that Brown did not greatly enjoy this arena, that Cameron was trying too hard, and Nick Clegg was thriving. In his opening statement, the Lib Dem leader looked down the camera lens and said, 'don't let anyone tell you the only choice is old politics – we can do something new, we can do something different this time.'[7]

The 90-minute debate proved to be a defining moment. Snap polls showed a victory for Clegg, prompting a huge surge of support. In the days which followed, YouGov had the Lib Dems on 34 per cent, with the Tories three points behind and Labour trailing in third.

Labour at first believed that what came to be known as 'Cleggmania' would help draw votes away from Cameron, but soon realised that it was also a threat to their own heartlands.

In the remaining two debates, Brown and Cameron did much better, landing blows on Clegg, though the Lib Dem leader remained an important figure in the election and began to be asked what he would do were there to be a hung parliament.

Specifically, the question was raised about the scenario in which Labour came third but won the most seats, a possibility under the electoral system and something Clegg found unacceptable. This was a blow to Brown and his team who, by now, believed their only real chance of staying in office was via a coalition with the Lib Dems.

In the days that followed, the path to victory became a little clearer, as Clegg said he might be able to work with Brown, but only if Labour did not finish third in terms of the popular vote.

Labour now had to consider how best to make the most of the days remaining until voting began. There was a gearshift away from the small gatherings Brown had been holding with supporters, often discussing issues in their front rooms. This approach had felt too stage-managed and did not get the prime minister seen by enough voters in person.

Though more walkabouts added some degree of spontaneity, such events were harder to control. That risk came to be embodied in the figure of Gillian Duffy, who heckled the prime minister during his visit to Rochdale on 29 April. In a discussion which followed, he carefully answered her concerns on a range of issues – notably about levels of immigration – and stated Labour's priorities on health, education and support for the less well-off.

The two departed with a handshake and mutual encouragement. Then, forgetting he was still wearing a broadcasting microphone, Brown was heard to describe the encounter as 'a disaster', calling Duffy 'this sort of bigoted woman'.[8] To Labour's horror, rolling news channels immediately began playing Brown's words.

With the fallout quickly escalating, the prime minister veered from his planned schedule to visit Duffy at home. After a 40-minute private meeting, Brown emerged to say he had misunderstood what had been put to him in their first encounter and had apologised. Nevertheless, what inevitably came to be known as 'Bigotgate' was hugely draining on Brown and his team.

The final week of campaigning saw a flurry of visits to marginal constituencies and Labour attempts to woo the Lib Dems and their voters. Ministers signalled the need to keep the Tories out of power while the home secretary, Alan Johnson, made it clear that coalitions were not to be feared.

The polls taken just before voting began all told much the same story – predicting a hung parliament, as had been the case at the outset. The bad news was the Tories looked like being the biggest party. Brown, too, was of that view, phoning the international development secretary, Douglas Alexander, the night before the election to apologise for the impending result.

What had been a topsy-turvy campaign held one further shock on election day when the former UKIP leader and candidate, Nigel Farage, survived a plane crash, after the light aircraft he had been travelling in nosedived into a field.

What was not widely known at 10 p.m., when voting ended, was that there had been an evening surge of people trying to cast their ballots. In places such as Sheffield, Birmingham, Manchester and parts of London, hundreds waiting outside polling stations were turned away as officials strictly followed the letter of the law.

Opening the BBC's coverage, David Dimbleby said it had been the most unpredictable election for a generation. He was one of a handful of people who knew the result of the exit poll. Based on a sample of 18,000 voters, it predicted the Conservatives would be the largest party in a hung parliament.

The first Labour spokesperson to appear on television, the party's deputy leader Harriet Harman, made the point that any deviation in the exit poll once actual votes were counted could see Gordon Brown remain as PM. Tellingly, she also made a subtle appeal to the Lib Dems, saying 'it's been clear that there is a general feeling that we need to change the voting system.'[9]

The first three results, all from the Sunderland area, showed swings to the Tories in safe Labour seats; but these were not uniform. As the night wore on, this became the pattern, Cameron's party achieving a smattering of success in taking some seats, but also in many cases not making it over the line.

At his own count in Fife, Brown increased his majority and echoed Harman's words, raising the prospect of electoral reform. Having spent time with local party workers, he flew to London, indicating to journalists he intended to remain in Downing Street.

Labour's expectation now was that Cameron would soon tip his party over 300 seats, but find it hard to muster another two dozen or so needed for even a bare majority in the Commons. On television and radio, Labour people began talking of progressive alliances, and the mood remained upbeat even though several ministers were losing their seats.

In Scotland Labour's vote share increased, while the Tories were heading for fourth place. However, the picture in Wales for Brown was poor, with the party losing four seats and falling to its lowest share of the vote since the Great War.

On the projected nationwide figures Labour and the Lib Dems together would be unable to form a majority, though with the confidence and supply assistance of some of the smaller nationalist parties it would theoretically be possible to govern. The complication was that the Conservatives and Lib Dems would jointly be able to form a working majority.

By the Friday morning after polling, Cameron had decided that his way forward was to try to form a coalition and to that end, and acting against convention by not waiting for Brown to see if he could forge an agreement with the Lib Dems, the Conservatives began talking to Clegg's party.

This effectively gave Cameron and his negotiators momentum. Brown did speak to Clegg by phone, but according to the Lib Dem leader, it went badly, with Clegg feeling as though he was treated too much as the potential junior partner.

Labour rightly felt that the majority of Lib Dem MPs would prefer a deal with them and that the two parties were relatively close in terms of shared values and outlook. However, it was also true that there were aligned policy areas between Cameron and Clegg, and that the Tory leader was prepared to make an offer which more or less matched Labour's.

Much of the wrangling came down to electoral reform, and when pushed the Tories offered a referendum on moving from first-past-the-post to the Alternative Vote system. This both matched and trumped Labour, because the electoral maths for a stable coalition seemed to favour a Tory/Lib Dem deal.

Labour did hold formal talks with the Lib Dems, and at one stage it looked as though things were progressing well. Brown even offered to stand down by the time of the Labour Conference in September after it was suggested he was a barrier to progress. Even this caused confusion for Clegg, who became nervous about who the next Labour leader might be and whether they would honour any coalition agreement.

Rightly or not, the Lib Dems came to believe that the Conservatives wanted them more. Also, by the Monday after the election senior Labour figures, including John Reid and David Blunkett, had joined prominent backbenchers in suggesting that a coalition was a poor idea.

Their argument was that Labour had been beaten, and it was best for the party to go into a period of opposition.

In the end Brown, knowing that his opponents were close to a deal, felt that any chance of staying in power had gone. He abruptly told Clegg on the afternoon of Tuesday 11 May that he could wait no longer and would resign. By that evening David Cameron had replaced him in Downing Street and would soon head up the first peacetime coalition government since the days of Ramsay MacDonald and the National Government of 1931.

It was a strange end to Labour's time in office stretching back to 1997: five days of uncertainty followed by a sudden and emotional departure. It had also been a bruising and difficult election for an exhausted party.

In an interview for this book, Gordon Brown reflected on Labour's 13 years in power and his role in the campaigns. 'The elections for which I chaired the main strategy group which often met daily were 1997, 2001 and 2005,' he said, adding 'to my regret I did not have time to chair the 2010 election strategy group.'

In each of Labour's victories, Brown makes clear the approach –as he puts it – 'our aim was to focus on the key issues, to prevent news media from turning against us, to get our key points across. But it was also strategic – to head off any potential difficulties and most important, to focus on our main themes.'

This encapsulates the core of Labour's strategy, but as the former prime minister points out, no two elections were quite the same. '1997 was about change, with change reflected in our key promises – 2001 was different, we started with "a lot done a lot to do," and that was to show where we had begun from five years earlier.'

'We then turned it (the campaign) into hospitals and schools first – because this is where we would focus our second term effects and of course we trebled NHS spending in cash terms with 8 per cent a year rises in the budget. We built new hospitals and also employed 30,000 new doctors.'

He also admits that Tony Blair's last election was fought under different circumstances. '2005 was difficult. I was brought in at the last minute. Originally, they had planned to have Alan Milburn [cabinet office minister] as chair of strategy but shifted when we were struggling in the campaign.'

Brown admits that the 2005 victory was won through a more defensive campaign than the two previous landslides. 'We had to deal with Iraq which saw the biggest rise in the Liberal vote, far bigger than 2010, but we focused on the economy and public services,'[10] he said.

Though public services remained strong by the time of the 2010 election, the economy had taken a pounding due to the financial crisis and voters simply began to look elsewhere for answers.

Many factors pushed Labour from office but the primary one was the unmovable obstacle of the parliamentary arithmetic. The final tally showed the Tories had 306 seats, while Labour fell to 258, down more than 90 on the previous total.

The Lib Dems, for all the exposure and excitement of the debates, were on 57, down five seats. Cameron and Clegg together could command 363 votes in the Commons, close to an 80-seat majority. While turnout was up to just over 65 per cent, Labour's share of the vote had dropped by over 6 per cent, a significant chunk of the electorate.

Considering these obstacles and without more left-leaning figures such as Paddy Ashdown, Charles Kennedy or Ming Campbell leading the Lib Dems, Labour was fighting an uphill battle, making a Tory/Lib Dem deal more likely from the outset. It was also true that the two main opposition parties were largely united, while Labour simmered with tensions.

Party staff and senior aides also felt that they had suffered from the lack of tight organisation, planning and cohesion which had served them so well at each successful turn since the darkness of the 1992 defeat.

The debates became the focal point, changing the rhythm of the campaign and injecting new life into the way the election was conducted. On this point, Labour suffered because it was not Brown's natural environment.

Brown only found his voice towards the end, but by then the damage had been done. For all that, while facing a hostile media Labour polled well enough to force a hung parliament. Had things gone differently in coalition discussions, the party might still have remained in office.

The fact that some senior figures were uneasy about a coalition, while the Tories and Lib Dems were hungry for power, also told its own story. Cameron played hard the idea that this was a change election and self-evidently Labour could no longer claim to be the biggest party. It was a case of fine margins though; had ten more seats been won, a majority with the Lib Dems could have been achieved.

It is also true that for a segment of the party there was something missing in 2010. For the first time since 1992, Tony Blair, Labour's serial election winner, was no longer at the helm. Conversely, had the damage caused to the former prime minister's standing by the Iraq war meant his political capital had been spent long ago?

Brown too had been in post, first as chancellor and then as PM, throughout Labour's period of rule, and to some degree there was a level of fatigue among voters about his messages.

At the same time, the Conservatives were no longer seen quite as much as the nasty or scandal-ridden party of old; they were also able to outspend Labour several times over during the campaign, and in Cameron voters perhaps saw something of the popular early Blair.

Labour had been unable to make the most of their successful management of the financial crash and how Brown had steered the economy away from disaster. The Tories knew that the Labour prime minister had won respect around the world for the action taken at this time, but also understood that were such a notion to take hold, it would likely have a terminal impact on their own election chances.

That Cameron was able to turn the financial crisis against Labour was a significant victory, and it shows just how vital strategic political communication is to all parties, especially in the fast-paced modern media era.

The Labour government was also seriously undermined by the sniping and plotting against Brown, much of it taking place just when Labour should have been pulling together to build out of the crash, as the economy turned upwards. Divided parties tend not to win elections. It was not just that Labour had been a long time in office, but now too many MPs had begun to look inward rather than out towards the country.

With a large measure of dignity Gordon Brown, accompanied by his wife Sarah and their two sons, strode hand in hand to the gates of Downing Street. Before departing, he spoke of human nature and its frailties, including his own, saying 'I loved the job for its potential to make this country I love fairer, more tolerant, more green, more democratic, more prosperous and more just – truly a greater Britain . . . above all, it was a privilege to serve.'[11]

With those words Labour slipped once more into opposition.

2010 General Election Result

Date of Election – 6 May

Overall Turnout – 65.1%

Labour

Candidates – 631

MPs – 258

Votes – 8,609,527

Percentage share of the vote – 29%

Result – Hung Parliament – Conservative/Lib Dem coalition

Highlight – The first peacetime coalition government in 80 years comes to power.

Chapter 31

2015 – On the Brink

'The 2015 election was never going to be easy'

Beckett Report[1]

Labour believed a return to power after one term in opposition was possible under the youthful Ed Miliband, but it was an era which began with one shock and would end with another.

Unusually for British politics, the date of the next general election was known years in advance thanks to the Fixed Term Parliaments Act, new legislation which all but removed the power of a prime minister to go to the country at a time of their choosing.

It was commonly expected that the election would take place on the first Thursday of May 2015, a factor which helped the Conservative/Lib Dem coalition to stay the course in office.

The defining characteristic of that government, and the years after Gordon Brown was replaced by David Cameron in Downing Street, was a series of austerity measures which hurt the weakest in British society.

These were imposed without any prior mention of them in either of the coalition parties' 2010 manifestos. The Conservatives had spoken only in vague terms of having 'a credible plan to eliminate the bulk of the structural deficit over a Parliament'.[2]

Soon after coming to office the chancellor, George Osborne, revealed reductions in public spending which would run to £83 billion. These included huge restrictions to welfare budgets, cancellations of school building programmes and deep cuts to local government, while increasing VAT to 20 per cent.

With interest rates historically low, these measures had the effect of contracting rather than growing the economy, and as a result homelessness grew, the use of food banks exploded and the working poor, women in particular, bore the brunt of the cuts.

The Coalition, driven by the Tories, were making a political choice as much as an economic one in going down the route of austerity. The challenge for Labour under its new leader was how to respond.

Gordon Brown had resigned in the days following the 2010 election when it became apparent a Tory/Lib Dem coalition was being formed. Harriet Harman, as deputy, took over on an interim basis.

Ed Miliband was one of five candidates in the race to succeed Brown – the others being Ed Balls, Diane Abbott, Andy Burnham and David Miliband, Ed's elder brother. After several rounds of voting, the field was whittled down to the two Miliband brothers. With strong trade union backing, Ed dramatically triumphed by just over 1 per cent in the run-off.

In victory, the 40-year-old former climate and energy secretary said 'I know we lost trust, I know we lost touch, I know we need to change. Today a new generation has taken charge of Labour . . .'[3] These were words designed to move decisively on from the New Labour era.

Labour at this stage was a badly bruised party, having lost office after 13 years. In the 2010 election, they had been unable to shake off the charge made by the Conservatives that by saving the banks in the crash of 2008, Labour bore responsibility for the ensuing deficit.

The Tories then continued to weaponise this as an issue under Miliband. The most prominent example came at Labour's own hands: Liam Byrne, the outgoing chief secretary to the Treasury had left a note for his successor which read 'I'm afraid there's no money . . . good luck!'.[4]

It had been intended as a joke, echoing Reggie Maudling, the departing Tory chancellor, who in 1964 cheerily apologised to Labour's Jim Callaghan for leaving the economy in a mess. Instead, it was used as a stick to beat Miliband and his team.

It was an era in which politics remained largely in campaigning mode well beyond the election and the formation of the Coalition, much of it powered by the turbulence caused by several referendums.

In May 2011, the Conservatives celebrated victory as plans to move from the first-past-the-post to the Alternative Vote system were trounced in a national poll. On the same day, voters in Scotland returned the Scottish National Party to power at Holyrood, the first majority government in the Scottish Parliament's history.

Labour fell to 37 seats, its worst showing at an election in Scotland for 80 years. The SNP was now able to demand a referendum on independence, having campaigned on the issue. This was granted the following year and slated for September 2014, not that the news made much of a splash at Westminster where the defining feature of politics remained the battle to reduce the deficit.

There was significant support among the public for that strategy and this gave Labour little room to deviate. Ed Balls, the shadow chancellor, did try to highlight problems with the government's approach saying they were moving too quickly and in so doing choking off growth and needlessly damaging public services.

Miliband, too, was keen to develop policies and take positions which presented his own idea of a socially democratic Britain. At the party conference in 2011, the Labour leader called for an end to what he termed 'fast buck' capitalism.[5] This was followed in 2013 by plans for a price freeze for gas and electricity bills, with the big energy firms being split up. In time there would also be proposals for a tax on homes worth over £2 million.

All of this was not only eye-catching but garnered Miliband the nickname 'Red Ed' – not always an affectionate title. His policies were popular, but voters still expressed doubts about the party's commitment to deficit reduction and seemed to buy the idea that the Coalition was clearing up a mess left by Gordon Brown.

Nevertheless, Labour retained a consistent lead in the opinion polls from early in the parliament until the beginning of 2015. In this, they were helped by a sharp fall in Lib Dem support after their catastrophic U-turn on abolishing tuition fees. What was kept very private in Labour circles was data showing that while David Cameron was more popular than his party, Miliband trailed Labour's own approval rating.

For Labour, the key objective was first to retain its 2010 voters while harvesting disaffected Lib Dems, as well as those disgruntled with the Tories over austerity. This came to be viewed as a '35 per cent strategy' by some commentators, though never formally endorsed as such by team Miliband.

It was something of a tightrope and the strategy divided opinion at the top of the party. The hope was that things would go smoothly in the years towards the election, and Miliband would be able to expose the government for their damaging policies.

When in 2012 the Labour MP, Eric Joyce, went on a violent rampage assaulting a Conservative MP and others in a Commons bar, it set off a chain reaction which would undermine Labour's chances of victory and define the party for years to come.

Joyce soon indicated he would stand down, but allegations of voting irregularity in his Falkirk seat led to a major dispute with Labour's biggest financial backer, Unite the Union.

Determined to be seen to act, Miliband ordered a review headed by Lord Ray Collins. He recommended new rules relating to unions and party members in selections, but also proposed dissolving the electoral college for Labour leadership elections, and so dramatically weaken union power by moving to a one-member one-vote system.

This enraged union leaders and the three biggest affiliates – GMB and Unison, along with Unite – substantially cut their funding to the party. In the year before the election, this hurt Labour's ability to push resources into marginal seats.

There were other factors which shaped the 2015 election, unseen in 2010 but which had a particularly negative effect on Labour. The first of these was the rise of UKIP, with its demand for withdrawal from the European Union and the claim that this was the only way to slam the door on rising levels of immigration.

In 2014, UKIP won the most votes and seats in Britain's elections to the EU Parliament. Though Labour gained seven seats, there was also the dawning realisation that UKIP not only presented a danger to the Tories, but that Labour's vote in many areas was also under threat at a general election which was only a year away.

Before that, Labour still had to navigate the autumn of 2014, a period which decisively shaped the path to the general election. Scotland's referendum on independence would take place on 18 September, with the question on the ballot paper being 'Should Scotland be an independent country?', and the options to vote simply Yes or No.

Labour under Miliband took a straightforward view that Scotland should remain inside the United Kingdom. The referendum campaign was at first a slow burn, but intensified in the weeks leading up to polling, with at least one poll putting the Yes campaign ahead.

This sparked panic at Westminster, not only in the Conservative and Unionist Party (to give the Tories their full title). Labour held a Shadow Cabinet meeting in Scotland and even sent 100 MPs to Glasgow by train to campaign, only to be greeted by a man in a rickshaw playing the Imperial March from Star Wars.

Miliband himself promised that a Labour government would not allow an independent Scotland to use the pound sterling and raised the spectre of inspection posts at the crossing into England, warning Scots that 'we would have to look at the issue of a border if you have different immigration policies'.[6]

Miliband needed to appeal across the United Kingdom and well knew the value of Scottish seats to his party in a general election. Though a reasonably comfortable victory followed, with the pro-Union parties securing 55 per cent of the vote, this presented a further problem.

For the first time, there was now a large and highly energised base of pro-independence Scots. In the SNP, 'Yes' voters had an obvious outlet for their frustrations and it was a party only too happy to point out that Labour had campaigned in alliance with the detested Tories under the 'Better Together' banner.

Suddenly, polls showed the SNP was likely to sweep the board not only at Holyrood but in a general election. Already spooked by the emerging threat from UKIP, the last thing Miliband needed was to be fighting on another front.

Days later, Miliband gave his keynote annual conference speech to delegates in Manchester. Speaking without an autocue for over an hour, the Labour leader set out his vision for the country, talking of better lives for working people and a Britain that could lead the world.

Miliband and his team hoped this would be the moment where he would show he was a prime minister in waiting. Coming off stage, he realised, as did political journalists, that he had failed to mention the burning issue of the £75 billion deficit as well as key passages on immigration.

The Conservatives quickly jumped on this with George Osborne tweeting 'Ed Miliband didn't mention the deficit once. Extraordinary. If you can't fix the economy you can't fund the NHS'.[7]

The Labour leader was understandably dejected and did his best to contain the damage by saying in subsequent TV interviews that his party would bring down the debt and that there would be no additional borrowing.

The story of the omitted parts of the speech played into a narrative – pushed by the Tories and sections of the media – that Miliband was a bright yet impractical politician out of touch with the real world. This treatment from the media took many forms, perhaps most memorably when Miliband was unflatteringly pictured eating a bacon sandwich.

Following the speech, there was criticism from both senior party figures and trade unionists. This had hardened by November with *The Observer* reporting that 20 shadow ministers were willing to call on Miliband to stand down. The paper, naming no names, claimed the rebels were drawn from across the party.

Like similar situations faced by Gordon Brown as prime minister, this quickly petered out, doubtless due to the proximity of the election, but also because in character Miliband was a conciliatory figure who brought Labour together.

The Conservatives revealed their first campaign billboard of 2015 on New Year's Day, with the message of staying on the right economic road. Miliband countered, trumpeting plans to hold four million conversations with voters rather than relying on posters paid for by big business.

In the weeks which followed, the Labour leader focused on shaping his message to the electorate. Unwilling to create hostages to fortune, Miliband told the BBC that he was not interested in deals with the SNP – who were still surging in the polls and likely to be the third party in the new parliament – but refused to rule it out absolutely.

This was a campaign theme the Tories would return to time and again, even when a formal arrangement with the nationalists was eventually rejected by Labour.

Miliband much preferred to highlight his five key pledges – 'A strong economic foundation', 'higher living standards for working families', 'an NHS with time to care', 'controls on immigration' and 'a country where the next generation can do better than the last'.[8] In addition there was a vow not to raise VAT and a cap on the profits private companies could make from the NHS.

The somewhat farcical controversy of this period was that the Miliband family home had two kitchens. More substantial was the news that Cameron would not serve a third term as PM and that Labour were again ahead in the polls.

At the end of March, Cameron announced that a general election would take place almost six weeks later, on Thursday 7 May. In a break with tradition the prime minister mentioned the Labour leader by name in his remarks, setting the tone for what would be a highly personalised campaign. Miliband, meanwhile, launched Labour's campaign at the site of the 2012 London Olympics, a move designed to show that the party had a positive upbeat vision for Britain.

Having brought the 2010 campaign to life, TV debates this time around were less dramatic and saw Miliband and Cameron directly face each other on one occasion only. Significantly, the SNP leader, Nicola Sturgeon, also did well in the debates and polling consistently put her party on course to sweep the board north of the border, taking seats Labour were relying on to achieve a majority.

Sturgeon made it clear she stood ready to play her part in deciding who was in power at Westminster, saying she would work with Labour to lock the Tories out of power, even if they were the biggest party. Understandably, Miliband rejected this assistance, though that did not stop the Conservatives depicting Miliband as literally being in the pocket of the SNP leader.

Labour's manifesto, revealed on 13 April, was framed around the message 'Britain only succeeds when working families succeed'.[9] The highlights were the banning of some zero hours contracts, freezing energy bills, reducing tuition fees and scrapping the so-called 'non-dom' tax status.

Voters were assured the entire platform had been fully costed and would be paid for without the need for extra borrowing. On the debt question, there was an explicit commitment to cut the deficit every year of the parliament.

Labour went a step further than other parties by also having a Women's Manifesto, spearheaded by Deputy Leader Harriet Harman, and utilising a pink minibus which toured marginal constituencies. This initiative, to woo some of the nine million women who had not voted in 2010, drew criticism that it was patronising and had echoes of a hen night.

Taken together, Labour's offer to the country was not as ambitious as Miliband might have envisaged when he had been elected, but he was a leader trying to make a distinctive pitch while facing threats across the board: from the Conservatives, UKIP and the SNP.

In this scenario, playing it safe was understandable, but it did not always work as intended. The party infuriated and depressed some of its activist base by releasing merchandising which included branded mugs promising controls on immigration.

There followed the strange case of the giant slab of limestone which was unveiled in a car park late in the campaign by Miliband himself. Labour's election promises had been carved onto it and the intention was to place it in the Downing Street garden in the event of a Labour victory. Though meant as a series of weighty and clear commitments, it was soon lampooned as the 'Ed-Stone' and 'Labour's tombstone'.

Still, in the final few days many across the Labour Party believed victory of some kind was within reach. The polls suggested the Tories were likely to be the largest party again but, with a significant increase in Labour seats, Miliband could hope to be at the head of an anti-Tory coalition.

Miliband himself had private doubts, and these were brutally realised when the exit poll confounded expectations, predicting the Conservatives would improve their standing and be just short of an overall majority on 316 seats.

For Labour, it was a bombshell moment: none of their internal predictions and indeed none of the national polls had the Tories on such high numbers. Staffers at Labour HQ stood with their hands over their mouths, unable to comprehend what was unfolding.

From his constituency home in Doncaster, Miliband spoke to senior aides and agreed that even a slight deviation in the exit poll would put Labour back in the game. It was a hope shared by others, notably the former Lib Dem leader, Paddy Ashdown, who declared that he would eat his hat live on TV if his party secured the measly 10 seats predicted.

The wait then began until actual results could be measured, with Harman telling broadcasters that it was difficult to know if the exit polls were correct. Peter Mandelson, Ed Balls and Yvette Cooper all then took to the airwaves raising the question about whether the Tories could command the support of the Commons without a majority.

Among the early declarations there were swings to Labour, but in Battersea, the first marginal result, the movement was to the Conservatives despite a big effort on the ground. At Nuneaton in the West Midlands the Tories doubled their majority and at this point Labour's top team knew that if the exit poll was wrong at all, it had underplayed the number of seats Cameron would win.

Miliband's thoughts now turned to resignation, with the picture in Scotland bleak for his party. Such was the movement to the Scottish nationalists they had to dampen expectations that a clean sweep of all the 59 seats would be achieved.

With huge swings – some as high as 35 per cent – Scottish Labour figures fell by the wayside one after another. Among them were Jim Murphy, the leader north of the border, Margaret Curran, the shadow Scottish secretary, and Douglas Alexander, who was in charge of Miliband's election campaign.

The final picture was devastating, with the SNP winning all but three seats, more than the combined total taken by the party in its entire history. Labour was reduced from 41 to just a single MP. This made Nicola Sturgeon's party the third largest at Westminster with the collapse of the Liberal Democrats. The former Coalition partners were left with only eight Commons members across the entire country.

Labour suffered the same fate, falling back to 232 MPs, a net loss of 26, winning just 30.4 per cent of the vote and just above the total of seats reached in 1987 when Margaret Thatcher had been at the height of her powers.

Cameron and the Conservatives were considerably strengthened with 330 seats, a gain of 24 which took them to an overall majority of 11 across the Commons. Not only had the Tories been the only UK-wide party able to build on the votes captured in 2010, but they had also achieved the rare feat of doing so as a governing party.

Such was the shock of the result it instantly reshaped British politics. By Friday lunchtime Clegg, Farage and Miliband had all announced their resignations, Miliband telling distraught party workers he was sorry to have overseen a defeat but adding 'we have come back before, and this party will come back again'.[10]

At his count hours earlier in Doncaster, the Labour leader had reflected to supporters that a surge of nationalism had washed over his party. It was undoubtedly the case, and in that atmosphere Labour simply could not get a hearing in Scotland.

'It was the year after the independence referendum, and there was a lot of people who said Labour had got into bed with the Tories,' is how Archie Dryburgh puts it. He was Labour's candidate against the only sitting Conservative MP in Scotland, running for the lowland seat of Dumfriesshire, Clydesdale and Tweedale.

As Dryburgh recalls, 'we went into the general election campaign on the back of what had been a loss for the independence parties but also on the back of a lot of stick for what we had done with the Tory party by being in Better Together.'

'I went in there expecting to lose but not by the amount that we did, and again that was because of independence. My campaign was based on getting people out of poverty, making sure the cost of living was not going to be a problem, that we had enough teachers, all the social values that I learned as a trade unionist.'

The constitutional question was something Labour simply could not evade, no matter how much they tried to argue otherwise. As Dryburgh puts it, 'I was hoping people had got over the independence issue, but they did blame Labour and there was a lot of Labour support-ers who wanted independence. It was the biggest issue on the doorstep and we weren't able to advertise our policies as well as we could have.'[11]

Labour in 2015 had a reasonable expectation of winning the election given it was not up against a Conservative party with a large majority, but taking on David Cameron, who had over the five preced-ing years had to govern from a Coalition position.

Added to this, the Conservative/Lib Dem partnership was deeply unpopular in parts of the country for implementing austerity and, in the case of Nick Clegg's party, for voting to increase tuition fees rather than scrap them as the party had previously promised.

For Labour, defeat came in many guises and the biggest single obstacle to victory was that throughout the life of the parliament, the party remained caught in the headlights of the financial crash of 2008, blamed for the downturn and the build-up of debt which followed.

'The defeat of 2010 had been heavy and although the economy had returned to growth, the aftermath of the global crash was a major feature of national life', was how the party's review into the 2015 defeat put it.[12] The Tories understood the force of this point, with Cameron brandishing the Liam Byrne letter at appearances throughout the campaign.

On top of this, from 2014 onwards, Labour found its vote being squeezed, first by UKIP over immigration and then by the SNP. According to the same review the sudden but then sustained spike in support for the Scottish nationalists 'made it impossible for us to be the biggest party'. If that were not enough, the collapse of the Lib Dems, who lost 27 seats to Cameron's party, 'enabled the Tories to gain an overall majority and keep us out of power'.[13]

To this can be added the perception that the Conservative leader – with his direct appeal to be allowed to finish the job he had started – appeared more likely to steer the UK back to economic health. In short, Cameron seemed to be a stronger contender to be prime minister.

Labour's strategy was to accept the need to reduce debt, but to do so at a rate which did not halt growth and which protected public services. This was a middle way – making Labour neither deficit deniers nor a full-blown anti-austerity party. Really though, the problem for Miliband and Balls was that no matter what they did, their main opponents would still blame them for the deficit because doing so was electoral gold dust.

In Scotland, Labour could not have argued for independence, being a UK-wide party and one which had long benefited from large numbers of Scottish Labour MPs at Westminster. Given that the referendum would be determined in large part by traditional Labour voters, the party might have performed better by carving out its own unique campaign and in so doing provide distance from the Tories.

It was a cruel irony that Labour did not bring about the referendum on Scotland's independence, but was most injured by its outcome. In 2015 it was all too easy for the Conservatives to alarm English voters by claiming that the SNP might not only prop up but control a minority Labour government.

Beyond this there were issues in Scotland and the north of England about how Labour had lost touch with its traditional base, most obviously in the form of near-dormant local parties and branches, an issue which certainly came to light during the referendum.

In September 2015, the Labour MP Jon Cruddas gave a speech suggesting Labour was 'dangerously out of touch with the electorate. It stands on the brink of becoming irrelevant to the majority of working people in the country.' To this diagnosis he added: 'the clock is ticking, and we had better change tack soon or face the consequences.'[14]

2015 General Election Result

Date of Election – 7 May

Overall Turnout 2015 – 66.2%

Labour

Candidates – 631

MPs – 232

Votes – 9,347,324

Percentage share of the vote – 30.4%

Result – Conservative majority

Highlight – The rise of the SNP destroys Labour's base in Scotland, and Ed Miliband's hopes of becoming Prime Minister.

Chapter 32

2017 – The Many Not the Few

'Rise, like Lions after slumber
In unvanquishable number!'

Percy Bysshe Shelley[1]

Labour went into this election more divided than at any time in the party's history, led by a figure from the far left, given almost no chance of success, and wholly unprepared for the battle to come.

Without a single ministerial or shadow post to his name in over 30 years in the Commons, Jeremy Corbyn had stormed to the leadership in September 2015 after Ed Miliband stepped down. Having begun as a 200–1 outsider, and only making it onto the ballot paper at the last moment, Corbyn's pitch was 'Straight Talking, Honest Politics' coupled with a radical agenda to change Britain.

Even in an era of political upheavals and upsets, Corbyn's victory stood out. Here was someone who had rebelled against his own party hundreds of times, often taking stances well outside the Labour mainstream. He had spoken to Sinn Féin at a time when the IRA remained active, he was pro-Palestinian, critical of NATO and a prominent Iraq War critic.

His victory was a quirk of history, the leadership election which brought him to prominence being held under new rules which watered down the power of MPs and affiliates. This was not only now a one-member one-vote system, it was also possible to sign up as a registered supporter and pay just £3 to be able to vote. It was via this route that over 100,000 people backed Corbyn.

Assisted by the Momentum campaigning group and their savvy use of online strategies, the Islington North MP won with almost 60 per cent of the 400,000 votes cast in the first round. It was an impressive mandate, marking a distinct shift leftwards in Labour's tides.

Tellingly, Corbyn won on an avowedly anti-austerity platform. It was this – particularly his forthright opposition to the Tory cuts implemented since 2010 – which began a wave of enthusiasm which would see the 66-year-old easily outpace his Shadow Cabinet opponents Liz Kendall, Yvette Cooper and Andy Burnham.

On becoming leader, Corbyn talked about ending the 'grotesque levels of inequality in our society', saying things had to change and that the Conservatives 'had used the economic crisis of 2008 to impose a terrible burden on the poorest people in this country'.[2]

This was not to everyone's taste. Shadow Health Minister Jamie Reed resigned while Corbyn was still giving his victory speech, and Cooper, Kendall, Rachel Reeves and other major figures said they would not serve under him. Soon this opposition spilled into open warfare at every level of the party, down to local branches which had grown exponentially as the Corbyn campaign took off.

From the start, there were obvious tensions between Corbyn's team in his parliamentary offices and long-standing staff at the party's Southside HQ in Victoria. Much of the Parliamentary Party (MPs and peers) had opposed his election and this made for a frosty and unsupportive atmosphere. Others took the view that Labour were the Official Opposition and therefore thought it best to serve, though Corbyn's core support in Parliament was limited to a small group.

It was not a situation which helped foster effective party discipline, a point highlighted in a Commons vote over whether the UK should extend airstrikes against Islamic State targets in Syria.

While Corbyn was opposed, his shadow foreign secretary, Hilary Benn, supported the military action. What followed left the frontbench looking ridiculously divided. Corbyn opened the parliamentary debate arguing against airstrikes, and Benn passionately closed it for Labour hours later, taking the opposite position.

Already there was a growing view that Corbyn was out of his depth and would lead Labour to an electoral hammering. Almost daily stories to this effect appeared in the media, often from unnamed Labour MPs, questioning not only what they saw as unrealistic policy positions, but also his lack of electability.

By the spring of 2016 another issue was emerging with complaints about alleged anti-Jewish racism. Concerns were raised regarding the conduct of a small minority in local party meetings, as well as online posts.

Labour tried to grasp this issue, appointing Shami Chakrabarti, the former boss of civil rights group Liberty, to conduct an inquiry. Her report contained several recommendations, concluding that the Labour Party is not overrun by anti-Semitism or other forms of racism but there is an 'occasionally toxic atmosphere'.[3]

The report's publication came amid a quickly escalating crisis for the Corbyn administration. On 23 June, the UK voted to leave the European Union in a knife-edge referendum; this prompted David Cameron to resign immediately as prime minister, having won a general election just 13 months earlier.

There was fury in Labour circles at the referendum result. Corbyn, not only as leader but as someone who had long expressed doubts about the concept of the EU, was the target of this ire. The suggestion from opponents was that although he had explicitly supported the case for Remain, his campaign efforts had been lukewarm at best.

There followed a wave of almost 40 resignations at Shadow Cabinet and Shadow Ministerial level, then a huge defeat in a confidence motion brought by the Parliamentary Party. No Labour leader had ever met such concerted opposition from his own MPs.

Corbyn's response was to tell thousands of his supporters gathered in Parliament Square: 'I was democratically elected leader of our party for a new kind of politics by 60 per cent of Labour members and supporters . . . I will not betray them by resigning. Today's vote by MPs has no constitutional legitimacy.'[4]

Buttressed by huge support among the membership and trade unions, he simply refused to stand aside, putting together a new Shadow team, doubling up across departments as necessary. He would soon be forced into another leadership contest by Shadow Work and Pensions Secretary Owen Smith. Corbyn won again and with an even greater mandate.

This came at a cost, though. Across the summer months of 2016, the public had again looked upon a party at war with itself. Corbyn's own approval ratings were dire, trailing far behind the popularity of the Labour brand and those of the new Tory prime minister, Theresa May.

She had come into office promising to be a one nation prime minister who would govern for the interests of the whole country. May also pledged that there would be no general election before 2020.

Her aim was to concentrate on implementing the vote to leave the European Union – now known as Brexit – as just what form this would take had been ill-defined by the referendum. It was an issue which would blaze through British politics with a growing intensity as the months progressed, sparking a widespread campaign for a second referendum and a legal challenge to leaving the EU.

All parties were troubled by the fallout of the Brexit vote and how to shape the future. Aware that Labour's support across the country was split between those who had voted Leave and Remain, John McDonnell, the shadow chancellor, sought to offer 'Not a Banker's Brexit for the lucky few, but a People's Brexit for the many.'[5]

By the end of 2016, with relative calm in Labour's ranks restored, senior figures began to tentatively plan ahead. With the Tories finding it increasingly difficult to navigate the Brexit process through Parliament given the small majority bequeathed from Cameron's time, Labour engaged both a polling company and a communications agency.

Crucially too, staff around the leadership began to think in terms of building a policy suite which would reflect Corbyn's priorities and, at the very least, transform the political debate. No one really believed that a general election was in the offing, but it was best to be ready. This soon proved to be a wise strategy.

In early 2017, May was delighted at her party's victory in the Copeland by-election. The rural west Cumbrian seat had been in Labour hands for 80 years and its capture seemed to prove to the prime minister that her government had broad appeal.

Around Easter, May and her husband had gone on a walking holiday in Wales, having made it clear only to a handful of very senior staff that she was now moving towards calling an election. On Easter Monday, 17 April, she phoned the queen to explain her plans.

All of this remained top secret, to the extent that the next day in Downing Street journalists simply did not know the nature of the unplanned statement the PM was about to give.

With virtually no warning, Britain was plunged into the first snap election since February 1974 under Ted Heath. Polling day was set for

8 June following a seven-week campaign. May told the public – 'if we do not hold a general election now . . . political game-playing will continue, and the negotiations with the European Union will reach their most difficult stage in the run-up to the next scheduled election.'[6]

The Conservatives held a polling lead in excess of 20 points over Labour, so the dangers of going to the country were considered minimal. Also, this was not a decision about Brexit alone: May also saw an opportunity to build a bigger Tory majority and move on from the Cameron era.

None of this would have happened without what May and her Cabinet felt to be a hopelessly weak and divided Labour Party. May's campaign guru, Lynton Crosby, framed the election around her, believing the Tory leader would be seen as strong and stable by the electorate, in stark contrast to Corbyn.

Many Labour MPs were left with a sense of impending doom and Labour's own polling was predicting disaster on an historic scale. The election could have been stopped by the provisions of the Fixed Term Parliaments Act, but fearing they would look weak and obstructive if they blocked it, Labour backbenchers allowed a Commons vote in favour of an election to sail through the House.

Labour now had to work at pace to prepare a manifesto, craft a campaign, select candidates and work out which seats were targets and which were to be defended. It was not all bad news though; this was the chance to produce an offer to the country which presented a different kind of political outlook.

Quickly the wheels began to move; staff working for the leadership abandoned Parliament, which was still sitting, and based themselves at the party's Southside building in Victoria. As if the situation were not challenging enough, local elections across swathes of England, plus the whole of Scotland and Wales, were also close at hand.

In those first days of campaigning Labour were able to utilise policies already being shaped for the locals. These included not only improvements in pay, conditions and rights for workers, but also the eye-catching promise of four more Bank Holidays a year.

The Labour leader seemed pleased at the prospect of the election, having spent much of the previous two years in campaign mode. While May's team fell back on tightly controlled small gatherings, Corbyn was often found addressing energetic public rallies, at times with audiences of thousands. At the outset, Corbyn's enthusiasm seemed novel and in time it would come to be a defining feature of the battle for power.

This was also true of the Labour slogan – 'For the Many, not the Few' – which was revealed in late April. The phrase can be found in part in the revamped Clause IV of the Party's constitution, but it has a long history of political use.

Its source was the radical poem *The Masque of Anarchy*, written by Shelley following the Peterloo Massacre of 1819. It was chosen for Labour's 2017 campaign because it succinctly captured the wide appeal Corbyn's team were tilting at, with the promise that there would be something for (almost) everyone under Labour.

That theory would shortly be tested in the local elections on 4 May. The results saw the Conservatives gain over 550 seats and take control of ten councils, while Labour recorded the worst performance by a leading opposition party in several decades.

While this seemed to point to a hammering in the forthcoming general election, the eminent polling guru, John Curtice, provided a lifeboat. 'Good, but perhaps not quite as good as the party would like. That seems to be the message for the Tories that emerged from the local ballot boxes . . .', he wrote, pointing out that the swing to May's party had been significantly lower than recent polling averages.[7]

This provided at least some hope that the Labour vote could hold up and that once they got into their stride, the rest of the campaign would create a positive feeling around the policies offered by Corbyn and his party.

The country would have sight of Labour's vision for government sooner than had been expected. Both *The Daily Telegraph* and the *Mirror* obtained a leaked draft of the manifesto, and on 11 May covered the story extensively.

Though at first causing consternation among those close to Corbyn, with allegations and counter-allegations about who had been responsible, it was soon clear that the leak had served only to give Labour more publicity for its policies.

The *Mirror*'s headline was 'Leaked Labour manifesto is a full-blooded socialist offer to Britain', with associate editor, Kevin Maguire, writing that the 'programme drips with exciting promises to build a better, decent, more prosperous country'.[8]

Five days later the official launch took place in Bradford, with Corbyn himself setting out plans including scrapping tuition fees, nationalising water companies and the railways, ending zero hours contracts, more free childcare and higher taxes for top earners. All of this was accompanied by a detailed booklet setting out how the measures would be paid for.

It was an ambitious package, with some observers characterising it as Milibandism on steroids – the kind of manifesto the previous leader might have dreamed about. For others, there were echoes of the failed radicalism of 1983 under Michael Foot.

Still, in the face of considerable pressure, Labour had at least conjured something which engaged hearts and minds. That same stress was being felt by the other parties, the Tories included.

The government was forced into a major U-turn after a complicated policy on reforming social care was badly received. Facing accusations that those requiring extensive care would lose their homes May tried to introduce changes to the manifesto policy then shrilly told the media 'nothing has changed, nothing has changed.'[9]

It was a moment which left May and her party looking chaotic and confused, rather than strong and stable. With polling suggesting the Tory lead had suddenly slumped to single figures, May was further weakened by her refusal to take part in a live television debate and a TV interview in which she bizarrely claimed that running through wheat fields was the naughtiest thing she had ever done.

In between, campaigning was halted for three days in tragic circumstances. A Manchester-born Islamist detonated a bomb at the end of a large Ariana Grande pop concert in the city, killing himself and 22 others. Hundreds more were injured, many of them young people, in one of the worst acts of terrorism seen in Britain.

With May being seen to take charge, making official statements and leading the response, the expectation was it would show the prime minister in her best light. Yet when the campaign restarted, it was Corbyn who seized the initiative.

In a speech the Labour leader blamed the bomber for his actions but also made the link between the Manchester outrage and British foreign policy – what he saw as a failed 'War on Terror' – as well as austerity. This drew sharp criticism from senior Conservatives, but polling showed many of the public had also joined the dots and agreed with Corbyn's analysis.

In the final days before the election, Labour activists in the cities were met with a wave of volunteers unlike anything seen in recent times, perhaps ever in the party's history. In some inner London seats the campaigning norms of door knocking and data gathering were abandoned, with people being told simply to go into the streets and tell anyone they found to vote Labour.

This reflected a wider mood, as Corbyn swept around the country being greeted by ever bigger crowds. At a music festival at Tranmere Rovers' football ground, thousands spontaneously began singing 'Oh Jeremy Corbyn' to the tune of the White Stripes' 'Seven Nation Army'.

Unlikely as it had seemed a few weeks earlier, this suggested the Labour leader was connecting with the country, just as he had with party members in his two leadership election campaigns.

All this stood in marked contrast with the picture in 2015, especially in more rural areas. Katherine Chibah was the Labour candidate in the greenbelt constituency of Hertford and Stortford outside London in both elections.

'I was selected in 2014, about a year before the election. We ran a really comprehensive campaign, we did lots of door knocking every week, we did street stalls,' she recalls. 'There was quite a lot of hostility towards Labour at the time and things were brought up on the doorstep about how Ed Miliband was in the SNP's pocket.'

'I thought Miliband was a really good leader. I think he was very honest, trying to be pragmatic and keep the wings of the party together. He was trying to provide honest answers to problems as he saw them. But people were saying "we don't know what Labour stands for".'

Fast forward two years, and Chibah was told to concentrate on neighbouring key seats and just run a skeleton campaign in her Tory-held constituency. 'It was such a different atmosphere,' she says, 'we did a street stall and we had people coming up to us – a lot of young people saying "we are going to vote Labour", they were so enthusiastic.'

'I remember older people coming up to us as well. I think it was the manifesto, it really caught people's imaginations. It was just so clear and so principled, people were crying out for that at that time.'

Chibah puts this down to national ideas capturing the public mood far more than local campaigns. As she explained: 'we only had time to do about two door knocking sessions and street stalls but the number of votes went up by over seven thousand, which seems absolutely unbelievable given the time before we had worked for a year and only managed to increase it by a tiny amount.'[10]

By this stage, late in the campaign the polls were mixed: some had the Tories with a large lead, others a small advantage; and though largely dismissed, some suggested a hung parliament was on the cards. On election night with voting about to end, senior Labour people began to get leaks that the exit poll would be positive, though it was unclear to what extent.

Moments later, the broadcasters revealed their projected figures. They indicated that Labour had deprived the Conservatives of their majority, though May's party was likely to remain the largest in Parliament. This prompted both celebration and dismay from some at Labour HQ. At his North London home, Corbyn and his closest aides hugged and wondered if he was about to become prime minister.

Labour's shadow foreign secretary, Emily Thornberry, told ITV that the figures suggested the Conservatives would have the first chance to form a government, but added that 'we are prepared to be the next government, we look forward to being the next government and implementing a highly popular manifesto.'[11]

At first it was unclear whether the exit poll was accurate. In the first few seats, all Labour holds, the Tories had done better than expected. At midnight, things began to crystallise as Swindon North was held by May's party, but with a swing to Labour. An hour later Labour held Darlington, a top Tory target, without their majority being troubled. The trick was repeated at Wrexham minutes later.

It was now beyond doubt that psephologists had been correct in their prediction. At this point Patrick Heneghan, Labour's campaigns chief, called Corbyn to tell him that having crunched the numbers May now had no chance of forming a majority.

At 3 a.m., the Labour leader went to his own declaration and having won handsomely told supporters 'I am very proud of the results that are coming in from all over the country', adding that people were voting for hope 'and turning their backs on austerity.'[12]

Corbyn made a direct call for May to resign, while the Tory leader looked bewildered and distressed at her Maidenhead count. Her great gamble had backfired, but she made no indication that she would be standing aside, again invoking the need for stability.

In total 70 seats changed hands; the Conservatives finished on 317, down 13 while Labour won 30 and ended up with 262 MPs. There was even a slight recovery for Corbyn's party in the former Scottish heartlands, where half a dozen seats were captured.

Overall, Labour's vote had shot up by a fraction under 10 per cent, the biggest single increase between two elections since 1945. The party took seats in Wales, London, Ipswich, Bristol, Brighton, Derby, Sheffield, Reading, Crewe and beyond.

Though an incredible result against all the odds, it was not a victory. The next day, May was back in Downing Street doing her utmost to make it seem like it was business as usual. Rivals for her job pledged support – they had good reason to do so.

In 2010, the electoral maths prevented Gordon Brown from going full throttle for a progressive coalition. In that election, Labour had come up short in terms of votes and seats, which then allowed the Tories to hug the Lib Dems very close. Corbyn, in 2017, would not have hesitated in building the necessary bridges with other parties, if it allowed him to push a left-wing Labour government into office.

Before June was out, May had secured the support of the Democratic Unionists from Northern Ireland. It was not a formal coalition, but a confidence and supply arrangement built on the promise of a further £1 billion for public services in Ulster.

The hard truth for Labour was that having been written off, the party had unexpectedly ridden the crest of a wave with popular policies of the left, but had still come up short. The Tories were significantly weakened, but opposition still beckoned for Corbyn.

Numerous former critics, among them Deputy Leader Tom Watson and Owen Smith, now sought to praise the Labour leader. 'Mr Corbyn has changed British politics and as such the Labour Party . . . is now a force to be reckoned with in this new parliament', was how James Landale put it for BBC News.[13]

For Labour, it had been a whirlwind few weeks which seemed to defy the rules of political gravity. Corbyn had gone into the election leading a party which had been tearing itself apart for two years. Theresa May's confidence in going to the country had in part been because Labour seemed in a state of disarray.

What she had not considered, or understood, when calling the election, was that Labour had more aces to play than their opponents. Policies, candidates and key messages are all needed well in advance. Even though the Tories held the levers of power they were not ready, and in that regard May's decision was a leveller and a personal disaster.

When it came to the vital matter of funding Labour was in the fortunate position of having strong support from the major unions, in particular Unite. The party's uncommonly healthy bank balance was also a by-product of the huge spikes in membership under Corbyn, a large and highly energised membership which the Tories could not match.

There was a strong mood in the country, especially among the young, that things had to change. This was not just a reaction to austerity, and tuition fees, but came from a general lack of hope in the future. Corbyn's commitment to social and economic justice smashed through the existing Westminster consensus.

Had they been paying attention, May and senior Tories would have seen that Labour's leader, though unorthodox, was able to move people. He had proved it twice to devastating effect in party leadership contests. The opposite was true of May.

In an era in which British general elections are ever more presidential in nature this proved crucial. May soon became a diminished figure, almost literally unable to carry the weight of the campaign. It was a point which did not go unnoticed by the poet laureate, Carol Ann Duffy, who wrote of May 'her body was a question mark'.[14]

For Labour the stars aligned: not only did they have the policies, but a leader who suited the moment. The key actors, the tumult of Brexit, the energising of the youth vote and the widespread use of social media as a campaign tool, all marked 2017 out as singular.

Laura Parker was Jeremy Corbyn's political secretary in 2017 before becoming the national co-ordinator of Momentum. Looking back, in an interview for this book, she believes Corbyn had a particular appeal to voters.

'The truth was here was a guy who talked about love, caring for people, inequality, compassion, homelessness and then odd little things like every child should have the chance to study a musical instrument – but not like some studied Blairite pamphlet. It was just so refreshing,' she said.

Parker is clear that Corbyn was seriously hobbled as leader without the whole party working with him. As she puts it: 'there was a failure to grab the core of the party machine, and this is all completely relevant to the election because in the end there was a parallel election campaign going on.'

'If you have two bits of the triangle – membership and machine or membership and PLP – you can probably just about survive with the third bit of the triangle being at odds with you. But if you have not got the PLP and not got the machine, then you haven't got your hands on the levers of power. So that was a massive structural limitation from day one.'

However, because there had already been a formal bid by MPs to get rid of their leader, Parker thinks there was built-in resilience around Corbyn and his team by the time of the 2017 election. 'We were always ready for a fight, that is the nature of politics, but we had been fighting since the minute Jeremy had won the leadership.'

'We never believed that the policies were as unpopular as the right-wing press would have you believe, or indeed the right wing of the Labour Party. We had a residual confidence and a core commitment and belief how we wanted to change the country.'

She thinks that there was a positive shift by voters during the campaign the more the Labour leader was heard. As she recalls 'people started to see in Jeremy what we had seen in Jeremy. He is a much better campaigner than he is leader of the Parliamentary Party.'

'You had six thousand people queuing in the rain in Gateshead to hear him speak and then you had the Tories with ten people from Conservative Central Office. So [Jeremy's] confidence grew and some people say that if we'd had a bit longer we would have done it.'

Parker stresses the success of a highly effective online campaign which was reaching millions of people via Facebook and other platforms. She is also in no doubt that the Tories helped Labour by trying to place the prime minister at the forefront of their campaign.

'May was a terrible and uninspiring candidate with no sort of personal warmth. That was a factor and people were tired of seven years of austerity . . . it was biting, and Corbyn did offer a very, very clear alternative.'

Aware that the campaign was going well, had the top Labour team gone as far as to plan for life in Downing Street? 'I think we were gob-smacked,' she says of the exit poll 'and then there was just this unfolding series of results, they just kept on rolling in.'

'I'm not sure we ever dared believe we would win, but we already knew that it was a victory of sorts, because we had not been routed and we had deprived the Tories of a majority. We were delighted, and relieved and to a large extent felt vindicated. If you think what Corbyn managed to do with the right-wing media against him and with the machinery of his own party against him, it's amazing.'

'It changed the political fortunes of the left for a time in Parliament because even the worst critics in the PLP had to admit that this was amazing. But what we really wanted to do was to change the country and to change the country we needed to win.'[15]

Just as with Neil Kinnock in 1992 it was revealed that Corbyn had come closer to victory than first realised. Kinnock had lost to John Major by fewer than 1,500 votes, the cumulative figure in seats which would have turned the election had people voted Labour rather than Tory.

In Corbyn's case, a switch of just over 2,000 votes to his party across half a dozen super marginal seats would have given the Labour leader the MPs needed. Then, with the help of smaller parties including the SNP and Lib Dems, Labour could have outvoted the Conservatives, even with the assistance of the DUP.

It would have been highly precarious, but Corbyn would have had the chance to go into Downing Street and make the changes he believed to be necessary – for the many.

2017 General Election Result

Date of Election – 8 June

Overall Turnout – 69.0 %

Labour

Candidates – 631

MPs – 262

Votes – 12,877,858

Percentage share of the vote – 40.0%

Result – Hung Parliament - Conservative minority

Highlight – The first snap election in over 40 years sees Labour's vote share rise by 10%.

Chapter 33

2019 – Cutting the Flowers

'You lost two and a half million voters in
two years, how do you do that?'

Emily Maitlis[1]

With Parliament barely functioning and autumn seeping into winter at the end of October 2019, Jeremy Corbyn announced that Labour had agreed to a general election which would take place in the run-up to Christmas.

Not since 1923 had the country been sent to the polls in the darkness of December. For Corbyn, the first Labour leader since Neil Kinnock to take his party into two successive general elections, this would either be the start of a new chapter in high office, or the full stop of a second defeat.

The coming of the election was a moment long anticipated, as Westminster grappled with the implementation of Brexit, the UK's fateful decision to leave the European Union. After two years of pandemonium in Parliament, the hope of the Conservative prime minister, Boris Johnson, was that he could use the ballot box to decisively shape Brexit and the politics of the looming new decade.

For Labour, this should have been the chance to build on its strong showing of 2017, but the issues facing the party's embattled and divided leadership had become challenging in the extreme.

None of this seemed to knock Corbyn's confidence. After his most senior MPs decided in favour of the Tory plan for an election, Labour's leader outwardly displayed a vigorous optimism, telling the media 'I'm absolutely looking forward to going to every part of the country with my wonderful Shadow Cabinet team . . . to give a message of hope where there isn't one with this government.'[2]

In reality, many in Labour were not at all happy. Johnson was a tough opponent, while the party was at odds over Brexit and anguished by long-standing accusations of anti-Jewish racism.

Yet the fact an election was taking place at all in 2019 was down to the dramatic surge under Corbyn two years earlier. Spearheaded by his energetic campaigning, Labour had deprived Theresa May of her majority; the Conservatives requiring a formal agreement with the Democratic Unionists to remain in office. The by-product of this new political reality was that the government now had less wriggle room in Parliament to conclude the Brexit process.

On this, the clock was ticking. May had triggered Article 50 of the Lisbon Treaty in March 2017 which allowed her only a two-year timeframe in which to fashion a Brexit deal. That summer, as talks with other countries were beginning about the nature of the UK's departure, Labour's leader strode triumphantly onto the stage at the Glastonbury Festival with tens of thousands chanting his name.

It was a moment of rock star adulation which again confirmed the popularity of Corbyn's message, especially with young people. His speech that day ranged across many themes, with calls for world peace, ending homelessness, hunger, poverty and the right of EU nationals to remain in the UK after Brexit.

While for Corbyn domestic issues seemed to be the main concern, it was the European question which was driving British politics. The hard-won capital Labour's leader had built up with the electorate in 2017 would all too soon be spent amid the coming political volatility.

Although the Conservatives were seriously split over Brexit between pro-Leave and pro-Remain wings, Labour had similar fractures. When it came to leaving the EU, or even the nature of that exit, opinion was divided across MPs, Lords, the Shadow Cabinet, the Leader's Office, membership, the trade unions and constituency parties.

Labour's leading lights correctly believed May was now a weak prime minister, hobbled without a majority and facing a restive party. What they did not know was how she could be defeated and replaced by Corbyn, with aides acutely aware that they still faced an internal Labour machine hostile to the leadership.

Emboldened by the unexpectedly positive result in 2017 – described by the BBC as 'the sweetest of defeats' – those closest to Corbyn could at least begin a process of change.[3] Labour's general secretary, Iain McNicol, was replaced by Unite's Jennie Formby, who was personally recruited by Corbyn and John McDonnell, the shadow chancellor.

There was a change in party structure with the appointment of dozens of community organisers, again with the expectation of an approaching election. These were pro-Corbyn Labour staffers imbedded in communities, and working on building up local campaigns.

That this could be done at all was down to the size of the membership which stood at half a million, making Labour one of the biggest political outfits in Western Europe. With this came an annual income of more than £15 million, and on top of that significant rolling donations from the unions.

The membership had been Corbyn's vanguard in the dark days of 2016 when his own MPs had mounted a failed coup. He had no wish to be at odds with his powerbase over the Brexit dilemma.

The rank and file of the party – and most of the electorate – were by this stage in favour of remaining in the EU, but many areas where

Labour was traditionally strong had voted to leave. The party was therefore left in a bind with key elements of its voting coalition pulling it in opposing directions.

This became clear as early as the summer of 2017, when 50 Labour MPs – a fifth of the party in the Commons – voted against the leadership and in favour of an amendment to the Queen's Speech calling for Britain to stay in the Single Market. Frontbenchers who did so were sacked, but this was a marker laid down by those implacably opposed to leaving the EU.

It led to more disputes and contortions, with the leadership keeping Brexit debates away from the floor of Labour's annual conference in September that year. By this stage, the party had also set out six tests to be met if it was to back any deal May managed to secure with Brussels.

Presented by Keir Starmer, as shadow Brexit secretary, these were vague enough to allow wriggle room if required. They focused on providing 'a strong and collaborative future relationship with the EU' and delivering 'the exact same benefits' gained via the single market and customs union.[4]

With the issue of Brexit dominating the Commons, MPs narrowly voted in favour of what was termed a 'meaningful vote' on any withdrawal agreement. Jeremy Corbyn then signalled Labour's intention to retain a close relationship with the EU customs union, to allow tariff-free access to markets.

At the same time, in early 2018, the People's Vote campaign took off. This was powered by a cross-party group of MPs and aimed to win widespread support in the country for a second referendum. As the Official Opposition and therefore the only organisation truly capable of overturning Brexit, Labour came under heavy pressure to back the campaign.

For the People's Vote the strategy was simple – push the Labour frontbench into a position in which they accepted the need for a second vote. To do so, they would use supporters at every level of the party, all suggesting that the greatest threat to Labour going into power was to shy away from putting the question of EU membership to the country once more.

Part of the problem was that this organisation was mainly led either by non-Labour figures or those within the party who were seen as being opposed to Corbyn. Within LOTO – the Labour Leader's Office – People's Vote was viewed as a proxy for destabilising Corbyn.

Across the Shadow Cabinet, there was little clarity on the way ahead on an issue which divided the party: Jon Trickett and Ian Lavery who represented northern English seats were pro-Brexit, while Keir Starmer and Emily Thornberry, both north London MPs, were avowedly pro-European. Others close to Corbyn warned him he risked an historic split, akin to that provoked by Ramsay MacDonald in 1931, if he backed a Tory Brexit.

The second half of 2018 saw things move in both main parties. In July the Brexit secretary David Davis and Boris Johnson, the foreign secretary, both resigned. The pair had been unhappy about the outcome of a Cabinet meeting at Chequers, the PM's country residence, during which it was agreed the UK would accept free trade with the EU and access to the Single Market.

Then, in a speech at a stormy annual conference in Liverpool in September, Keir Starmer warned May that if her government was unable to reach a Brexit deal, Labour would step in. It would do so, the shadow Brexit secretary proclaimed, either via a general election or by campaigning for a public vote on the terms of that departure.

Then came the unscripted coda which both infuriated and delighted delegates, Starmer announcing that 'nobody is ruling out

Remain as an option.'[5] Though Corbyn and others tried to clarify these remarks, the affair simply sowed further confusion and division in the party and beyond.

One of the problems was that LOTO seemed happy to retain an all-options stance. This was fence sitting, though not without reason, given the way Brexit was likely to split the Labour vote.

In January 2019, the prime minister suffered the largest defeat for a government in Commons history over the Brexit Withdrawal Agreement. Labour responded by tabling a no confidence vote, which May won, albeit with assistance from the fringe DUP. In March, she was again defeated when a second meaningful vote was held and soon promised to resign in return for MPs voting through her plans.

Across April and May 2019, the government reached out to Labour to hold talks about finding common ground on the way forward. This was facilitated by the EU granting an October extension to the Article 50 process. Though the discussions were cordial and made some progress, they ended without a deal, Corbyn citing what he called the government's 'increasing weakness and instability'.[6]

What Labour's team had worked out was that May could give no assurances – there was every likelihood that she would be replaced by a new Tory prime minister who would rip up any agreement which had been reached. It was a point highlighted by her party's performance in the elections to the EU Parliament.

Though Britain was in the process of exiting the EU, these were required while the country formally remained a member. For the Conservatives the results were poor, with the party finishing fifth. Framed by Brexit, it was also a disaster for Labour who were beaten into third place by the Brexit Party and the Lib Dems.

The next day, 24 May, an emotional Theresa May announced she was standing down, citing her regret at being unable to deliver Brexit.

By late July, her place had been taken by Boris Johnson. Jeremy Corbyn was now up against his third Tory leader.

It soon became obvious that Johnson did not share his predecessor's cautious approach. At the height of the Brexit crisis, Johnson attempted to impose a long suspension of Parliament to stop what Brexiteer MPs saw as undue influence by the Remain camp on the leaving process.

Though the Supreme Court ruled against the prime minister, he then went on to say that he would rather die in a ditch than oversee another extension to the Brexit deadline.

From this point on, it looked as though the government was prepared to execute a No-Deal or 'cliff edge' Brexit. Then, in late October, Johnson reached for an early general election as a means of breaking the Parliamentary logjam. Like May in 2017, he was seeking to conjure more Tory MPs via the ballot box.

By this stage, Labour was committed to negotiating a new Brexit deal within six months of coming to power, which would then be put to the country in a confirmatory public vote. With the electorate polarised, this stance did nothing to address the growing anger in Labour Leave areas. MPs in these seats were now desperate to get any Brexit deal possible over the line.

Until this point, Jeremy Corbyn had resisted all talk of an election, at least until the possibility of a No-Deal Brexit had been removed. When the EU then agreed to a further delay, until the end of January 2020, things shifted.

No longer could the tide pushed by Johnson be held back. With the pro-EU Scottish Nationalists and Liberal Democrats also now calling for an election Labour could hardly shy away. Making the announcement, Corbyn promised 'the most ambitious and radical campaign for real change our country has ever seen.'[7]

On 29 October, the Commons voted overwhelmingly in favour of setting aside the Fixed Term Parliaments Act and a general election was scheduled for 12 December. Most Labour activists and MPs knew they faced a struggle to maximise the party's vote in the cold days of a winter campaign with minds already turning to Christmas and the holiday season.

Also, what began as a trickle of accusations of anti-Semitism under Corbyn had turned into a flood in the two years from 2017 to 2019. Relations with many Jewish communities and long-established groups, such as the Jewish Labour Movement, plummeted to the point where trust was shattered.

This not only generated a mountain of negative coverage which rolled on across days and weeks – with Corbyn often criticised for past remarks and social media posts – it was also polarising, taking the party close to breaking point.

Some Corbyn supporters were adamant that claims of anti-Jewish racism were being used by hostile political and media figures to tarnish the leadership. Data from the party showed that there had been a few hundred complaints of anti-Semitism relating to Labour members, amounting to 0.1 per cent of the membership.

Nevertheless, campaigners who felt they had genuine grievances were incensed at any downplaying of the scale of the problem, and the fact that Corbyn and his team were unable to draw a line under the issue was highly problematic.

For some MPs all of this, plus Brexit, was too much. Across 2018, there had been growing chatter at Westminster about the prospect of a new 'centrist' party emerging. In February 2019, seven Labour backbenchers resigned to form what was initially called The Independent Group, also including four former Conservative MPs.

On any measure, then, the 2019 election was unlikely to be one favourable to Labour. Memories of 2017 were fresh enough to drive activists, who again came out in their thousands, many believing their work on the ground could be enough to tip the party into power.

As in 2017, Corbyn and his team read the signs and had been preparing for the prospect of an election since the summer. In 2019, they would face a different proposition. The Conservatives, backed by large donations, had updated their party apparatus and campaigning machine. Also, they were now ahead of Labour on social media and targeted online advertising.

While Labour's strains and divisions were all too clear, the Tories were united and determined to run an effective campaign. They began with a commanding lead in the polls and a leader more popular than his opposite number.

From the start, Boris Johnson began hammering home the message that it was time to 'get Brexit done'.[8] The focus was on Leave-leaning seats, especially across the Midlands and the North of England.

Here, in many instances, the Tories had spotted that there had been a rise in votes for their party in 2017, despite the seats returning Labour MPs. These were the constituencies which would come to be dubbed the 'Red Wall' – traditional working-class communities where discontent with Labour had been growing long before the Brexit referendum.

Labour's pitch to the electorate was that they had a once in a generation chance to change the country. It was a framing which deliberately aimed to move the focus away from Brexit, fighting squarely on domestic policy, a strategy which had been so effective two years earlier.

The campaign began badly when the party was mysteriously hit by a cyber-attack on its computers at the Southside HQ. This came on top of rising tensions about who was running and organising the campaign, Labour staffers or Corbyn's people. Meanwhile, the Momentum group was also organising volunteers and pumping out its own online content.

The issue of anti-Semitism continued to flare, with two former Labour MPs, long opposed to Corbyn, saying they would be voting Conservative and urging Labour voters to follow suit. This was followed by a front-page splash by the *Jewish Chronicle* also urging Britons to reject Corbyn, claiming that anti-Semitism in the party had been 'inspired by its leader'.[9]

In response, Labour said it was dealing with complaints at speed, using new disciplinary processes and an education programme to raise awareness of the issue. However, in the context of the election, the damage was done: no party hoping to go into government could reasonably do so under the cloud of alleged racism.

Labour again trusted that their manifesto 'It's Time For Real Change' would chime with the public. This was split into several chapters covering 'A Green Industrial Revolution', 'Rebuild our Public Services', 'Tackle Poverty and Inequality', 'The Final Say on Brexit', 'A New Internationalism'.[10]

There were numerous policies including a £400 billion National Transformation Fund, £250 billion for green transition, a National Education Service, more police, council housing and the nationalisation of water, energy and the railways, as well as free broadband across the country.

Going well beyond the 2017 platform, it stood as an offer which would have taken Britain decisively in a different direction to the journey the country had been on in the previous 40 years.

Corbyn finished his address at the manifesto launch in Birmingham by quoting the words of the Nobel Prize-winning Chilean poet, Pablo Neruda: 'You can cut all the flowers, but you cannot keep Spring from coming,' he said. It was a strikingly lyrical means of depicting change, which few other British political leaders would have used.[11]

Johnson, for his part, stuck to more obvious metaphors: suggesting he had a Brexit deal which was 'oven ready', often citing the idea of slamming this in a microwave and being seen with all manner of food – including pies, doughnuts and fish.[12]

Johnson, too, was evasive in the campaign. There was huge controversy, and no little anger from Labour, when, despite giving assurances, the prime minister then refused to take part in a one-to-one prime time BBC interview with Andrew Neil.

This unwillingness to undergo the forensic questioning other party leaders had already been exposed to was compounded by Johnson at one point pocketing a journalist's phone and, on another occasion, avoiding further inquisition by appearing to retreat to a walk-in fridge.

While Corbyn's team worried about their prospects under an avalanche of negative publicity, they knew their man had to take his key message to as many voters as possible. This included the claim that the future of the NHS post-Brexit had been on the table in trade talks with the United States.

The final few days remained fraught for Labour, with Nigel Farage's Brexit Party reversing its stance and committing not to stand candidates in any of the seats the Tories had won in 2017. It was a period which saw further attacks on Corbyn by Johnson, who claimed the Labour leader was weak on terrorism and had dithered over Brexit.

Voting took place during a long day of downpours across much of the country, with even more wintry conditions in parts of Scotland. This was a gloomy picture for Labour in particular, the Tories having grown ever more confident of victory.

Unlike two years earlier, the exit poll revealed on television at 10 p.m. was met with silence among Labour's senior team watching in

Islington. The projection was that the party would have its worst night since the days of the National Government in 1935.

The Tories were predicted to be on target for a majority of over 80 seats, with Labour dropping below 200 and great swathes of the much-discussed Red Wall – including Blyth Valley, Workington, Bolsover and even Tony Blair's old seat of Sedgefield – turning blue.

By 3.30 a.m., Jeremy Corbyn had been re-elected as MP for Islington North and announced he would resign as Labour leader once a successor was in place. Corbyn felt normal politics had been obscured by Brexit and vowed to 'continue the cause for socialism, for social justice and for a society based on the needs of all rather than the greed of a few'.[13]

Final figures showed Labour with 202 MPs and the Conservatives on 365, giving them a sizable majority of 81, but short of the outright landslide territory which they had hoped for. While traditional Labour areas in parts of England had turned away, in Scotland the nationalists had been resurgent, leaving Labour with just one seat, the position it had found itself in after the defeat of 2015.

In sharp contrast to 2017, senior party figures and media commentators were quick to pin what was a calamitous defeat on Corbyn. As he had been two years earlier, McDonnell was sent out to bat for Labour in the TV studios on the night, and the shadow chancellor made no attempt to run away from the impending defeat.

In an interview for this book, McDonnell said there had been several factors behind Labour's election loss, the main one being the wrangling over leaving the EU.

'It was a Brexit election and there was no way you could manage the Brexit issue within the party successfully. Overwhelming Labour Remain voters – 70 per cent Remainers, party members 80 or

90 per cent – yet we are representing constituencies that voted Brexit,' he reflected.

This had left him seriously worried that Labour was facing an irrevocable split. The political reality was obvious in McDonnell's view: 'all the polling that was coming out was basically demonstrating every time we moved towards a more Brexit position, we lost sizable support, and that sizable support was a lot of our core activist support. So, we were losing our electoral machine as well.'

'So then if you move towards a more Remain position you have then lost a lot of vote support, if you like, in certain constituencies. It was an impossible position. We tried to reconcile; we tried every compromise position you could think of . . . it was just unmanageable.'

In the summer of 2019, McDonnell had been worried by internal polling showing the Tories were likely to win a majority of 150 seats. Labour then simply tried to consolidate its core vote, knowing that an election was likely.

The party was also conscious of the role the media would play when that election was called. As McDonnell put it: 'they had two years more to do character assassination on Jeremy (Corbyn) and it was pulverising. Even Neil (Kinnock), even Ed (Miliband) hadn't experienced anything like this.'

The hoped-for diversion was the offer being made to the public: 'the manifesto was great,' McDonnell said, 'but the way we campaigned on it, throwing out policy and policy in those weeks, enabled them (the Tories and media) to build it up into a lack of credibility.'

He speaks openly about how he feels the media operates towards Labour, by which he means the Tories being given greater latitude. One point which highlights this for McDonnell is the way Johnson wriggled out of the interview with Neil. 'I was so angry, so angry about that.

Jeremy's interview with Andrew Neil was a difficult one to say the least, and then Johnson avoided it and got away with it.'

As for anti-Semitism he believes 'the issue was, did we get ahead of it quickly enough? We tried but we failed, as simple as that. And we now know part of that failure was because as Martin Forde revealed [in a major independent report commissioned by the party post Corbyn] within the bureaucracy itself the disciplinary process was being used for factional purposes.'

McDonnell feels that the party machine inherited in 2015 refused to clarify whether, and at what speed, the recommendations of the 2016 Chakrabarti Report were being implemented. These were changes to improve Labour's disciplinary and complaints processes, as well as a new body to advise on issues, including legal matters.

'I was asking at Shadow Cabinet "had the system been set up, was the legal panel in place, how many cases are we dealing with?" We weren't getting responses on that, and we should have really kicked some arse as a result of it very early on, despite everything Jeremy tried to do. After that then it just snowballed completely out of control. Every interview we went on it (anti-Semitism) was raised.'

Though McDonnell recognises both the seriousness of anti-Semitism and the damage done to Labour in these years, he feels Brexit still dominated and was 'an issue which enabled a traditional right-wing demagogue – Johnson – to use all those nationalist prejudices and mobilise them'.

Labour's job, of course, was to counter how the Tories used Brexit as a tool for division. McDonnell acknowledged this, saying 'how do you overcome that? Well, it's traditional political education all the way through and that is what we need to do now as well.'

'So, you try to build a robust movement that can argue the case. We got some way there to a certain extent, but it was just overwhelming really.' It is a straightforward, honest, answer which at the same time sums up the Corbyn years and extends beyond, to face the future.[14]

2019 General Election Result

Date of Election – 12 December

Overall Turnout – 67.3%

Labour

Candidates – 631

MPs – 202

Votes – 10,295,912

Percentage share of the vote – 32.1%

Result – Conservative government

Highlight – Labour slumps to its lowest number of MPs since the 1930s.

Chapter 34

2024 – All Change

'From now on, you have a government unburdened by doctrine, guided only by the determination to serve your interest.'[1]

Keir Starmer

Landslide is no longer the appropriate word for what Labour achieved in the 2024 general election: it was more an earthquake, which reduced the Conservative Party to rubble. Labour, whose vote share did not actually advance hugely, reaped the benefits of years of careful preparation, of weeks of focused campaigning, leavened with a good dose of anti-Tory tactical voting, to emerge with a monumental victory.

In every part of the country Labour advanced, emerging victorious with a total of 411 seats. The scale of the achievement put the new prime minister, Sir Keir Starmer, into government with a Commons majority of 174, just shy of the figure achieved by Tony Blair in 1997, and comfortably more than that enjoyed by Clement Attlee at the end of the Second World War.

It was a victory which swept the Conservatives from office on the back of their worst ever result, vindicating strategies Starmer had employed that took Labour well beyond its comfort zone.

One example of Starmer's quest to broaden Labour's appeal came in October 2020, when he stomped through the Wiltshire fields of the leader of the National Farmers' Union. It was hardly home turf for the party, and it highlighted a core idea from which there would be no deviation: speak the language of those in the towns and villages of England which knit their way into the great urban centres, and from there success would flow.

Labour also pushed hard to portray itself as a patriotic party. Delegates sang the British national anthem at the annual conference for the first time in 2022. The union flag replaced the red rose as the party's ubiquitous motif: at Labour's national HQ, on party leaflets, membership cards; and flanking Starmer at almost every speech he made. Perhaps all this was a means of moving the party beyond the Brexit schism of the preceding years, or simply a way of harvesting votes in areas which had turned away in 2019. There was a sense also that some in charge of Labour – Morgan McSweeney, Labour's campaign director, and his Labour Together group – felt that this was terrain on which the party belonged.

Strategically, these populist touches could hardly be said to please everyone, but they did little harm to Labour's chances of appearing as a government-in-waiting after the Conservatives collapsed mid-Parliament.

With public trust in the Tories shattered, Labour and Keir Starmer went into the general election of 2024 more confident of victory than at any time since 2001. In late May, shortly after losing close to 500 seats in the English local elections, the prime minister, Rishi Sunak, decided to go to the country and seek a new term in office.

Standing in the pouring rain in Downing Street, Sunak revealed his plan for a six-week campaign, culminating in polling on 4 July. Tory MPs were left astonished and angry at the sudden announcement, and the widespread expectation of the political classes was that an era which had begun with a 2010 sweetheart deal between the Tories and the Liberal Democrats was closing.

Starmer and his Shadow Cabinet had been demanding an election for months and when it arrived Deputy Leader Angela Rayner set the tone, saying 'this is our chance to kick weak Rishi Sunak and his incompetent, chaotic circus out'.[2]

Ramming the message home on day one of the campaign proper, Starmer told his party: 'Change. That is what this general election is about. This is the moment we have been working towards. We must come together to beat the Tories and deliver a Labour government to change Britain for the better'.[3]

There were echoes here of Harold Wilson in the 1960s, the idea of turning Britain around after long years of corrosive Tory rule and harnessing the country's future potential. Starmer spoke less in terms of policies and more of his 'Missions', a means – as he saw it – of fixing long-term problems in the economy, the NHS, green energy supply, education and anti-social behaviour.

Beyond the obvious mantra of change, what all of this meant in real policy terms was harder to pin down, with journalists asking when they would see more substance to flesh out these themes. The game, though, as far as a cautious Labour Party was concerned was not to miss what had become an open goal, with a return to power seeming to be so close at hand.

Starmer's refrain had long been that under his leadership, Labour was no longer the party of Jeremy Corbyn. In a very real sense, this was true. In late 2020 Corbyn had been suspended, then quickly reinstated. But without his having the whip returned, he was unable to sit as a Labour MP. The reason for this was the former leader's response to an investigation into Labour's handling of complaints of anti-Jewish racism by some party supporters during his time in charge.

In 2024, he would stand as an independent in his Islington North seat, a strange set of circumstances for a man who had led Labour over five turbulent years. Other MPs from the left also felt they were being pushed aside. A major row about the future of one of them, Diane Abbott, dominated the first week of Labour's campaign before she was finally given the green light to stand as a candidate.

The sudden calling of the election also precipitated a rush to set in place candidates before the nomination deadline. This saw the high-profile deselection of Faiza Shaheen, another left-wing candidate in north-east London, while several Starmer loyalists on Labour's ruling National Executive were picked at the last minute to stand in rock-solid safe seats.

The approach of the Labour leadership to the party's left wing has been a frequent point of contention across different eras: Neil Kinnock won a high-profile fight with Militant in the 1980s; Tony Blair and Gordon Brown both accepted, and at times worked with, the broad left inside Labour; the same was largely true of Clem Attlee and Hugh Gaitskell with the Bevanites; while Harold Wilson made a point of striving for unity.

The truth is that every Labour leader gets to define the party in their own image. Though historically there are restrictions on this in the form of the annual conference, the NEC and the unions, the power of the leadership has been growing ever since the days of Ramsay MacDonald and Arthur Henderson in the early twentieth century.

Elected as MP for Holborn and St Pancras in 2015, Keir Starmer – named after Labour's first leader, Keir Hardie – took the reins in April 2020, the vacancy arising after Corbyn stood down after having twice failed to take Labour into power.

A former human rights lawyer and director of public prosecutions, Starmer had instantly become the front runner, having played a prominent role on the front bench as the shadow secretary for exiting the European Union.

His campaign, crafted by McSweeney, was powered by members from across the party who saw him as a unifying force who could build on Corbyn's anti-austerity pro-public services offer. In the leadership campaign, Starmer vowed to retain the radicalism of the Corbyn years and end the factionalism which had blighted the party.

He also promised to deal with the anti-Semitism crisis which had beset Labour and focus on returning to government as soon as possible. As Starmer put it on taking up the post: 'Where that requires change, we will change. Where that requires us to rethink, we will rethink.'[4]

Few senior party or trade union figures believed it possible that Labour would be close to power within one electoral cycle of the 2019 defeat, when Boris Johnson had won the biggest Conservative majority since Margaret Thatcher in 1987.

A further handicap to Labour was that their new leader had been crowned during the first months of the Coronavirus pandemic, an issue which would dominate national life and politics with numerous restrictions for two years. During this period Starmer found it difficult to gain traction, be heard by the public at large and stop the Conservatives painting him as someone who wished to keep Britain in a state of lockdown.

So frustrated was the Labour leader that after local election losses and defeat in the Hartlepool by-election in 2021, he considered standing down. Three months later the turning point came, as Labour scraped home in the Batley and Spen by-election by a margin of 300 votes.

As much as Starmer desired to reform his party while holding the exit door open to those unhappy with his direction of travel, elsewhere events were unfolding which would prove pivotal to Labour's chances of success.

Boris Johnson resigned as prime minister in July 2022, rocked by a series of scandals. First came 'Partygate' – gatherings at Downing Street during the Covid lockdowns which contravened the regulations the rest of the country was living under.

The saga dogged his government, damaging the Conservatives, who lost almost 500 council seats in the 2022 local elections. Then, when Johnson promoted the Tory MP Chris Pincher as his deputy chief whip, despite knowing he faced multiple sexual assault allegations, the party turned on the prime minister, forcing him from office.

It was a moment from which the Tories struggled to recover. Not only had they lost a proven election winner, but his replacement, Liz Truss, lasted a mere 45 days in office. On 20 October, she resigned in the wake of a disastrous 'mini budget' which spooked the markets, led to a run on sterling and pushed up mortgage rates against a backdrop of soaring inflation.

Truss's leadership rival, Rishi Sunak, took over in Downing Street with Jeremy Hunt as his chancellor, but as with the 1992 'Black Wednesday' calamity, when Britain was suddenly forced out of the European Exchange Rate Mechanism, any claims the Tories had to be competent stewards of the economy had perished.

Just as John Smith and then Tony Blair had benefited from the fallout from this ERM debacle, which had seen the Conservative government spending billions trying to prop up a faltering pound, so now Starmer and his shadow chancellor, Rachel Reeves, were able to present Labour as sound on the economy.

What Reeves would constantly refer to as their 'fiscal rules' acted as the bedrock of Labour's policy to keep the economy balanced. They were also used as a shield to blunt claims by opponents that Labour would again be a tax-and-spend party.

The fiscal rules were contentious with some sections of Labour, having been cited as the reason for watering down, or refusing to adopt, a range of policies including abolishing tuition fees, green investment targets, lifting the two-child benefit cap and nationalising key areas of industry.

Yet what could not be overlooked was that following Truss's brief tenure in office, the polls barely ever moved in the Conservatives' favour. Having been in front since late 2021, Labour was often ahead by 20 points or more.

Starmer presided over the dominant political force in the land and, though the party had not wholly been at peace with itself since 2019, in contrast to the Conservatives, Labour looked highly professional and credible. The party spoke of national renewal, its ambition to 'get Britain's future back', and Labour being 'back in the service of working people'.[5]

In 1979 Jim Callaghan identified a generational sea change against Labour. Now the tide had turned in Labour's favour. Reflecting general public opinion, the press reported an anti-Conservative feeling across the country. Regardless, shadow ministers were careful not to be seen to be taking the electorate for granted, always prefacing their remarks in the media with phrases such as 'if Labour has the privilege of forming the next government'.[6]

In an unusually long campaign Labour also had to guard against complacency and apathy, in a bid to maximize its vote. Just as in 1970 with the unexpected loss to Ted Heath, this election would be held during a major international football tournament, the European Championship, with England expected to do well and Scotland also featuring, prompting fears that a focus on football might turn the electorate's attention away from politics.

One issue which had been of concern earlier in the year was the deep anger felt across Labour's urban base about the huge civilian death toll in Gaza because of Israel's military response to the Hamas terrorist attacks in October 2023. For many, not only Muslim voters, the party had been too slow to support calls for a ceasefire. There had already been a political cost to this, with Labour losing the Rochdale by-election to George Galloway in February 2024.

For Labour the campaign was generally a very smooth and disciplined affair. As the days wore on, and the weather warmed (a little) Starmer remained the focus, appearing daily and tirelessly at campaign events up and down the country.

He had shown hesitation in the first televised debate on ITV on 4 June when the prime minister repeatedly claimed Labour would raise taxes by £2,000 per working household. Over the following days, the Office for Statistics Regulation – the UK's official statistics watchdog – and the BBC both suggested Sunak's figures could be seen as misleading.

Starmer went further, saying the prime minister 'knew he was lying'.[7] It was an important moment, and one which demonstrated that Labour would shut down spurious attacks on their taxation plans such as those which had so damaged Neil Kinnock's chances in 1992.

Starmer's efforts to appear responsible on the economy were reinforced when he explicitly ruled out any increases to income tax, national insurance and VAT. At the launch of the Labour manifesto on 13 June in Manchester, these tunes and some familiar others were played again. Starmer spoke of growing the economy, of wealth creation, new rights for workers and bringing the railways back into public hands.

Notably, he pledged that under a Labour government there would be no return to austerity and that Britain had the chance to take a different path. Critics, though, pointed out that there had been a quiet acceptance of existing spending plans which were likely to see year-on-year cuts in some government departments of between 2 to 3.5 per cent.

The manifesto itself – dubbed by insiders a 'short campaigning document' – was simply titled 'Change', that one word featuring on the cover beside a picture of a serious-looking Starmer. The Conservative manifesto had no images of Sunak on its cover, instead containing only the slogans 'Clear Plan, Bold Action, Secure Future'.[8] At its heart were plans for lower taxes and reducing immigration levels. Having gone from 'It's Time For Real Change' in 2019 as a manifesto slogan, it seemed that Labour had finally mastered the art of encapsulating its message in one brief word or phrase, but that the Conservatives had forgotten it.

A fortnight from election day, with some polls showing Starmer's party set to win more than 450 seats, senior Tories began to warn against Labour achieving what they termed a 'supermajority'. Political commentators immediately sensed the underlying message: the Conservatives were tacitly accepting a Labour victory and appealing to voters to limit the scale of defeat.

In calling the election when he did, Sunak had hoped that the first signs of a possible economic recovery, with inflation at its lowest for almost three years (the Consumer Prices Index was running at 2.3 per cent in April), would allow his party to creep over 30 per cent in the polls and close the gap with Labour.

What Sunak had not foreseen was the return of arch-Brexiteer Nigel Farage as leader of Reform UK, and with it a major boost in the polls for that party. In the 2019 election Farage had removed Brexit Party candidates from all seats then held by the Conservatives, while at the same time going full throttle against Labour.

In 2024, in contrast, Labour seemed likely to be the chief beneficiaries of Farage's re-emergence. It was a moment which signposted the potential of an historic split on the right of British politics, a mirror image of the SDP/Labour rupture of the 1980s.

From the outset the Tory campaign was chaotic and error prone, with Sunak at times flirting with ridicule and at others prompting outright anger. The prime minister was first widely derided for a plan, never previously mentioned, to bring back mandatory national service for 18-year-olds. Not only did this seem wildly unpopular, but it allowed Labour the opportunity to say it was an uncosted pledge running to several billion pounds.

In early June, Sunak made a catastrophic decision to leave the D-Day 80th anniversary commemorations early to give a political interview. Keir Starmer, in contrast, remained in France looking for all the world as though he were already prime minister. It was a moment which not only riled sections of the media normally sympathetic to the Conservatives, but also angered veterans and the wider public, forcing Sunak into an apology.

A major scandal then erupted over allegations that bets had been placed on the date of the election by those who may have had inside information. The Gambling Commission began an investigation which, in the main, centered on several Conservative candidates, Tory officials and police officers.

In the meantime, Labour remained focused and largely untroubled. Prominently featured alongside the leader himself were Rachel Reeves, Angela Rayner, Wes Streeting and Pat McFadden, who was national campaign co-ordinator and a pivotal figure close to Starmer.

Across the country, Labour strategists concentrated on what they termed 'battleground' and 'non-battleground' areas. With most constituencies modified by boundary changes, more than 250 seats were identified which could be won, compared with just over 20 which merited defensive resources.

In short, Labour was on the front foot, driving into areas which had become winnable, or which the party believed should have been won in 2019. To execute this, many candidates and activists were explicitly told how and where they could campaign. Not always a happy arrangement, this left prospective MPs dividing their time between twinned seats the party was sending them to, while trying to retain some visibility in their own area.

There was also a marked difference with the two previous election campaigns of 2017 and 2019. Those had seen no shortage of committed volunteers, very often from the left of the party, but in 2024 Labour was working with a somewhat reduced ground operation, often making the most of local councillors and longstanding active members. Despite a reduction in numbers, the party knew it could still more than compete with the Conservatives on the streets and doorsteps.

The other element was the so-called 'air war' across the media and wider communications outlets. In this area, Starmer's party was boosted by the endorsement of *The Economist*, *The Sunday Times* and *The Sun* newspapers, in each case for the first time since 2005.

Campaign messages were pushed out to voters most prominently on social media, including TikTok, where the parties hoped to appeal to young and first-time voters. Labour also moved quickly to buy up online advertising space, even in traditionally hostile newspapers, dominating these during the closing days of the campaign.

This was a confident move from a confident party, but one which required significant expenditure. That Labour under Starmer was able to afford this was because now it could rely not only on trade union contributions but – in contrast to the Miliband and Corbyn eras – it was also benefiting from a significant rise in large private donations from super-wealthy individuals.

None of this stopped the party asking for small donations from members, with emails and text messages being pumped out often twice daily. These appeals came from David Evans, the party's general secretary, Angela Rayner, Starmer and others.

The day before the election, Mel Stride, a Tory cabinet minister, admitted that his party was set to be defeated, while Suella Braverman, the former home secretary, raised the prospect of the Tories ceasing to exist as a meaningful political entity.

Both Keir Starmer and Rishi Sunak went to vote with their wives, the Labour leader being greeted by several well-wishers. The expectation in almost every quarter was that Labour would win handsomely.

However, at 5 p.m., the party gave its members a scare, sending out a text message which read 'DO NOT SHARE 100 seats look too close to call', and urgently asking for more volunteers.[9] Whatever the motive, it underscored how party strategists were leaving nothing to chance in their efforts to maximize the vote.

The exit poll, released at 10 p.m., revealed the UK was heading for a seismic political shift. Labour was projected to have won 410 seats, a majority of 170. Though senior Labour figures, including Angela Rayner, did all they could during their television appearances to mask their delight at what was still just a projection, in truth it was a moment of unbridled celebration across the party and wider Labour movement.

The exit poll was confirmation that the polls had been right not only for weeks but many months, with the Conservatives expected to win in just 131 constituencies. According to the psephologists, the Liberal Democrats would comfortably again be the third party in the Commons.

When results began to come in, they were broadly in line with these expectations, and before dawn broke Sunak revealed that he had called the Labour leader to congratulate him on his victory, one which made Starmer Labour's seventh prime minister and just the fifth to win from opposition.

The final picture showed only a slight deviation from the exit poll. Labour would have 411 seats in the new House of Commons, an increase of 209, while the Conservatives sank to their worst result in modern history with just 121 MPs. Outside the era of the National

Government in the 1930s, this left the Tories with the lowest number of seats for a second party in over 200 years.

Labour strengthened in Wales and roared again in Scotland, gaining 36 seats there, ending the Westminster dominance of the Scottish National Party which had been in place since 2015.

Not all results went Labour's way. Jeremy Corbyn won comfortably in Islington North, where he stood as an independent, describing the result as 'a warning to the incoming government that dissent cannot be crushed without consequences'.[10]

Although Rochdale was retaken, independents who stood on a platform of highlighting the issue of Gaza had a good night, taking four seats from Labour, including that of the shadow paymaster general, Jonathan Ashworth, and coming close to unseating several others. Ashworth was not the only high-profile loss: Thangam Debbonaire, the shadow culture secretary, was defeated by the Green Party in Bristol.

In keeping with British politics since 2010, the overall results demonstrated an increasing volatility in the electorate. Not only had there been a sharp movement from Tory to Labour, but Reform had surged to five seats, with Farage winning in Clacton.

In an interview for this book on the weekend following the election Thangam Debbonaire reflected on the unpredictability of the electorate and the dangers for Labour. As she put it 'the volatility is everywhere, the volatility isn't just in Bristol Central, I think it is everywhere. It may have different sentiment, but it has possibly similar sort of outputs in terms of dissatisfaction with politics as usual.'

'For those of us who lost and those who had a very difficult fight I think there are lessons [for Labour] to learn electorally, politically and in terms of public discourse.'

Debbonaire's concern is how Labour deals in government with the emerging threat to its base from not only the Greens, but also from

Reform and independent candidates who have proven it is possible to make their mark using a single issue, in this case the conflict in the Middle East.

She remains proud of her own efforts to bring about a Labour government, resolute in support for Keir Starmer and his task of changing Britain. Her hope is that Labour will be able to 'tell a new story and sing a new song'; doing so, she believes, 'can start to bring the country back together and then start peeling away the more divisive forces that do surround us'.[11]

Much of what Debbonaire is concerned with reflects the oddness of the numbers in this election. While the country had resolved to rid itself of a deeply unpopular government, only 60 per cent of the electorate had taken part, a low turnout figure last witnessed in 2001.

Labour won with just 33.7 per cent of the vote, a tiny increase on its share in 2019 and well down on the 2017 figure. Just 9.7 million people voted Labour, down from the 10.3 million in what had been an historic defeat under Corbyn.

Immediately after the election Sir John Curtice, the polling guru who had overseen the exit poll, wrote that 'in the most disproportional electoral outcome in British electoral history, Labour's strength in the new House of Commons is a heavily exaggerated reflection of the party's limited popularity in the country'.[12]

Understandably, 2019 is often cited as a dismal episode for Labour, but crucially the party then had been able to win enough seats to retain an effective strength in Parliament, far stronger than the Conservatives, bruised by the rise of Reform, find themselves in 2024.

Labour's task in 2019 was to build from its low base, using that as a platform for future elections. This it did successfully, in part because of the unique relationship between the party at all levels and the unions from which it draws such strength.

After what had not really been a deeply ideological election for the party, the question now is no longer about how Labour wins, but rather what it does with victory and how it pivots from the idea of change to its delivery.

Having walked up Downing Street with his wife Victoria, and having stopped to speak to friends, family and colleagues in an echo of 1997, Starmer addressed the country for the first time as prime minister, saying 'You have given us a clear mandate, and we will use it to deliver change, to restore service and respect to politics. End the era of noisy performance. Tread more lightly on your lives and unite our country.'

'With respect and humility, I invite you all to join this government of service in the mission of national renewal. Our work is urgent, and we begin it today.'[13]

It was a message designed to reach all parts of the country, including former Tory heartlands, with the reiteration of the 'invitation to join the government' message so prominently used by David Cameron in the Conservative manifesto of 2010. Quite understandably, Labour was keen to make the point that they now occupied swathes of former Conservative territory and had no intention of retreating from there in the coming years.

Yet just as it was in 1945, the basic political desire remains among the population – the country still wants food, work and homes, educational opportunity and much else. Only when these issues have been addressed will people feel their country has turned a corner and Labour has truly offered them sight of a brighter future.

That is the huge task Keir Starmer and his ministers face, now that they occupy the corridors of power, the great offices of state and sit together at the Cabinet table for the first time in 14 long years in the wilderness.

2024 General Election Result

Date of Election – 4 July

Overall Turnout – 59.7%

Labour

Candidates – 631

MPs – 411

Votes – 9,708,716

Percentage share of the vote – 33.7%

Result – Labour government

Highlight – Labour wins a huge landslide – the fifth in the party's history, but on an historically low share of the vote. Keir Starmer becomes the seventh Labour Prime Minister.

ACKNOWLEDGEMENTS

Without the kindness and encouragement of many people this book would never have seen the light of day.

As ever, I'd be nothing without my wife Lindsey who offered endless patience and considerable support. I am also grateful to my agent, David Luxton, who believed in this project from the off and was always a calm and reassuring presence.

It has been my good fortune to work with the brilliant team at Elliot and Thompson – with thanks to Amy Greaves, Claire Maxwell, Pippa Crane and especially my publisher, Katie Bond, who saw the book as clearly as I had and remained both enthusiastic and wise as we navigated our way to publication. I'd also like to thank Philip Parker for his admirable editing skills and my friend Peter Schiazza for his photography.

Most of the people I approached for interview were forthcoming and understood the value of telling Labour's story from their first-hand experiences. I'm deeply indebted to all who gave their time so generously.

My son Aidan made many helpful suggestions during our discussions on long walks, while my friend Rhianna Louise offered insights into publishing and inspired me to press ahead in the early days.

Others dear to me were supportive and on hand with thoughtful comments as I progressed – among them Cliff Graham, Jason Hall, David McVittie, Raphael Honigstein, Hugo Cornejo, Carmel Nolan, Rachel Jupp, Jonathan Wald, Mike Collett, Simon Thomson, Mike Crook, Sian Jones and Liz Warren Corney.

The staff at the Bishopsgate Library were incredibly helpful, similarly Russell and the archivists at the People's History Museum in Manchester, David Tobin at Walden Books and the Labour History Group.

This volume builds on the efforts of numerous other journalists and academics who have preserved our election stories over many previous decades and I took much inspiration from the writer, broadcaster and fellow pond swimmer, Steve Richards, who has deep knowledge of the Labour Party and politics beyond.

My eternal thanks to all.

Endnotes

Introduction

1 The many not the few – https://labourlist.org/2014/04/keir-hardies-sunshineof-socialism-speech-full-text/
2 Alastair Campbell – interview with the author.
3 Gordon Brown's maiden speech – https://www.theyworkforyou.com/debates/?id=1983-07-27a.1226.0&
4 Keir Hardie – sunshine of socialism – https://labourlist.org/2014/04/keirhardies-sunshine-of-socialism-speech-full-text/

1893 – A Distinct Labour group

1 Clement Attlee – Francis Williams, *Fifty Years March* p. 5
2 The Labour Party – https://labour.org.uk/
3 Alfred H. Havighurst, *Britain in Transition* p. 15
4 Keir Hardie – quoted in *The Guardian* – https://www.theguardian.com/politics/2020/feb/28/founding-of-the-labour-party-1900

1900 – The Khaki Two

1 Labour manifesto 1900 en rule http://labourmanifesto.com/1900/1900-labour-manifesto.shtml
2 *The Guardian* – https://www.theguardian.com/politics/2020/feb/28/founding-of-the-labour-party-1900
3 Henry Pelling, *A Short History of the Labour Party* p. 10
4 Keir Hardie's *Speeches and Writings* p. 104
5 *South Wales Daily Post* quoted in Nation Cymru – https://nation.cymru/culture/the-true-story-of-how-merthyr-elected-keir-hardie-as-labours-first-mp/
6 *Labour Leader* newspaper – Sunday 27 October 1900 https://www.britishnewspaperarchive.co.uk/viewer/bl/0002734/19001027/058/0008
7 Iain Dale (edited), *Labour Party General Election Manifestos 1900–1997* p. 8

1906 – A New Party in Parliament

1 Labour Party annual conference report 1906 – quoted from *The Book of the Labour Party* Vol.full point. I p. 141

2   Keir Hardie via A. K. Russell, *Liberal Landslide* p. 209
3   *Labour Party General Election Manifestos* 1900–1997 p. 10
4   Quoted from Ralph Miliband, *Parliamentary Socialism* p. 20
5   Kenneth Morgan, Liberal History https://liberalhistory.org.uk/wp-content/uploads/2015/07/51-Morgan-1906-Blissful-Dawn.pdf
6   Philip Snowden via A. K. Russell, *Liberal Landslide* p. 209

1910 (January) – Does Labour Count?
1   Arthur Henderson – *Durham Chronicle*, 6 January 1911
2   David Lloyd George – quoted in Alfred H. Havighurst, *Britain in Transition* p. 96
3   Ibid. – p. 98
4   Parliament website – https://publications.parliament.uk/pa/ld200506/ldselect/ldconst/141/14104.htm
5   The Labour Party General Election manifesto January 1910 – http://www.labour-party.org.uk/manifestos/1910/jan/1910-jan-labour-manifesto.shtml
6   House of Lords 21 December 1909 via – https://www.historyandpolicy.org/policy-papers/papers/the-osborne-judgement-of-1909-trade-union-funding-of-political-parties-in-h
7   Herbert Asquith – Liberal Manifesto 1910 – http://www.libdems.co.uk/manifestos/1910/jan/january-1910-liberal-manifesto.shtml
8   In his biography 'Keir Hardie', Iain McLean (P140) says that KH had bitterly told the 1910 conference of the ILP that 'At the present time the Labour Party has almost ceased to count.'

1910 (December) – Labour Clears the Way
1   Labour leaflet number 49 – quoted from – Keith Laybourn, *The Labour Party 1881-1951* p. 69
2   David Lloyd George – quoted in the *Yorkshire Observer*, November 12 1910 – https://blogs.bodleian.ox.ac.uk/archivesandmanuscripts/2011/09/23/100-years-ago-constitutional-crisis-and-the-parliament-act-of-1911/
3   *James Ramsay MacDonald and the Problem of the Independence of the Labour Party, 1910-1914* – https://www.jstor.org/stable/1905942?read-now=1&seq=3#page_scan_tab_contents
4   Conservative Party manifesto December 1910 – http://www.conservativemanifesto.com/1910/dec/december-1910-conservative-manifesto.shtml#:~:text=They%20have%20selected%20the%20season,which%20keeps%20them%20in%20office

5   Labour party manifesto – http://www.labour-party.org.uk/
manifestos/1910/dec/1910-dec-labour-manifesto.shtml

1918 – Everything Changes

1   J. A. Hobson https://spartacus-educational.com/PRgeorge.htm

2   Arthur Henderson, Labour Party Conference 1917 – quoted in Alfred H.
Havighurst, *Britain in Transition* p. 138

3   History Today https://www.historytoday.com/archive/labour-party-and-
clause-four-1918-1995

4   Labour manifesto, 1918 – http://www.labour-party.org.uk/
manifestos/1918/1918-labour-manifesto.shtml

5   Herbert Tracey, *Book of the Labour Party*, Vol. I, p. 232

1922 – Unrest and Development

1   J. R. Clynes – *Halifax Evening Courier* 11 February 1919

2   Beatrice Webb – Henry Pelling *A Short History of the Labour Party* p. 46

3   Labour Party manifesto 1922, Dennis Kavanagh & Iain Dale, *Labour Party
General Election Manifestos 1900-1997*, p. 19

4   Labour Party Annual Report 1921

5   Alfred H. Havighurst, *Britain in Transition* p. 160

6   Conservative Party manifesto 1922 – http://www.conservativemanifesto.
com/1922/1922-conservative-manifesto.shtml

1923 – Fail or Succeed – Labour in Government

1   *The English Review* – quoted in Ralph Miliband, *Parliamentary Socialism*
p. 99

2   Annual Register via Gov.UK – https://history.blog.gov.uk/2014/01/22/
whats-the-context-britains-first-labour-government-takes-office-22-
january-1924/

3   David Marquand, *Ramsay MacDonald* p. 256

4   Labour Party manifesto 1923 http://www.labour-party.org.uk/
manifestos/1923/1923-labour-manifesto.shtml

5   Ibid.

6   David Lloyd George – https://www.expressandstar.com/news/
politics/2018/11/23/a-fit-country-for-heroes-100-years-since-lloyd-
georges-legendary-wolverhampton-speech/

7   Winston Churchill, quoted in Ralph Miliband, *Parliamentary Socialism*
p. 99

8   The Guardian 22 January 1924 – https://www.theguardian.com/politics/2024/jan/22/ramsay-macdonald-forms-britains-first-labour-government-1924

9   J. R. Clynes, *Memoirs*

1924 – Red October

1   Ramsay MacDonald, quoted in the *Daily News* (London) – Tuesday 28 October 1924 https://www.britishnewspaperarchive.co.uk/viewer/bl/0003212/19241028/205/0001

2   The Campbell Case – N. D. Siederer https://www.proquest.com/openview/88b785657a047e5ca5c3fe6c69471d1c/1?pq-origsite=gscholar&cbl=1819031

3   Ramsay MacDonald quoted in Ralph Miliband, *Parliamentary Socialism* p. 115

4   James Maxton – quoted in Martin Pugh, *Speak for Britain* p. 184

5   *The Daily Mail* via Warwick Digital Collections https://wdc.contentdm.oclc.org/digital/collection/russian/id/2595/

6   Labour Party Manifesto 1924 – http://www.labour-party.org.uk/manifestos/1924/1924-labour-manifesto.shtml

7   Conservative Party Manifesto 1924 — http://www.conservativemanifesto.com/1924/1924-conservative-manifesto.shtml

1929 – Striking Back

1   *The Scotsman* 1 June 1929

2   Ramsay MacDonald 1929 Radio address — https://www.youtube.com/watch?v=h3_RsaNzau4

3   Historic UK — https://www.historic-uk.com/HistoryUK/HistoryofBritain/General-Strike-1926/

4   *The Daily Mail* 6 May 1926 – https://wdc.contentdm.oclc.org/digital/collection/strike/id/80

5   Ramsay MacDonald quoted in Ralph Miliband, *Parliamentary Socialism* p. 135

6   Ramsay MacDonald – Hansard https://hansard.parliament.uk/Commons/1926-05-13/debates/d1b280f9-a9f0-4337-bdba-3a1378fb3afa/GeneralStrikeMrMacdonaldSSpeech

7   Stanley Baldwin — The British General Election 1929 Report – CQ Researcher https://library.cqpress.com/cqresearcher/document.php?id=cqresrre1929050600

8   *The Daily Mail* – Quoted in Martin Pugh, *Speak for Britain* p. 199

9   Philip Snowden quoted in *The Scotsman* 1 June 1929

10   Ramsay MacDonald via British Movietone News – https://www.youtube.com/watch?v=kuP_mUMbMTs

1931 – Depression and Betrayal

1   John Wheatley quoted in Martin Pugh, *Speak for Britain* – p. 184.

2   Philip Snowden via https://www.billjaneway.com/the-1931-sterling-crisis

3   Ramsay MacDonald – quoted in Ralph Miliband, *Parliamentary Socialism* p. 176

4   George V's private secretary quoted in Alfred Havighurst, *Britain in Transition* p. 223

5   Ramsay MacDonald quoted in Ralph Miliband, *Parliamentary Socialism* p. 161

6   Anti MacDonald rhyme – quoted in Keith Laybourn, *The Labour Party 1881–1951*

7   Philip Snowden – quoted in Martin Pugh, *Speak for Britain* p. 215

1935 – The Rising Tide

1   Labour Party manifesto 1935 – http://www.labour-party.org.uk/manifestos/1935/1935-labour-manifesto.shtml

2   Independent Labour Party, quoted via Ralph Miliband, *Parliamentary Socialism* p. 194

3   Labour annual conference – via Alfred Havighurst, *Britain in Transition* p. 243

4   New Statesman and Nation – quoted in Alfred H. Havighurst, *Britain in Transition* p. 249

5   *A Life on the Left: George Lansbury (1859–1940): A Case Study in Recent Labour Biography*, John Shepherd – https://www.jstor.org/stable/27516003?read-now=1&seq=15#page_scan_tab_contents

6   Stanley Baldwin via British Paramount News – https://www.youtube.com/watch?v=-q0jw8PlJB4

7   Clement Attlee – Ibid.

8   *Daily Mirror* – 14 November 1935 – https://www.britishnewspaperarchive.co.uk/viewer/bl/0000560/19351114/093/0011)

9   Clement Attlee – *Northern Daily Mail* Saturday 16 November 1935 – https://www.britishnewspaperarchive.co.uk/viewer/bl/0000378/19351116/139/0005

1945 – Winning the Peace

1   J. B. Priestley – quoted in Alfred Havighurst, *Britain in Transition* p. 243

2   Leo Amery quoted in Kenneth Harris, *Attlee* p. 166

3   Beveridge Report – https://www.sochealth.co.uk/national-health-service/public-health-and-wellbeing/beveridge-report/

4   *The Times* 2 December 1945 and the *Economist* 5 December 1945 – quoted in Alfred Havighurst *Britain in Transition* p. 331

5   Ellen Wilkinson Quoted in *Labour Party Report 1945* – Published by Transport House. Chairman's Address – Ellen Wilkinson MP p. 80

6   Labour Party manifesto 1945 – http://www.labour-party.org.uk/manifestos/1945/1945-labour-manifesto.shtml

7   Ibid.

8   Churchill Pathé News – https://www.gresham.ac.uk/watch-now/general-election-1945

9   *New York Time*s – Friday 27 July 1945

10 *Evening Standard* – https://twitter.com/fisherandrew79/status/1551839672942346240

11 *Daily Mirror* – https://www.agefotostock.com/age/en/details-photo/1945-daily-mirror-front-page-reporting-clement-atlee-wins-british-general-election-for-labour/MEV-11113233

12 Attlee and King George VI quoted in Francis Beckett, *Clem Attlee*

13 Attlee quoted in Kenneth Morgan, *Labour People* p. 135

14 Denis Healey – BBC The 1945 General Election – https://www.youtube.com/watch/SWXtbg3gUJw

15 *Daily Mirror*, quoted in Martin Pugh, *Speak for Britain* p. 276

16 Harold Macmillan via History Extra – https://www.historyextra.com/period/second-world-war/ask-your-father-the-general-election-of-1945/

17 Churchill via Gresham College 1945 general election lecture – https://www.gresham.ac.uk/watch-now/general-election-1945

18 Clement Attlee quoted from British Pathé News – https://www.youtube.com/watch?v=oBnbXgl-_pU

1950 – A Sharp Kick in the Pants

1   The Red Flag https://www.marxists.org/subject/art/music/lyrics/en/red-flag.htm

2   Nye Bevan – *Hansard House of Commons Debates*, vol. 422, cols. 43–63, 30 April 1946

3   Ernest Bevin quoted in Alfred Havighurst, *Britain in Transition* p. 409

4   Hartley Shawcross – *Hansard House of Commons Debates 02 April 1946 vol 421*, cc1112–217

5   Labour manifesto 1950 – http://www.labour-party.org.uk/manifestos/1950/1950-labour-manifesto.shtml

6   Winston Churchill – https://winstonchurchill.org/publications/churchill-bulletin/bulletin-075-sep-2014/churchills-1950-election-message-on-film/

7   Mr Cube Tate and Lyle via the *Financial Times* – https://www.ft.com/content/001e0dc6-2503-11df-a189-00144feab49a

8   Clement Attlee – Alfred Havighurst, *Britain in Transition* p. 430

9   Nye Bevan – https://www.mojologic.com.au/speech-10-aneurin-bevin-they-are-lower-than-vermin/

10 Clement Attlee quoted in Kenneth Harris, *Attlee* p. 446

11 Herbert Morrison – quoted in The Critic https://thecritic.co.uk/masters-no-more-clement-attlee-and-the-revolt-of-the-suburbs/

1951 – Forward or Backwards

1   Nye Bevan via *The Guardian* https://www.theguardian.com/politics/2003/jul/29/comment.labour

2   Clement Attlee – *The New Statesman* – quoted in Kenneth Harris, *Attlee* p. 486

3   Nye Bevan – https://licc.org.uk/resources/nhs/

4   Hugh Gaitskell – via Tides of History – https://tidesofhistory.com/2020/05/07/nye-bevan-quits-the-dawn-of-labours-divisive-decade/

5   *Daily Express* via Ralph Miliband, *Parliamentary Socialism* p. 314

6   British Pathé – Britain to Vote https://www.youtube.com/watch?v=f4BlCJAY2dU

7   *British Journal of Sociology*, Sept 1962 – quoted in Michael Lynch, *Britain 1900–57*

8   Conservative Manifesto 1951 – http://www.conservativemanifesto.com/1951/1951-conservative-manifesto.shtml

9   Labour Manifesto 1951, http://www.labour-party.org.uk/manifestos/1951/1951-labour-manifesto.shtml

10 Ibid.

11 Richard Crossman – the *New Statesman*, 19 April 1963

12 Winston Churchill quoted in – Kenneth Morgan, *Labour in Power, 1945–1951*, p. 412

1955 – Fighting Snow White

1   Rab Butler quoted in Michael Lynch *Britain 1900–57* p. 221

2   Anthony Eden quoted in *The Scotsman* 16 April 1955

3   Clement Attlee via the Press Association Wednesday April 20, 1955 –
    https://www.britishnewspaperarchive.co.uk/viewer/bl/0000769/
    19550420/010/0001

4   Sir Winston Churchill via Politico – https://www.politico.com/story/
    2019/04/05/winston-churchill-resigns-1955-1250726

5   Lord Cherwell – quoted in David Marquand, *Britain Since 1918* p. 153

6   *Lancaster Guardian* – https://www.lancasterguardian.co.uk/heritage-and-
    retro/retro/labour-party-conference-in-morecambe-70-years-ago-was-
    rowdy-affair-3845495

7   Manny Shinwell quoted – https://www.bbc.co.uk/news/special/politics97/
    background/pastelec/ge55.shtml

8   Attlee quoted in Kenneth Harris, *Attlee* p. 533

9   Ibid.

10 BBC TV Sir Anthony Eden takes questions from the press – https://www.
    youtube.com/watch?v=Kq-_Bpl6Oy8&t=3s

11 Ibid.

12 BBC TV coverage – https://www.youtube.com/watch?v=i1IvM-VKqL8

13 Ibid.

14 Clement Attlee – quoted in Kenneth Harris, *Attlee* p. 534

1959 – The Struggle Continues

1   Clement Attlee – quoted in Kenneth Harris, *Attlee* p. 537

2   Nye Bevan quoted – https://www.bbc.co.uk/programmes/p01b77rk

3   Harold Macmillan quoted via BBC – http://news.bbc.co.uk/onthisday/hi/
    dates/stories/january/10/newsid_3783000/3783251.stm

4   Harold Macmillan – Guardian obituary –https://www.theguardian.com/
    politics/1986/dec/30/obituaries

5   Nye Bevan – https://www.theguardian.com/politics/2015/sep/25/10-best-
    labour-conference-speeches-andrew-rawnsley

6   Harold Wilson – see Andrew Thorpe *A History of the British Labour Party*
    p. 150

7   Quoted via BBC Politics – https://www.bbc.co.uk/news/special/
    politics97/background/pastelec/ge59.shtml

8   1959 General Election posters – via David Butler and Richard Rose, *The
    British General Election of 1959*

9   Labour Party election broadcast – see You Tube (timecode – 08.00)
    https://www.youtube.com/watch?v=NeOidaboxM4

10   Nye Bevan quoted – *The Independent* – https://www.independent.co.uk/
     voices/sleight-of-hand-from-a-wouldbe-chancellor-1284336.html

11   Hugh Gaitskell quoted – BBC TV election night 1959 part II –
     https://www.youtube.com/watch?v=UOv79m389_w

12   Ibid – Gaitskell BBC 1959 coverage Pt3 Timed – 7.12 ends –
     https://www.youtube.com/watch?v=K7IOe0hG5E8

1964 – The New Britain

1   Harold Wilson via *The Guardian* – https://www.theguardian.com/
     century/1960-1969/Story/0,,105651,00.html

2   Clause IV quoted in http://www.labourcounts.com/Clause_four_
     comparisons.htm

3   Nye Bevan – via Tribune – https://tribunemag.co.uk/2020/03/tides-of-
     history

4   Hugh Gaitskell – quoted via *The Guardian* https://www.theguardian.com/
     politics/2001/sep/19/labourconference.labour

5   The BBC reporting on Gaitskell's death http://news.bbc.co.uk/onthisday/
     low/dates/stories/january/18/newsid_3376000/3376971.stm

6   Harold Wilson – see Wright and Carter, *The People's Party*, p. 100

7   Harold Wilson – quoted in Alfred Havighurst, *Britain in Transition* p. 502

8   Labour posters see V&A – https://collections.vam.ac.uk/item/O548127/
     lets-go-with-labour-and-poster-boswell-james/

9   Douglas-Home – *The New York Times* 16 September 1964 – https://www.
     nytimes.com/1964/09/18/archives/rise-in-prosperity-pledged-by-home.
     html

10   BBC Election Coverage 1964 – Part 8 see timecode 1.hr 02 mins
     https://www.youtube.com/watch?v=7V7vdCfMDYg

11   *The Guardian* – https://www.theguardian.com/politics/1964/oct/17/
     electionspast.past

1966 – Time for Decision

1   Labour Party manifesto 1966 – http://www.labour-party.org.uk/
     manifestos/1966/1966-labour-manifesto.shtml

2   Harold Wilson, conference speech 1965 – http://www.
     britishpoliticalspeech.org/speech-archive.htm?speech=163

3   Wilson on BBC TV– https://www.britishpathe.com/asset/222510/

4   Ted Heath – Ibid.

5   Smethwick campaign slogan – https://www.theguardian.com/world/2014/
     oct/15/britains-most-racist-election-smethwick-50-years-on

6 Quintin Hogg via the Hecklers – Joseph Strick – https://www.youtube.com/watch?v=wRjDusinQdc

7 Bob McKenzie – BBC TV 1966 election (33.10) https://www.youtube.com/watch?v=3j_Ms4g_wd8

8 BBC TV 1966 election (33.10) https://www.bbc.co.uk/iplayer/episode/b0075011/1966-general-election-part-1

9 David Butler – Ibid. – 1 hr 24 minutes

10 Ted Heath –Ibid. – 6 hrs 32 minutes

11 Harold Wilson – https://www.theguardian.com/politics/1966/apr/01/past

1970 – Now Britain's Strong

1 Marcia Williams – quoted in Nick Thomas-Symonds, *Harold Wilson The Winner* p. 318

2 Harold Wilson – https://commonslibrary.parliament.uk/pound-in-your-pocket-devaluation-50-years-on/

3 Ted Heath – Conservative Manifesto 1970 – http://www.conservativemanifesto.com/1970/1970-conservative-manifesto.shtml

4 BBC election night 1970 https://www.bbc.co.uk/programmes/b00v9jg

5 Harold Wilson – Ibid.

6 *Evening Standard* – via Butler and Pinto-Duschinsky, *The British General Election of 1970* p. 144

7 Tony Crosland – https://www.theguardian.com/football/blog/2010/apr/21/world-cup-1970-harold-wilson

8 Harold Wilson – https://www.bbc.co.uk/iplayer/episode/m000kf80/bbc-election-1970-part-2

1974 (February) – Yesterday's Men?

1 Harold Wilson – https://www.youtube.com/watch?v=z9WfwLG086Y0830

2 *Yesterday's Men* documentary BBC 1971 – https://www.youtube.com/watch?v=AVKJ--_UwRY

3 Harold Wilson – Quoted in Martin Pugh, *Speak for Britain* p. 346

4 Harold Wilson – Quoted in Butler and Kavanagh *British General Election Feb 1974* p. 74

5 Labour manifesto Feb 1974 – http://www.labour-party.org.uk/manifestos/1974/feb/1974-feb-labour-manifesto.shtml

6 Ibid.

7 Roy Jenkins – see Steve Richards, *The Prime Ministers*

8   Jeremy Thorpe – see AP archive 14.40 – https://www.youtube.com/watch?v=z9WfwLG086Y

9   Alastair Burnet BBC election 74 – https://www.youtube.com/watch?v=RnYbBr5tOsI

10 Harold Wilson – Ibid. 1 hr 40 mins

11 Harold Wilson – AP[19] – https://www.youtube.com/watch?v=KpfyJiaWZCk

1974 (October) – A Bumpy Ride

1   Harold Wilson – see Nick Thomas-Symonds, *The Winner* p. 363

2   Barbara Castle – https://www.bbc.co.uk/news/uk-politics-32844483

3   https://api.parliament.uk/historic-hansard/commons/1974/mar/12/queens-speech

4   Ted Heath – Butler and Kavanagh, *The British General Election of October 1974*

5   Harold Wilson – election broadcast – 18 September 1974, via BBC Radio 4 https://www.facebook.com/watch/?v=10158449654750459

6   Labour manifesto Oct 1974 – http://www.labour-party.org.uk/manifestos/1974/oct/1974-oct-labour-manifesto.shtml

7   Conservative election material – Butler and Kavanagh, *The British General Election of October 1974* p. 128

8   Harold Wilson – https://www.bbc.co.uk/news/special/politics97/background/pastelec/ge74oct.shtml

9   Harold Wilson – BBC Election coverage Oct 1974 – https://www.youtube.com/watch?v=8jefOrpP9tE – 3hrs 43

1979 – Sea Change

1   Tony Benn, *The Benn Diaries* p. 473

2   Barbara Castle quoted in Alfred Havighurst, *Britain in Transition* p. 569

3   Willie Ross – https://news.stv.tv/feature/jim-sillars-looking-back-at-60-years-of-agitation

4   Jim Callaghan Leader's speech Labour Conference 1976 – http://www.britishpoliticalspeech.org/speech-archive.htm?speech=174

5   Jim Callaghan – see John Shepherd – https://www.thefreelibrary.com/Labor+wasn%27t+working%3A+John+Shepherd+looks+back+thirty+years+to+the...-a0191856361

6   Tony Benn – *The Benn Diaries* – https://www.jstor.org/stable/j.ctvnb7r7q

7   Margaret Thatcher – Conservative Party Broadcast – 17 January 1979 – https://www.youtube.com/watch?v=Txsslou33HQ

8   BBC TV Tonight – 9.00 minutes – 28 March 1979 – https://www.youtube.com/watch?v=ZqzIZVJOQdk

9   Harold Wilson, *Final Term* p. 242 – Epilogue

10   Labour party manifesto 1979 – http://www.labour-party.org.uk/manifestos/1979/1979-labour-manifesto.shtml

11   Conservative Party Manifesto 1979 – http://www.conservativemanifesto.com/1979/1979-conservative-manifesto.shtml

12   BBC News – https://www.bbc.co.uk/news/uk-politics-10377842

13   Bernard Donoughue – interview with the author

1983 – The New Hope

1   'Stand Down Margaret' is a song by British band The Beat on their debut studio album *I Just Can't Stop It* released on 23 May 1980 by Go-Feet Records in the UK and by Sire Records in the US

2   Labour manifesto – see *The Guardian* – Wednesday 30 March 30, 1983 – https://uploads.guim.co.uk/2017/05/12/footmanifesto.jpeg

3   The Limehouse declaration — http://www.liberalhistory.org.uk/wp-content/uploads/2014/10/LimehouseDeclaration.pdf

4   Denis Healey – see Channel 4 News – https://www.channel4.com/news/denis-healey-dies-aged-98

5   Economists letter to *The Times* on monetarism — https://www.margaretthatcher.org/document/121217

6   Margaret Thatcher speech to Conservative Conference — https://www.margaretthatcher.org/document/104431

7   Butler and Kavanagh, *The British General Election of October 1983*, p 82

8   Labour Party manifesto 1983 – http://www.labour-party.org.uk/manifestos/1983/1983-labour-manifesto.shtml

9   Ibid.

10   Gerald Kaufman via *The Telegraph* – https://www.telegraph.co.uk/news/politics/7362487/Michael-Foot-Labours-1983-general-election-manifesto-and-the-longest-suicide-in-history.html

11   Lord Hailsham – See *Washington Post* 21 May 1983 https://www.washingtonpost.com/archive/politics/1983/05/21/labor-candidate-foot-turns-few-heads-in-hustings/d208e49c-e10f-4757-899c-a178ad1639ae/

12   Denis Healey – See *New York Times* 3 June 1983 – https://www.nytimes.com/1983/06/03/world/labor-makes-issue-of-falkland-war.html

13   Michael Foot – see *Liverpool Echo* 9 June 1983 — https://www.britishnewspaperarchive.co.uk/viewer/bl/0000271/19830609/002/0001

14   Michael Foot via – Butler and Kavanagh, *The British General Election of October 1983* p. 85

15   Margaret Thatcher – BBC 1983 election coverage 1.15 – https://www.youtube.com/watch?v=W7HYevqFHCc

16   Neil Kinnock – ITV election coverage 2,51 timecode

1987 – The Dream Ticket

1   Labour Party manifesto 1987 – http://www.labour-party.org.uk/manifestos/1987/1987-labour-manifesto.shtml

2   TV AM coverage – 12 June 1987 – https://www.youtube.com/watch?v=P0p5r_ibGT4

3   Neil Kinnock – Speech to Labour Conference, 2 October 1983 reported in *Labour Party Annual Conference Report 1983*, p. 30

4   Queen Elizabeth – https://www.independent.co.uk/life-style/royal-family/queen-elizabeth-battle-orgreave-police-miners-b2397160.html

5   Neil Kinnock – interview with the author

6   Kinnock speech – Labour Conference 1 October 1985 — http://www.britishpoliticalspeech.org/speech-archive.htm?speech=191

7   Tory election slogan – https://www.telegraph.co.uk/news/2021/06/11/untold-story-margaret-thatchers-1987-election-wobble-day/

8   ITV election night coverage – https://www.youtube.com/watch?v=0kX12RryLec

9   John Smith see BBC election coverage – https://www.youtube.com/watch?v=bVahD8xWoxo

10   Butler and Kavanagh, *The British General Election of 1987* p. 267

11   Neil Kinnock interview with the author

12   Ibid.

1992 – Well All Right!

1   Labour's 1992 Manifesto opened with Adrian Henri's poem *Winter Ending* (http://www.labour-party.org.uk/manifestos/1992/1992-labour-manifesto.shtml) from *Not Fade Away: Poems 1989–1994* by Adrian Henri published by Bloodaxe Books Ltd, 1994. Copyright © Adrian Henri. Reproduced by permission of the Estate c/o Rogers, Coleridge & White Ltd., 20 Powis Mews, London W11 1JN

2   Tony Benn quoted in *The Times* 15 September 1987

3   Sir Geoffrey Howe – https://www.britpolitics.co.uk/speeches-sir-geoffrey-howe-resignation/

4   Margaret Thatcher written resignation statement – https://www.margaret thatcher.org/document/108254

5   Neil Kinnock interview with the author

6   Jack Cunningham – https://www.latimes.com/archives/la-xpm-1991-05-03-mn-1028-story.html

7   Neil Kinnock interview with the author

8   *The Sun* 9 April 1992 – https://www.theguardian.com/politics/pictures/image/0,9353,-10104389507,00.html

9   Neil Kinnock interview with the author

10 David Dimbleby – https://www.youtube.com/watch?v=5rQELMwCVW4

11 Neil Kinnock interview with the author

12 Ibid.

1997 – A New Dawn

1   'Things Can Only Get Better' is a song by Northern Irish musical group D:Ream. It was written by Peter Cunnah and Jamie Petrie and released in 1993 by Magnet Records on the group's debut album, *D:Ream On Volume 1*. On Wednesday 22 May 2024, 'Things Can Only Get Better' again made political news headlines when protestors sang it during Rishi Sunak's General Election announcement.

2   Tony Blair – https://www.youtube.com/watch?v=8bldWwrgS_E

3   Neil Kinnock – resignation speech https://www.theguardian.com/politics/2015/apr/14/neil-kinnock-resigns-labour-leader

4   John Smith to Labour Conference 1993 – https://www.theguardian.com/politics/1993/sep/30/labour.uk

5   John Smith – https://www.bbc.com/news/uk-wales-politics-41847718

6   Tony Blair – https://www.theguardian.com/politics/from-the-archive-blog/2015/apr/29/clause-four-labour-party-tony-blair-20-1995

7   Joy Johnson – interview with the author

8   Tony Blair – https://www.deseret.com/1997/3/17/19300987/let-s-vote-major-calls-an-election

9   Labour Election manifesto 1997– http://www.labour-party.org.uk/manifestos/1997/1997-labour-manifesto.shtml

10 Tony Blair – BBC Election night 1997 – part 2 – 46 mins – https://www.youtube.com/watch?v=_XoMKIP5lFg

11 John Major – https://www.youtube.com/watch?v=YbUWY8u1UJ8 1hr 02 mins

12 Tony Blair – https://www.youtube.com/watch?v=8bldWwrgS_E

13 Clare Short – interview with the author

14   Peter Mandelson – https://www.youtube.com/watch?v=yax-pI8hZWA 0057 timecode

15   Tony Blair – https://www.youtube.com/watch?v=AbhTVJz09G0

2001 – The Quiet Landslide

1   Tony Blair, *A Journey*

2   Tony Blair – https://www.bbc.co.uk/news/special/politics97/diana/ blairreact.html

3   Peter Kilfoyle – http://news.bbc.co.uk/1/hi/uk_politics/625784.stm

4   Aide to William Hague – https://www.telegraph.co.uk/news/ uknews/1355767/Labour-poll-lead-collapses-in-wake-of-petrol-crisis.html

5   Mark Seddon – Interview with the author

6   Sharon Storer – http://news.bbc.co.uk/news/vote2001/hi/english/ newsid_1334000/1334131.stm

7   Lady Thatcher – https://www.margaretthatcher.org/document/108389

8   Tory tax cuts poster – *The Guardian* – https://www.theguardian.com/ politics/election2001/poster/0,,462990,00.html

9   Gordon Brown– http://news.bbc.co.uk/news/vote2001/low/english/ newsid_1373000/1373023.stm

10   Tony Blair – https://edition.cnn.com/2001/WORLD/europe/06/08/ uk.election.05/index.html

11   Mark Seddon – Interview with the author

2005 – We Can Unite Again

1   Andrew Marr http://news.bbc.co.uk/1/hi/uk_politics/vote_2005/ frontpage/4523201.stm

2   CBS News – https://www.youtube.com/watch?v=9eTzV7HvKHU

3   Tony Blair – https://www.theguardian.com/uk/2003/feb/15/politics. politicalnews

4   Robin Cook – via Hansard – https://publications.parliament.uk/pa/ cm200203/cmhansrd/vo030317/debtext/30317-33.htm

5   Lord Puttnam – via *New York Times* https://www.nytimes. com/2004/05/10/world/the-struggle-for-iraq-britain-blair-offers-an-apology-for-abuses-by-soldiers.html

6   Gordon Brown – Robert Peston via *The Daily Telegraph* – https://www. telegraph.co.uk/news/uknews/1480740/There-is-nothing-that-you-could-say-to-me-now-that-I-could-ever-believe.html

7   Michael Howard – via *The Daily Mail* – https://www.dailymail.co.uk/news/article-343798/Howard-We-offer-alternative-Blairs-smirking-politics.html

8   Labour election poster – http://news.bbc.co.uk/1/hi/uk_politics/vote_2005/frontpage/4503405.stm

9   Conservative Election poster via *The Independent* – https://www.independent.co.uk/news/uk/politics/tory-election-poster-sparks-complaints-of-racism-from-students-and-teachers-531552.html

10 Tony Blair – via BBC News - http://news.bbc.co.uk/1/hi/uk_politics/vote_2005/frontpage/4471115.stm

11 *The Sun* – https://www.theguardian.com/media/gallery/2009/sep/30/the-sun-labour-conservatives-front-pages

12 Reg Keys via BBC News – http://news.bbc.co.uk/1/hi/uk_politics/vote_2005/frontpage/4506283.stm

13 Tony Blair – ITV election night coverage part 5 – 20 minutes. https://www.youtube.com/watch?v=q4QqdX5PPFA

14 Alistair Campbell – Interview with the author.

2010 – A Privilege to Serve

1   Tony Blair – via Hansard – https://hansard.parliament.uk/Commons/2007-06-27/debates/07062782000011/PrimeMinister

2   Gordon Brown via BBC –http://news.bbc.co.uk/1/hi/uk_politics/6245682.stm

3   David Cameron – via *The Guardian* – https://www.theguardian.com/politics/2008/mar/12/budget.conservatives

4   James Parnell – https://www.theguardian.com/politics/2009/jun/04/james-purnell-resigns-gordon-brown-cabinet

5   Alistair Darling – via BBC – http://news.bbc.co.uk/1/hi/uk_politics/8584163.stm

6   Labour election poster via *The Guardian* – https://www.theguardian.com/politics/2010/apr/02/david-cameron-gene-hunt-labour-poster

7   Nick Clegg – ITV leader's debate – https://www.youtube.com/watch?v=rk5HvJmy_yg

8   Gordon Brown – via Sky News – https://www.youtube.com/watch?v=yEReCN9gO14

9   Harriet Harman – via BBC election night coverage 2010, 11 mins in https://www.youtube.com/watch?v=UGrSaUc3Mro

10 Gordon Brown – interview with the author.

11   Gordon Brown – http://news.bbc.co.uk/1/hi/uk_politics/election_2010/
     8675913.stm

2015 – On the Brink

1   The Beckett Report – p. 4 – https://www.markpack.org.uk/files/2016/01/
     Learning-the-lessons-from-defeat-taskforce-report-Margaret-Beckett-report-
     into-Labour-2015-general-election-defeat.pdf
2   Conservative Party manifesto 2010 – https://general-election-2010.co.uk/
     2010-general-election-manifestos/Conservative-Party-Manifesto-2010.pdf
3   Ed Miliband – https://www.channel4.com/news/ed-miliband-is-new-
     labour-leader
4   Liam Byrne – https://www.itv.com/news/2015-05-10/labours-liam-byrne-
     admits-shame-at-no-money-letter
5   Ed Miliband via *The Guardian* – https://www.theguardian.com/politics/
     2011/sep/28/end-fast-buck-culture-miliband
6   Ed Miliband via Reuters – https://www.reuters.com/article/
     idUSKBN0F21XB/
7   George Osborne – https://www.bbc.co.uk/news/uk-politics-29335450
8   Labour's 2105 pledge card – https://www.bbc.co.uk/news/uk-politics-
     31885907
9   Labour manifesto 2015 – https://www.bbc.co.uk/news/election-2015-
     32284159
10   Ed Miliband resignation speech – https://www.theguardian.com/politics/
     2015/may/08/ed-miliband-to-resign-as-labour-leader
11   Archie Dryburgh – interview with the author
12   Learning the lessons from defeat, Labour Report – https://www.markpack.
     org.uk/files/2016/01/Learning-the-lessons-from-defeat-taskforce-report-
     Margaret-Beckett-report-into-Labour-2015-general-election-defeat.pdf
13   Ibid.
14   Jon Cruddas – https://labourlist.org/2015/08/labour-stands-on-the-brink-
     of-becoming-irrelevant-to-the-majority-of-working-people/

2017 – The Many Not the Few

1   *The Masque of Anarchy* – Percy Bysshe Shelley
2   Jeremy Corbyn – https://www.youtube.com/watch?v=wB8EMRgVV1U
3   Chakrabarti Report – https://www.bbc.co.uk/news/uk-politics-36672022
4   Jeremy Corbyn via *Belfast Telegraph* – https://www.belfasttelegraph.co.uk/
     news/jeremy-corbyn-will-not-betray-supporters-by-resigning-after-no-
     confidence-vote/34839220.html

5   John McDonnell – https://labourlist.org/2016/10/mcdonnell-dont-let-the-tories-deliver-a-bankers-brexit/?amp

6   Theresa May – https://time.com/4744216/read-theresa-may-statement-general-election/

7   Professor John Curtice – https://www.independent.co.uk/voices/local-election-2017-latest-analysis-john-curtice-tory-landslide-general-election-a7720801.html

8   *Daily Mirror*, Kevin Maguire – https://www.mirror.co.uk/news/politics/leaked-labour-manifesto-full-blooded-10398536

9   Theresa May – https://www.theguardian.com/society/2017/may/22/theresa-may-u-turn-on-dementia-tax-cap-social-care-conservative-manifesto

10 Katherine Chibah, interview with the author

11 Emily Thornberry – via ITV – https://www.youtube.com/watch?v=D4jNO_UCDHc

12 Jeremy Corbyn at his count – https://www.youtube.com/watch?v=1PXnD5jEa-A

13 James Landale BBC – https://www.bbc.co.uk/news/election-2017-40219339

14 'Campaign' by Carol Ann Duffy – *The Guardian* – https://www.theguardian.com/books/2017/jun/10/campaign-a-poem-by-carol-ann-duffy-exclusively-for-the-guardian

15 Laura Parker, interview with the author

2019 – Cutting the Flowers

1   Emily Maitlis, via *The Daily Express* – https://www.express.co.uk/news/uk/1216776/BBC-Emily-Maitlis-Momentum-Jeremy-Corbyn-Labour-update-latest

2   Jeremy Corbyn – via *The Guardian* – https://www.theguardian.com/politics/2019/oct/29/downing-street-signals-compromise-on-potential-general-election-date

3   BBC News – https://www.bbc.co.uk/news/election-2017-40219339

4   Keir Starmer – Labour List – https://labourlist.org/2017/03/keir-starmer-labour-has-six-tests-for-brexit-if-theyre-not-met-we-wont-back-the-final-deal-in-parliament/

5   Keir Starmer – via Sky News – https://news.sky.com/story/labour-conference-sir-keir-starmer-insists-nobody-is-ruling-out-remain-as-an-option-11508213

6   Jeremy Corbyn – via BBC News – https://www.bbc.co.uk/news/uk-politics-48304867

7   Jeremy Corbyn – via *The Guardian* https://www.theguardian.com/politics/2019/oct/29/downing-street-signals-compromise-on-potential-general-election-date

8   Boris Johnson – via *The Guardian* https://www.theguardian.com/politics/video/2019/nov/06/boris-johnson-pledges-to-get-brexit-done-within-weeks-of-re-election-video

9   *The Jewish Chronicle* – https://www.thejc.com/lets-talk/leaders/to-all-our-fellow-british-citizens-xzvf1ms6

10 Labour Manifesto 2019 – https://ucrel.lancs.ac.uk/wmatrix/ukmanifestos2019/localpdf/Labour.pdf

11 Labour Press Office – https://labourlist.org/2019/11/labours-manifesto-launch-its-time-for-real-change/

12 Conservative Party – via Facebook – https://www.facebook.com/watch/?v=845444842570629

13 Jeremy Corbyn – https://www.youtube.com/watch?v=aksFr0xyTPI

14 John McDonnell – Interview with the author

2024 – All Change

1   Keir Starmer – UK government official transcript – https://www.gov.uk/government/speeches/keir-starmers-first-speech-as-prime-minister-5-july-2024

2   Angela Rayner via email to Labour Party members (23/05/2024)

3   Keir Starmer email to Labour Party members – (22/05/2024)

4   Keir Starmer via the *Guardian* – https://www.theguardian.com/politics/2020/apr/04/keir-starmer-wins-labour-leadership-election

5   The Labour Party – https://labour.org.uk/wp-content/uploads/2024/04/Lets-Get-Britains-Future-Back.pdf

6   David Lammy – https://www.davidlammy.co.uk/fabian-society-speech/

7   Keir Starmer – BBC News – https://www.bbc.co.uk/news/articles/c3ggr85dremo

8   Conservative Party manifesto 2024 – https://manifesto.conservatives.com/

9   Labour Party text message – 4/07/2024

10 Jeremy Corbyn – https://www.dailymail.co.uk/news/article-13605647/Jeremy-Corbyn-warns-Sir-Keir-Starmer-dissent-crushed-without-consequences-WINNING-Islington-North.html

11 Thangam Debbonaire – interview with the author

12 Sir John Curtice – https://www.thetimes.com/uk/politics/article/john-curtice-general-election-labour-victory-results-7cpgvbrcs

13 Keir Starmer – https://www.gov.uk/government/speeches/keir-starmers-first-speech-as-prime-minister-5-july-2024

Labour Leaders and their Constituencies

(Constituency of each leader cited at the time they took up the post.)

Keir Starmer – 2020–present
Constituency – Holborn and St Pancras
Born – 1962

Jeremy Corbyn – 2015–2020
Constituency – Islington North
Born – 1949

Ed Miliband – 2010–2015
Constituency – Doncaster North
Born – 1969

Gordon Brown – 2007–2010
Labour Prime Minister – 2007–2010
Constituency – Kirkcaldy and Cowdenbeath
Born – 1951

Tony Blair – 1994–2007
Labour Prime Minister – 1997–2007
Constituency – Sedgefield
Born – 1953

John Smith – 1992–1994
Constituency – Monklands East
Born 1938 died 1994

Neil Kinnock – 1983–1992
Constituency – Islwyn
Born – 1942

Michael Foot – 1980–1983
Constituency – Ebbw Vale
Born 1913 – died 2010

Jim Callaghan – 1976–1980
Labour Prime Minister –1976–1979
Constituency – Cardiff South
Born 1912 – died 2005

Harold Wilson – 1963–1976
Labour Prime Minister – 1964–1970 and 1974–1976
Constituency – Huyton
Born 1916 – died 1995

Hugh Gaitskell – 1955–1963
Constituency – Leeds South
Born 1906 – died 1963

Clement Attlee – 1935–1955
Labour Prime Minister – 1945–1951
Constituency – Limehouse
Born 1883 – died 1967

George Lansbury – 1932–1935
Constituency – Bow and Bromley
Born 1859 – died 1940

Arthur Henderson – (August) 1931–(October) 1932
Constituency – Burnley
Born and died (see below)

Ramsay MacDonald – 1922– (August) 1931
Labour Prime Minister – 1924 and 1929–1931
Constituency – Aberavon
Born and died (see below)

J R Clynes – (February) 1921–(November) 1922
Constituency – Manchester Platting
Born 1869 – died 1949

William Adamson – 1917–1921
Constituency – Western Fife
Born 1863 – died 1936

Arthur Henderson – 1914–1917
Constituency – Barnard Castle
Born and died (see below)

Ramsay MacDonald – 1911–(August) 1914
Constituency – Leicester
Born 1866 – died 1937

George Barnes – 1910–1911
Constituency – Glasgow Blackfriars and Hutchesontown
Born 1859 – died 1940

Arthur Henderson – 1908–1910
Constituency – Barnard Castle
Born 1863 – died 1935

Keir Hardie – 1906–1908
Constituency – Merthyr Tydfil
Born 1856 – died 1915

Chair of the Labour Representation Committee
1905–1906 – Arthur Henderson
1904–1905 – David Shackleton
1903–1904 – John Hodge
1902–1903 – Richard Bell
1901–1902 – Allen Gee
1900–1901 – Frederick Rogers.

The following served as acting leader of the Labour Party

Margaret Beckett
May to July 1994

Harriet Harman
May to September 2010
May to September 2015

George Brown
January to February 1963

Herbert Morrison
December 1955

Index

9/11 terrorist attacks (2001) 270,
270–1

A

Abbott, Diane 301, 350
Adamson, William 34, 40, 42
Afghanistan 270, 271
al-Qaeda 270, 271
Alexander, Douglas 263, 292, 310
Alliance, SDP–Liberal 210, 214–15,
220, 226
Amalgamated Society of Railway
Servants union 18–19
anti-Semitism 276, 317, 333, 339, 341,
345
Article 50 (Lisbon Treaty) 333, 337
Ashdown, Paddy 237, 239, 296, 309
Ashworth, Jonathan 359
Asquith, Herbert 28, 31–2, 33, 35, 60
atomic bomb testing 142
Attlee, Clement 1, 104–7
    1945 election 88–9, 347
    1950 election 101, 102–3
    1951 election 104, 111
    1955 election 118
    attacks on 119, 121
    becomes PM 92
    Bevanites and 350
    Campbell on 2–3
    Churchill and 87, 118
    Labour leader 78–80, 81, 84
    on party history 11
    as PM 97, 98, 103
    Potsdam Conference 88
    resigns 111, 123
    returns 113–14
    on top men 123
    War Ministry 84
Attlee, Violet 101, 118

Auriol, Vincent 106
austerity 96, 300–1, 303, 312, 326,
330

B

Baldwin, Stanley
    1929 election 65
    becomes leader 49, 52
    joint manifesto 79
    as PM 63, 78, 81
Balfour, Arthur 21, 33
Balls, Ed 301, 302, 309, 312
banking crisis (2007) 285–6
Bank of England 71, 135, 146, 157,
259, 281
Barnes, George 32
Batley and Spen by-election (2021) 351
Beckett, Margaret 185, 300
Beckett Report (2016) 300
Bell, Martin 253, 254
Bell, Richard 16
Benn, Hilary 317
Benn, Tony
    1979 election 198
    Cabinet member 178
    challenges Kinnock 231
    on Conservatives 189
    EEC and 190
    Healey and 206
    TV broadcasts 129
    Wilson and 169
Bevan, Aneurin 'Nye' 106–7, 116–17
    Cabinet member 95, 124
    Clause IV and 134
    Conservatives and 104, 119
    death 134
    on Gaitskell 130
    'In Place of Fear' 159
    visit to Moscow 126

Bevanites 116–17, 350
Beveridge Report (1942) 86, 90
Bevin, Ernest 78, 85, 97, 98, 105
'Big Loaf, Small Loaf' campaign (1906) 21
'The Big Society' 290
bin Laden, Osama 271
'Black Friday' (1921) 44
'Black Wednesday' (1992) 247–8, 255, 352
Blair, Cherie 255, 257, 277
Blair, Tony
    9/11 attacks 270–1
    1997 election 1, 245, 252–8, 347
    2001 election 259, 262–9
    2005 election 275–81, 296
    broad left and 350
    Brown and 248, 268, 274–5
    Campbell on 2–3
    future leader 246
    Iraq dossier 271
    Iraq invasion 297
    Kosovo Albanians 261
    Labour leader 248–51, 352
    Major and 254–5
    Marr on 270
    as PM 2, 274–5, 281
    resigns 283
    speeches 258
    Thatcher and 249, 266
Blairites 257, 287
Blears, Hazel 287
Blunkett, David 263, 294
Boer War 15, 18
Bonar Law, Andrew 35, 45, 49
Bondfield, Margaret 59, 68
Booth, Charles 12
Booth-Clibborn, Edward 197
Braverman, Suella 357–8
Brexit 318–20, 332–46, 337, 348
Brexit Party 337, 342, 355
Brezhnev, Leonid 148
Brighton bombing (1984) 220
British Empire 21, 97, 135
British Telecom 220

Brittan, Leon 222
Brown, George 137, 150, 156, 162
Brown, Gordon
    2001 election 262–3, 266–7, 268
    2005 election 277, 281
    2010 election 289–388
    'Bigotgate' 291–2
    Blair and 248–9, 268, 274–5
    broad left and 350
    Budgets 259, 275
    campaign roles 295–6
    chancellor 259, 260, 273
    financial crash (2008) 4
    maiden speech 5
    as PM 2
    possible leader 241, 283
    shadow chancellor 246, 251
    speeches 283–4, 288, 298
Bryant and May match strike (1888) 12
Budgets
    1900s 26, 27, 31
    1920s 55, 65
    1931 70
    1950s 107, 114
    1966 151
    1974 179
    1981 207
    2000s 259, 275
    2010 288–9
    mini Budgets 180
Burnet, Alastair 173, 225
Burnham, Andy 301, 316
Bush, George W. 270, 271, 272
Butler, David 152
Butler, Rab 86, 99, 113, 114
by-elections
    1920s 65
    1960s–1970s 135–6, 139, 148, 157, 168
    1980s–1990s 206, 208, 222, 232, 234, 248
    2010s–2020s 287, 319, 351, 354
    National Government success 79
    numbers of 42
Byrne, Liam 301, 312

C

Cable and Wireless 94
Callaghan, Jim 202
  1966 election 150
  1979 election 195–202
  chancellor 156, 157, 302
  death 275
  foreign secretary 178
  interviews 198
  'little-Budget' 151
  as MP 90
  as PM 190–202, 353
  possible leader 137
  speeches 191
  stands down 205
Cameron, David 285, 286, 289–98, 303, 311–13, 317, 361
Campbell, Alastair 2–3, 250–1, 263, 275, 281
Campbell-Bannerman, Henry 21, 22
Campbell, J. R. 57–8, 59
Campbell, Ming 296
Castle, Barbara
  Cabinet member 159, 169, 178
  Clause IV and 134
  as MP 90
  NEC member 117
  on Thatcher 189
central banks 156
Chakrabarti, Shami 317
Chamberlain, Joseph 21
Chamberlain, Neville 84, 92
Chelmsford, Lord 53
Cherwell, Lord 115
Chibah, Katherine 324–5
Chile 179
China 142
Churchill, Winston
  1945 election 89
  1950 election 100
  Attlee and 3, 87, 118
  chancellor 62–3, 65
  on the Labour Party 112
  loses seat 52
  as PM 86, 88, 106, 110, 114
  Potsdam Conference 88–9
  radio broadcasts 92
  War Ministry 84–5
City, the 71, 222
Clegg, Nick 288, 290–1, 310
Clinton, Bill 265
Clynes, J. R. 42, 48, 52, 54
Co-operative Movement 38
coalitions 293–8, 326–7
  Con–Lib 294–5, 297, 300–2
  informal Con–DUP 327
  Lab–Lib 24, 192
  Lib–Con 35, 37–8, 45
  see also National Government
Cold War 97, 107
Collins, Lord Ray 303
Common Market, European
  see European Economic Community (EEC)
Commonwealth countries 97, 105, 135, 141, 150, 151
Communist Party of Great Britain 44, 56, 58
Conservative Party
  1900 election 15–16
  1906 election 20
  1910 elections 29
  1918 election 35, 38
  1920s elections 45, 46, 49–50, 59–60, 66–7
  1930s elections 74, 80
  1945 election 88, 89, 92
  1950 election 100, 101, 102
  1951 election 108, 110–12
  1955 election 120–1
  1959 election 130–2
  1960s elections 138–9, 141–3, 148–54
  1970 election 159–65, 353
  1974 elections 169–75, 181–8
  1979 election 195–202
  1983 election 210–16
  1987 election 217, 222–9, 351
  1990s elections 237–43, 245
  2000s elections 262–9, 276–81

Conservative Party (continued)
2010s election 289–98, 307–13, 319–31
2019 election 340–6, 351
2024 election 347, 354–61
2024 result 362
1922 Committee 186
'Action Not Words' 151
advertising campaigns 129, 182, 196, 215, 236, 276, 277, 306–7
beliefs 11
'A Better Tomorrow' 160
'The Big Society' 290
collapse of 348, 352
donations 340
by-elections 135, 148, 157, 168, 208, 232, 234, 248, 287, 319
ERM debacle 352
European Parliament 220, 232, 337
'The Industrial Charter: ...' 99
local elections 260
manifestos
1929 66
1950s 101, 108–9, 128
1960s–1970s 151, 160, 181, 196
1980s–1990s 224, 237, 253
2000s–2010s 265, 277, 290, 323
2010s 361
2019 355
2024 355
mass council seat loss (2022) 352
municipal elections 99
'Partygate' and other scandals 351–2
Putting Britain Right Ahead 148, 151
reserve party funds 99
strongholds 4–5
Consumer Prices Index 355
Cook, Robin 263, 272
Cooper, Yvette 309, 316
Corbyn, Jeremy 4, 315–31, 332–46, 349–50, 351, 359
Coronavirus pandemic 351–2
'Coupon Election' (1918) 38, 40
Cousins, Frank 156

Cripps, Sir Stafford 46, 79, 85, 98, 105, 106
Crooks, Will 33
Crosby, Lynton 320
Crosland, Anthony 127, 163, 178
Crossman, Richard 111–12, 117
Cruddas, Jon 313
Cudlipp, Hugh 119
Cunningham, Andrew 179
Cunningham, Jack 234
Curran, Margaret 310
Curtice, John 321
Curtice, Sir John 360

D

Daily Express 50, 107, 119, 199
Daily Herald 51, 91
Daily Mail 58, 63, 213
Daily Mirror 80, 91, 109, 119, 121, 159, 199, 322
Daily Telegraph 224, 261, 286, 322
Dalton, Hugh 46, 98, 102
Dalyell, Tam 272
Darling, Alistair 285, 286, 288–9
Davis, David 336
Dawes Plan (1924) 56
Day, Robin 216
D-Day 80th anniversary commemorations (2024) 356
de Gaulle, Charles 140, 157
de Valera, Éamon 40
Debbonaire, Thangam 359–60
Democratic Unionist Party (DUP) 327, 330, 337
devolution 194–5, 260
Dewar, Donald 263
Diamond, Anne 217
Diana, Princess of Wales 260
Dimbleby, David 240, 292
Dimbleby, Richard 120, 142
Donoughue, Bernard 201–2
'Double Member' constituencies 17
Douglas-Home, Alec 137, 138, 140–3, 147
D:Ream 245, 252, 255

Driberg, Tom 117
Dryburgh, Archie 311
du Cann, Edward 186
Duffy, Carol Ann 328
Duffy, Gillian 291–2
Duncan Smith, Iain 274
Dunwoody, Gwyneth 152

E

Ecclestone, Bernie 260
Economic Affairs, Department for 146
Economic Affairs, Ministry 139
economic crisis (2008) 316
Economist 128, 357
Eden, Sir Anthony 113, 114, 118–19,
    124–5, 131
Education Act (1902) 21
Education Act (1944) 86
education, secondary 128, 140
Egypt 124
Eisenhower, Dwight 124
electoral map 89, 99
Elizabeth II 114, 219
English Review, The 48
Equal Franchise Act (1928) 65
European Championship, UEFA (2024)
    353
European Economic Community
    (EEC)
    division over 169
    Labour Party and 205
    leaving 170
    proposed entry 140, 143, 151, 156,
        168
    referendum 190–1
    renegotiations 178, 184
European Parliament 220, 232, 287,
    337
European Union
    customs union 335
    euro 261, 265
    referendum 317–18
Evans, Craig 265
Evans, David 357
Evening Standard 162

Exchange Rate Mechanism (ERM)
    247–8, 255, 352
exchange rate, monetary 157, 167
exit polls
    1970s–1980s 161–2, 173, 185, 225
    2000s–2010s 279, 292–3, 325–6,
        330, 342–3
    2024 358
expenses, MP 287

F

Fabian Society 16
facts, key (Labour history) 7–9
Falklands War (1982) 208, 213, 215
Farage, Nigel 292, 310, 342, 355, 359
Financial Times 240, 266
Fixed Term Parliaments Act (2011)
    300, 320, 339
'Flapper Election' (1929) 66
foot and mouth disease (2001/2010)
    262, 265, 284
Foot, Michael 90, 169, 178, 198, 205,
    208–15
Foot, Sir Dingle 162
Formby, Jennie 334
fox hunting 281
France 192
free trade 21, 49–50, 51
Freedom of Information (FOI) 281
Freeman, John 106
Friedman, Milton 207
Frost, David 224
fuel duty 261, 265
Future of Socialism, The (Crosland) 127

G

Gaitskell, Hugh
    Bevanites and 350
    chancellor 106–7
    Clause IV and 134
    concedes defeat 131, 132
    death 137
    Labour leader 123–4, 124, 128–32
    visit to Moscow 126
    Wilson and 134–5

Galloway, George 354
Gallup 88, 248
Gambling Commission 356
Gaza 353–4, 359, 360
general elections
    1900 2, 15–16
    1900 result 19
    1906 20, 28
    1906 result 25
    1910 26, 28, 32–3
    1910 results 30, 34
    1918 35, 37–8
    1918 result 41
    1922 45
    1922 result 47
    1923 50
    1923 result 54
    1924 2, 55, 58–388
    1924 result 61
    1929 67, 68
    1929 result 68
    1931 69, 73–388
    1935 2, 78–82
    1935 result 82
    1945 2, 84, 88
    1945 result 93
    1950 98–103
    1950 result 103
    1951 104–12
    1951 result 112
    1955 113, 118–21
    1955 result 122
    1959 125–6, 130–2
    1959 result 132
    1964 133
    1964 result 144
    1966 148–54
    1966 result 154
    1970 159–65, 353
    1970 result 165
    1974 166, 169–75, 177–88
    1974 results 176, 188
    1979 195–202
    1979 result 203
    1983 204
    1983 result 216
    1987 223–9
    1987 result 229
    1992 5, 235–43, 354
    1992 result 244
    1997 251–8, 259
    1997 result 258
    2001 259, 262–9
    2001 result 269
    2005 275–81
    2005 result 282
    2010 4, 288–98
    2010 result 299
    2015 307–13
    2015 result 314
    2017 4, 319–31, 357
    2017 result 331
    2019 1, 332, 340–6, 351, 355, 357
    2019 result 346
    2024 1, 347
General Strike (1926) 63–4
George V 32, 52, 53, 71, 78
George VI 89, 103, 105
Germany 35, 36, 37–8, 45, 84, 192
Gladstone, Herbert 23
Gold Standard 62, 72
Goldsmith, Sir James 254, 278
Good Friday Agreement (1998) 260, 281
Gordon Walker, Patrick 150
Gould, Bryan 223
Gould, Philip 251, 263, 275
Gow, Ian 232
Great Depression (1929–39) 70
Great War (1914–18) 35–6, 38
Greater London Council (GLC) 139
Green Party 359
Greenwood, Arthur 84, 86
Griffiths, Peter 150
Guardian, The 16, 143
Guilty Men ('Cato') 91

H

Hague, William 261, 266, 267, 268
Hailsham, Lord 211

Haldane, Viscount 53
Hamas 353–4, 360
Hamilton, Neil 253, 254
Hardie, Keir
  1906 election 20, 23
  Great War and 36
  ILP and 13, 18
  Labour leader 24, 30
  LRC and 13, 16–17
  Starmer named after 350
  'sunshine of socialism' 6
Harman, Harriet 293, 301, 308, 309
Hartlepool by-election (2021) 351
Hattersley, Roy 198, 218, 223, 239
Healey, Denis
  1979 election 198
  1983 election 212
  Benn and 206
  Budgets 179
  chancellor 169, 178, 192
  Conference speech 90–1
  EEC referendum 191
  fear of 205, 208
  mini-Budgets 180
Heath, Ted
  1970 election 159–65, 353
  1974 elections 166, 170–5,
    177–88
  party leader 148–54, 166–8
  Powell and 158
  replaced by Thatcher 189
Hecklers, The (US documentary) 150
Henderson, Arthur
  1906 election 23
  1910 elections 28
  1923 election 54
  Home Office 52
  Labour leader 14, 35–6, 39, 41, 73,
    350
  loses seat 39, 42, 76
  regains seat 42, 78
  on the Tory Party 26
Heneghan, Patrick 326
Henri, Adrian 230
Heseltine, Michael 222, 233

Hewitt, Patricia 288
Hitler, Adolf 77, 84, 91–2
Hobson, J. A. 35
Hogg, Quintin 150
Hoon, Geoff 288
Housing Act (1924) 55
Howard, Michael 274, 275, 276, 277,
  278
Howe, Geoffrey 207, 210, 232–3
Hudson, Hugh 224
Human Rights Act (1998) 281
hung parliaments 174, 292
Hunt, Jeremy 352
Hussein, Saddam 271
Hutton Report (2004) 273
hydrogen bomb (H-Bomb) 117, 118

I

immigration 277–8, 279, 312
immigration levels 150
Import Duties Act (1932) 77
'In Place of Strife' (1969 White Paper)
  159
Independent Group, The 339
Independent Labour Party (ILP) 13,
  16, 45, 49, 77, 83
Industrial Relations Act (1971) 177
inflation 167, 179, 181, 184, 190, 263,
  274, 355
International Monetary Fund (IMF)
  156, 192
IRA 220, 232
Iran 271
Iraq 270, 271
Iraq invasion (2003) 271–3, 276, 278,
  279–80, 281
Ireland 97
Irish Home Rule 15, 21, 33
Irish nationalists 195
Irish Parliamentary Party 29, 39
Iron and Steel Act (1949) 100, 106,
  109, 139
Israel 353–4, 360
Italo-Abyssinian War (1935–37) 78,
  83

J

Japan 86
Jarrow Hunger March (1936) 83
Jenkins, Roy
  1983 election 214
  Cabinet member 178, 184
  as chancellor 159, 169
  EEC referendum 191
  founds SDP 205–6
  on Heath 171–2
  loses seat 226
  returns 206
Jewish Chronicle 341
John Paul II, Pope 275
Johnson, Alan 287, 292
Johnson, Boris 332, 336, 338, 342–6,
    351–2
Johnson, Joy 250
Johnson, Lyndon 147
Joseph, Sir Keith 184
Jowett, Fred 16, 53
Joyce, Eric 303

K

Kaufman, Gerald 210
Keeler, Christine 136
Kelly, Dr David 273
Kendall, Liz 316
Kennedy, Charles 276, 278, 296
Keynes, John Maynard 63
Keys, Reg 279
Khaki Election (1900) 15
Khrushchev, Nikita 142
Kilfoyle, Peter 261
Kinnock, Glenys 240, 242
Kinnock, Neil 5
  1983 election 223–9
  1992 election 238–43, 330, 354
  Benn challenges 231
  interviews 224
  'Kinnock the Movie' 224
  Labour leader 216, 218, 221, 233–4,
    237, 238
  Militants and 350
  modernising agenda 230

  resigns 245–6
  Scargill and 220
  Smith and 235
  speeches 221
  on Thatcher 213
Korean War (1950–53) 107, 109,
    111–12
Kosovo War (1998–99) 261

L

Labour Party
  1900 election 2
  1906 result 20, 25
  1910 elections 26
  1910 results 30, 34
  1918 election 35, 38–9
  1918 result 41
  1922 election 45
  1922 result 47
  1923 election 50–1
  1923 result 54
  1924 election 2, 58–60
  1924 result 61
  1929 election 65, 66, 66–7
  1929 result 68
  1931 election 69, 73–4
  1931 result 75
  1935 election 2, 76, 80, 81, 83
  1935 result 82
  1945 election 2, 89–90, 92
  1945 result 93
  1950 election 99–100, 102
  1950 result 103
  1951 election 110–12
  1951 result 112
  1955 election 120
  1955 result 122
  1959 election 130–2
  1959 result 132
  1964 election 141–3
  1964 result 144
  1966 election 148–54
  1966 result 154
  1970 election 159–65
  1970 result 165

1974 elections 169–75, 181–8
1974 results 176, 188
1979 election 195–202
1979 result 203
1983 election 209–16
1983 result 216
1987 election 217, 223–9
1987 result 229
1992 election 5, 238–43, 354
1992 result 244
1997 election 1, 245
1997 result 259
2001 election 262–9
2001 result 269
2005 election 275–81
2005 result 282
2010 election 4, 289–98
2010 result 299
2015 election 307–13
2015 result 314
2017 election 319–31, 357
2017 result 331
2019 election 1, 340–6, 357
2019 result 346
2024 election 1, 347–61
2024 result 362
advertising campaigns 181–2, 276, 284
anti-Semitism 276, 349, 351
Book of the Labour Party 39
'Britain will win with Labour' 224
by-elections 148, 168, 208, 222, 232, 248, 287, 319, 354
Campaign Strategy Committee 219
Clause IV 36–7, 44, 134, 249, 321
Conferences 20, 77, 78, 86–7, 90, 117, 133, 159, 191, 204, 234, 284, 288, 348, 350
European Parliament 220, 232, 337
'fiscal rules' 352–3
'A Future Fair For All' 289–90
income and donations 334
'It's Time For Real Change' 341
'It's Time to Get Britain Working Again' 237

'Labour and the Nation' 64–5
'The Labour Way is the Better Way' 195
leaflets 31
'Let us work together …' 170–1
local elections 260
LRC and 23–4
manifestos
  1910s 32–3, 38
  1920s–1930s 43, 51, 76
  1940s–1950s 87–8, 90, 116, 128, 129–30
  1960s–1970s 139–40, 145, 150, 160, 170–1, 181, 195
  1980s 209–10, 214–15, 217, 224
  1990s 230, 237, 253
  2000s 264, 265, 277
  2010s 284, 289–90, 308, 322, 341
  2024 354–5
mass rallies 139, 238–9, 243
media operation 250–1
membership 64, 251, 334
municipal elections 158
National Plan 146, 156
'The New Hope for Britain' 209
'Now Britain's strong – let's make it great to live in!' 160
power of the leadership 350
press conferences 252
private donations to 250, 260
programmes for government 2–3
progress of 43
'The Red Flag' 53, 67, 77, 94
slogans 128, 139, 181–2, 321
'For Socialism and Peace' policy programme 78
special conference 205
splits in 116
'Time for Decision' 150
TV broadcasts 129
victory rally 254
Wilson's review 126–7
Women's Manifesto 308

Labour Representation Committee
    (LRC) 16–388
  1900 election 16, 267
  1906 election 20, 22–4
  founded 13, 16
  manifestos 15, 22
  renamed Labour Party 23–4
Labour Together group 348
Lamont, Norman 235, 247
Landale, James 327
Lansbury, George 14, 34, 42, 74, 76, 78
Lavery, Ian 336
Lawson, Nigel 222
League of Nations 36, 51, 78, 79
Lee, Jennie 162
Letwin, Oliver 276
Lib-Lab MPs 13, 17, 28
Liberal Democrats 254, 276, 303
  1992 election 237
  2010 election 288, 290–8
  2015 election 312
  2017 election 330
  2019 election 338
  2024 election 358
  by-elections 232, 248
  European Parliament 337
  Iraq War and 278, 279
Liberal Party 11, 21–2, 45
  1900s–1910 elections 20, 21, 22–3,
    26–8, 29, 38, 40
  1920s elections 50, 60, 67
  1950s elections 100, 110, 111, 120,
    121
  1964 election 142
  1970s elections 172, 174, 175, 183,
    186
  by-elections 135
  Labour supplants 3
  Lib–Lab pact 192
  LRC and 13–14, 17
  manifestos 50
  minority government 21
  National Government 74, 180
  reforms 26
  split in 40, 45, 51

trade unions and 13
Wilson and 145
Liberal Unionist Party 15, 21, 29
Liverpool, Lord 226
Livingstone, Ken 261
Lloyd George, David
  1918 election 38
  becomes PM 37
  chancellor 26, 27
  Germany and 45
  Labour and 40
  as PM 51
  privatisation 44
  on Tory Peers 31
  on voters 24
local elections 117, 139, 260, 262,
    320–1, 352
London County Council 76, 79, 99
London Dock Strike (1889) 12
London Evening Standard 127
Lords, House of 26–7, 28–9, 31–2
  reform 281

M

Maastricht Treaty (1992) 235
McDonnell, John 283, 319, 334, 343–4
MacDonald, Ramsay 3
  1900 election 16
  1906 election 23–4
  1910 elections 32
  1923 election 51–4
  1929 election 67–8
  Chairman 34
  expelled 76
  Great War and 36
  ILP and 13
  Labour leader 14, 62, 350
  loses seat 39, 42, 80
  LRC and 18, 23
  as PM 55–8, 60, 67–8, 70–5
  regains seat 48–9
  resigns 72
  speeches 22, 71
  on strikes 64
McKenzie, Bob 152

MacLaine, Shirley 211
Macleod, Iain 143
Macmillan, Harold
    1959 election 127, 131
    becomes PM 125–6
    future leader 92
    as PM 135
    resigns 136
    sacks MPs 136
Macmillan, Hugh 53
McNicol, Iain 334
Maguire, Kevin 322
Maitlis, Emily 332
Major, John
    1992 election 233–7, 239–43, 245,
        330
    1997 election 251–8
    Blair and 254–5
    as PM 247–8
    Smith and 247
    soapbox campaign 237–8, 239, 253
    'Social Chapter' 235
Manchester Arena bombing (2017) 323
Mandelson, Peter 219, 250, 257, 260,
    262, 309
Manningham Mills strike (1891) 12
Marr, Andrew 270
Marshall Plan, US 97
Martin, Michael 287
Maudling, Reggie 302
Maxton, James 57
May, Theresa 318–31, 336–7
McFadden, Pat 356
McSweeney, Morgan 348, 351
Memorandum on War Aims (1917) 36
Mikardo, Ian 117
Milburn, Alan 296
Miliband, David 287, 301
Miliband, Ed 300–3, 305–13, 315,
    324
Militant Labour 208, 221, 224, 227
Miners' Federation 28–9, 63
Mineworkers, National Union of
    (NUM) 168, 170, 171, 219–20
Momentum 316, 328, 341

Morrison, Herbert
    Attlee and 105
    'Big Five' 98
    loses seat 59
    possible leader 79, 123
    Tories and 102
    War Ministry 85
mortgage rates 184
municipal elections 99, 158
Murdoch, Rupert 251
Murphy, Jim 310
Mussolini, Benito 77, 92

N

Nasser, Col Gamal Abdel 124
National candidates 73
National Coal Board 94
National Enterprise Board 169
National Executive Committee (NEC)
        209–10
    Bevanites and 117
    candidate selection 23, 350
    influence of 37, 87, 219
    MacDonald and 51, 68
    Wilson and 149
National Farmers' Union 347
National Freight Authority 151
National Government 73–5, 79–80
    1935 election 80, 81
    possibility of 180, 183, 184
National Health Service (NHS) 95–6,
        106–7
    future of 212, 342
    Miliband and 307
    prescription charges 146
    spending on 273, 295–6, 306
    state of 264
    under Labour 281
    'War of Jennifer's Ear' 238
National Insurance 95, 251, 273, 289,
        354
National Labour 73, 74, 79, 80
National Ports Authority 151
nationalisation 44–5, 91, 94–5, 100,
        116–17, 128, 139

Neil, Andrew 342, 344
Neruda, Pablo 341–2
New Labour 249–58, 259–69, 270–81
New Statesman and Nation 77
Newsnight (BBC) 224
Nissan car company 213
'Nixon shock' (1971) 167
North Atlantic Treaty Organization (NATO) 97, 224, 315
North Korea 271
Northern Ireland 158, 260, 281, 327
nuclear disarmament 205, 224

O

Obama, Barack 286
Observer, The 306
oil embargo 167
oil prices 168
OPEC 167
Open University 151
Operation ROBOT 115
Osborne, George 289, 300–1
Osborne Judgement (1909) 28, 32, 34, 64
Owen, David 205–6, 218

P

Parker, Laura 328–31
Parliament Bill (1910) 31–2
Parliamentary Labour Party (PLP) 33, 37, 51, 329
Parmoor, Lord 53
peace marches 271–2
People, The 226–7
People's Vote campaign 335–6
Peston, Robert 274
Phillips, Morgan 120, 152
Pincher, Chris 352
Plaid Cymru 174, 195
Poland 84
Poll Tax 232–3, 234, 274
Poplar Rates Rebellion (1921) 76
Portillo, Michael 254
Powell, Enoch 158, 170, 173
Prescott, John 263, 264–5

Priestley, J. B. 83
privatisation 44, 220, 227, 237
Profumo, John 136
protectionism 20, 22, 49, 70, 77
Purnell, James 287
Puttnam, Lord 272

Q

Queen's Speech 145, 178, 335
Question Time Special (BBC) 278

R

radio broadcasts 57, 92, 104
rationing, end of 116, 119
Rayner, Angela 349, 356, 357, 358
recessions 167, 230, 286
Red Wall seats 340, 343
Redundancy Payments Act (1965) 147
Reed, Jamie 316
Reeves, Rachel 316, 352, 356
Referendum Party 254
referendums 184, 190–1, 194–5, 260, 302, 304–5
Reform Act, Third (1885) 12
Reform UK 355, 359, 360
regional planning 169
Reid, John 294
Rent Act (1965) 147
Representation of the People Act (1918) 37
Retail Price Index 198
Rhodesia (*now* Zimbabwe) 147
riots, inner-city 207
Robertson, John 191
Robinson, Geoffrey 260
Rochdale by-election (2024) 354
Rodgers, Bill 205–6
Rolls-Royce 167
Ross, Willie 191
Russia 43, 53, 91

S

Saatchi & Saatchi 196, 236
Salisbury, Lord 15
Scargill, Arthur 220

Scotland 359
  1987 election 226
  2010 election 293
  2019 election 342
  devolution 194, 260, 302, 304–5
  local elections 320
Scotland Act (1978) 194
Scotsman, The 62
Scottish Labour Party 105, 191, 310, 326
Scottish National Party (SNP) 359
  1974 elections 174, 185, 186
  1979 election 199
  2015 election 310
  2017 election 330
  2019 election 338
  deals with 306–7
  devolution and 194, 302, 304–5
  E. Miliband and 324
  by-elections 158, 168
  success of 312
SDP/Labour rupture (1980s) 355
SDP–Liberal Alliance
  see Alliance, SDP–Liberal
Seamen, National Union of 155–6
Second World War (1939–45) 84–6
Secret Intelligence Service 58
Seddon, Mark 263–4, 269
Select Committees 158
'Selsdon Man' 160
Shackleton, David 24
Shaheen, Faiza 350
Shawcross, Sir Hartley 98
Shelley, Percy Bysshe 315, 321
Shinwell, Manny 59, 80, 118
Shore, Peter 178, 198
Short, Clare 256–7, 263
Sillars, Jim 191
Single Market 335, 336
Sinn Féin 39–40
Six-Day War (1967) 156
Smith, Ian 147
Smith, John
  death 247, 274
  Kinnock on 241
  Labour leader 246–7, 256, 352
  shadow chancellor 235, 235–6
  on Thatcher 225
Smith, Owen 318, 327
Smith, T. Dan 179
Snowden, Philip
  1900 election 16
  1906 election 23
  1929 election 66, 68
  1931 election 73, 74
  chancellor 52, 55, 70
social care reform 323
Social Democratic Federation 16
Social Democratic Party (SDP) 205–6, 207, 215, 218, 227
South Africa 178
South Wales Daily Post 17
Soviet Union 56, 58, 59, 60, 97, 124
Spanish Civil War (1936–39) 83
Spectator 143
Starmer, Keir 1, 2–3, 4, 335, 336–7, 347–61
Starmer, Victoria 361
Statistics Regulation, Office for 354
Steel, David 214
sterling crises 96–7, 145–6, 156, 157, 167, 192
'Stop-Go' economics 140
Storer, Sharon 264
Straw, Jack 264
Streeting, Wes 356
Strick, Joseph 150
Stride, Mel 357
strikes 12, 18–19, 63–4
  Ford workers 193
  miners' 166, 168, 170, 171
  NUM 219–20
  'winter of discontent' 193–4
Sturgeon, Nicola 307–8
Suez Crisis (1956) 124, 131–2
Sun, The 193, 199, 227, 239, 242, 251, 266, 278, 288, 357
Sunak, Rishi 348, 349, 352, 355–61
Sunday Times, The 357

T

Taff Vale Railway Company 18–19, 28
Taliban, the 271
Tate and Lyle 100
Taverne, Dick 185
taxation
    1950s–1960s 126, 135, 140
    1970s–1980s 179, 222, 232
    1990s 234–7, 251, 281, 354
    2000s 259, 265, 281
    2010s 284–5
    2020s 354
Technology, Ministry for 140, 146, 156
terrorism 220, 270, 270–1, 284, 323
Thatcher, Margaret
    1979 election 195–202
    1983 election 204
    1987 election 217–29
    as PM 202, 351
    Blair and 249, 266
    economy and 231
    Europe and 265
    interviews 225
    mortgage rates and 184
    newspaper headliner 217
    party leader 189
    speeches 194, 200, 207
Thomas, Jimmy 52, 54, 68, 80
Thornberry, Emily 325, 336
Thorpe, Jeremy 172, 174, 183
three-day working week 168
TikTok 357
Times, The 20, 134, 207, 266, 278
Tonight (BBC) 195
Tory Party 11
trade deficit 156, 164, 171, 305
Trade Disputes and Trade Union Act (1927) 64
Trade Union Act (1913) 37
Trades Disputes Act (1906) 27
Trades Union Congress (TUC)
    Blair and 271
    Callaghan and 193
    Daily Herald 51

General Council 71
General Strike 63, 64
LRC and 13, 19
MacDonald and 51
'Social Contract' and 184, 187, 190
Wilson and 169
trades unions
    Clause IV 134
    Collins' Review 303
    Labour leadership and 350
    LRC and 22
    membership 12, 44
    nationalisation of mines/railway 44–5
    see also strikes
Transport and General Workers' Union 156
Trickett, Jon 336
Triple Alliance 44
Truss, Liz 4, 352, 353
tuition fees, university 273
turnouts
    1940s–1950s 89, 101, 102, 120
    1960s–1970s 153, 162, 187
    1980s–1990s 214, 243
    2000s–2010s 267, 280, 296
    2024 360
TV broadcasts
    1955 election 119–20
    1959 election 129, 131
    1964 election 141–2
    1966 election 152
    devaluation of pound 157

U

UKIP (United Kingdom Independence Party) 287, 292, 312
Ulster Unionist Party 174, 175
UN Refugee Convention 278
unemployment 1, 62–5, 69–75, 263, 286
    1920s–1930s 44, 77
    1970s–1980s 191, 198, 205, 207, 210–12
    1990s 230

United Nations (UN) 97, 124, 261
United States 69–70, 97, 271, 286
Upper Clyde Shipbuilders, Glasgow
	167

V
VAT 354
Vietnam War (1955–75) 147, 158
voting age 158

W
Wakefield, Anthony 278
Wales 194, 226, 260, 273, 293, 320,
	359
Wall Street Crash (1929) 69
war debt 96
War Ministry 84
'War of Jennifer's Ear' 238
Watson, Tom 327
Webb, Beatrice 42
Webb, Sidney 52
'Welfare State' 95–6
Westland Helicopters 222
Wheatley, John 53, 55, 69
Whigs 11
Wilkinson, Ellen 86–7, 98
Williams, Marcia 155, 198
Williams, Shirley 178, 184, 198, 200,
	205–6
Wilson, Harold
	1966 election 145–54
	1970 election 159–65
	becomes PM 142, 143
	becomes PM again 175
	Campbell on 2–3
	character 151
	Clause IV and 134
	on the Conservative Party 133
	on devolution 195
	on Douglas-Home 140
	EEC application 156
	fading 169

	Gaitskell and 134–5
	on inflation 166
	Labour leader 137–9
	as MP 90, 106
	NEC and 117
	as PM 1, 2, 4, 155, 177–88, 349
	resigns 189–90
	'Social Contract' 171, 177, 183,
		187, 190
	speeches 139, 183
	Thatcher and 198
	Wilson Review 126–7
Wilson, Mary 148, 160, 198
Wilson, Woodrow 36
'winter of discontent' (1978–79) 193
Withdrawal Agreement (Brexit) 335,
	337
women
	austerity and 301
	Co-op movement 38
	Conservative Party and 103
	Eden and 118
	given the vote 37, 65–6
	Labour Party and 43, 132, 153
	Liberal Party and 172
	pitching to 58
	striking 12
	in war 273
	Welfare State and 95
	Women's Manifesto 308
Worcester, Bob 243
Workers' Weekly 56
World Cups 161, 163

Y
Yesterday's Men (BBC documentary)
	169
YouGov 290

Z
Zinoviev, Grigory 58
Zinoviev Letter 58, 59, 60

DOUGLAS BEATTIE is an award-winning journalist and author. Having worked for numerous media outlets including BBC News, Scottish Television and the Press Association, he has spent the past decade inside the Labour Party and trade unions, most recently as a media and political director.

Twice elected as a Labour councillor, he stood for Parliament for Scottish Labour in 2017. He grew up in Langholm in Dumfriesshire, studied politics at Glasgow University and now lives in London.

Douglas Beattie is fascinated by the history of tribal divisions, one of his previous books being an acclaimed study of British football derbies, *The Rivals Game: Inside the British Derby*.